Praise for *Church Mergers: A Gui*

"Tracing the imaginary journey of several churches, Bandy and Brooks offer up a compelling argument for twenty-first-century church mergers. This book is also good for any church needing revitalization, even if it isn't a candidate for a merger."

—Bill Easum, founder and president of The Effective Church Group

"Just when many would see a potential church merger as really 'giving up' on a church's future, Bandy and Brooks see the potential of merger as 'giving over' to God's mission by reaching out to new people in new places, in new ways, and with new vision. Bandy's works are a staple of my coaching and church consulting work, and the clear step-by-step process offered in *Church Mergers* is the resource we have been looking for. Bandy and Brooks address every question and every hope for God-sized possibilities."

—Lucinda S. Holmes, InConnexion Coaching and Consulting, LLC

"Mergers have become an increasingly popular approach for churches in distress. Unfortunately, mergers are too often promoted for survival rather than strategic reasons. In *Church Mergers*, Bandy and Brooks have provided a way to think through the strategic necessities of a merger. Using their combined experience in creative ministry and expertise in church demographic and lifestyle analysis, they show the reader how mergers can be used to develop approaches to ministry that can result in disciple making churches. This book is for pastors, denominational leaders, and church members who are considering mergers."

—Dan Jackson, Director of New Church Development, Florida Annual Conference of the United Methodist Church

"Only master-level coaches could have written this book. Packed with detailed strategies, incisive wisdom, and myth-busting data, *Church Mergers* is the *Fodor's Guide* to a new beginning in ministry."

—Sally Morgenthaler, author of *Worship Evangelism*

"Bandy and Brooks thoroughly unpack the perils and promise of church mergers. This essential guidebook will lead churches contemplating merger toward clarity of purpose and vision so that they gain traction in fulfilling their God-ordained mission. This is an absolute must read resource for judicatory leaders as well as pastors and laity involved in church mergers."

—Douglas Ruffle, Interim Associate General Secretary/ Executive Director—Path 1, New Church Starts, Discipleship Ministries

CHURCH MERGERS

A Guidebook for Missional Change

THOMAS G. BANDY AND PAGE M. BROOKS

An Alban Institute Book

ROWMAN & LITTLEFIELD
Lanham • Boulder • New York • London

Published by Rowman & Littlefield
A wholly owned subsidary of The Rowman & Littlefield Publishing Group, Inc.
4501 Forbes Boulevard, Suite 200, Lanham, Maryland 20706
www.rowman.com

Unit A, Whitacre Mews, 26-34 Stannary Street, London SE11 4AB, United Kingdom

British Library Cataloguing in Publication Information Available

Library of Congress Cataloging-in-Publication Data

Names: Bandy, Thomas G., 1950– author.
Title: Church mergers : a guidebook for missional change / Thomas G. Bandy and Page M. Brooks.
Description: Lanham : Rowman & Littlefield, 2016. | "An Alban Institute Book" — title page. | Includes bibliographical references and index.
Identifiers: LCCN 2016032734 (print) | LCCN 2016033692 (ebook) | ISBN 9781566997942 (cloth : alk. paper) | ISBN 9781566997959 (pbk. : alk. paper) | ISBN 9781566997966 (electronic)
Subjects: LCSH: Christian union.
Classification: LCC BX8.3 .B36 2016 (print) | LCC BX8.3 (ebook) | DDC 280/.042—dc23
LC record available at https://lccn.loc.gov/2016032734

♾™ The paper used in this publication meets the minimum requirements of American National Standard for Information Sciences—Permanence of Paper for Printed Library Materials, ANSI/NISO Z39.48-1992.

Printed in the United States of America

CONTENTS

Stage 3: A New Beginning

Essential Information

Why Merge? **1**

The decision for merger is about growing the church and changing the world . . . and not just survival.

The very idea of merger sends tremors of anxiety through a church. That anxiety is often negative—*What might we lose?*—or positive—*What might we gain?* In the past, the negative anxiety has usually been uppermost in the minds and hearts of church members. In the boom times of Christendom, when congregations multiplied in a culture favorable to faith, "merger" was synonymous with "failure." Today, however, the positive anxiety is often uppermost in church leaders' minds and hearts. In these lean times of post-Christendom, when congregations struggle to just hold their own in a culture suspicious of faith, "merger" has become synonymous with "opportunity."

Exploring the motivations of churches for merger will help leaders understand and prepare for the stress of changes to come. Anxiety is usually a mix of negative and positive feelings. In order for merger to be successful, people must primarily see it as an opportunity and a sign of faithful vitality.

Churches initially raise the question about merger because they are either experiencing a *panic attack* or a *kairos moment*. Admittedly, it is sometimes hard to tell the difference.

Most churches raise the question about merger or some other drastic option for congregational life and mission because they are experiencing a panic attack. A panic attack for an individual person occurs when he or she is suddenly overwhelmed by problems. Every aspect of life is a mess, one thing impacts another, and the person doesn't know where to even begin to sort out the problems.

A panic attack for churches is similar. Even when a church is well aware of looming issues, problems suddenly converge all at once. The panic may be precipitated by a financial crisis, natural disaster, death in the church family, disability of the pastor, or other major event. But often it is actually precipitated by a relatively small event that sets off a cascading effect on other church programs. In one church, all it took was a breakdown in kitchen appliances. This caused the cancellation of a community dinner, which contributed to a year-end deficit; and the crisis involved a safety inspection, which in turn caused a municipal inquiry about fire safety. Meanwhile, it also precipitated a quarrel between the matriarchs of the two leading church families, which led to lower worship attendance, which caused the pastor to request disability leave. It all happened in four weeks. The resulting panic attack led church people to ask: *Is it time for a merger?*

Sometimes, however, the question is raised out of a kairos moment. *Kairos* is a New Testament word that describes an unexpected moment of divine revelation that changes everything for the good. It is stressful, but it is positive. The greatest kairos moment is Christ himself. Paul says, "While we were still weak, at the *right time* Christ died for the ungodly" (Romans 5:6 New Revised Standard Version [NRSV]).[1] Interestingly, Paul even saw the impending shipwreck on his journey to Rome as a kairos moment (Acts 27:9–10). He discerns signs of God's positive action in even the most trying circumstances:

> For [God] says, "At an *acceptable time* I have listened to you, and on a day of salvation I have helped you." See, now is the acceptable time; see, now is the day of salvation! We are putting no obstacle in anyone's way, so that no fault may be found with our ministry, but as servants of God we have commended ourselves in every way: through great endurance, in afflictions, hardships, calamities, beatings, imprisonments, riots, labors, sleepless nights, hunger; by purity, knowledge, patience, kindness, holiness of spirit, genuine love, truthful speech, and the power of God; with the weapons of righteousness for the right hand and for the left; in honor and dishonor, in ill repute and good repute. . . . We have spoken frankly to you Corinthians; our heart is wide open to you. There is no restriction in our affections, but only in yours. (2 Corinthians 6:2–12)

Churches can interpret misfortune and stress in an entirely different light, as Paul did. They can see misfortune as an opportunity and even as an act of God that decisively changes the course of a congregation to walk more faithfully with God.

For example, the series of hurricanes that devastated the Gulf Coast in 2005 not only damaged church buildings but also shattered church infrastructures because so many church members and leaders were scattered as refugees away from home. Yet many churches in Slidell, New Orleans, Baton Rouge, and other small communities in Louisiana eventually realized that this was a kairos moment. Many of the usual differences between traditions, neighborhoods, races, and ethnicities were literally "washed away," and Christians came together in mutual support in extraordinary ways. Many small churches found new opportunities to both grow membership and bless neighborhoods through mergers and other collaborations.

Unfortunately, churches can go back and forth between panic attacks and kairos moments. Immediately after the hurricanes of 2005, church leaders experienced a panic attack. The magnitude and complexity of both church and community redevelopment were overwhelming. It took almost a year for many churches to see the disaster as a kairos moment. This did not take away their grief but did refocus their anxiety. They saw an opportunity to make radical changes to communities and congregations for the better. Mergers, partnerships, and outreach ministries sprang up in unexpected and exciting ways. However, by 2009 the window of opportunity began to close again. Once some of the immediate issues had been resolved, leadership attitudes went backward. Instead of experiencing a kairos moment, they reverted to panic attack. Changes might have been positive, but churches began to realize that the changes were also permanent. There was no going back to the old ways in the old days.

The attitude with which a person poses a question about drastic change makes a huge difference to the eventual outcome.

When the question is driven by a panic attack, the subsequent conversation becomes remarkably self-centered and fractious. Churches frequently rely on internal surveys to discover membership likes and dislikes. Inevitably, factions emerge. Bureaucracies grow. Committees multiply. Votes are taken, retaken, set aside, and taken again. Even if the congregation decides to merge, it cannot decide with whom to merge, because each faction has its own favorite partner. Very often, once the immediate crises are resolved or at least under control, the church reverses course and fails to follow through with the original plan. Panic attacks focus attention on maintaining the status quo.

When the question is driven by a kairos moment, the subsequent conversation is focused on God, God's purpose, and the opportunities to bless the communities beyond the church. Churches rely on prayer. Networks emerge. Partnerships grow. Outreach multiplies. Votes do not need to be second-guessed because there is greater clarity about mission goals. Leaders are trusted to do whatever it takes to achieve those goals. Even when immediate crises ease, the congregation does not hesitate to follow through with its original plan. Kairos moments focus attention on achieving mission results.

When leaders ask if it is time for drastic action, the first thing churches must do is test the attitude behind the question. If this is a panic attack, then any plans for radical action (mergers or other options for congregational life and mission) will almost certainly fail. Most mergers are driven by panic attacks. Most of these mergers fail. The few that do succeed can rarely be sustained, because the whole becomes less than the sum of the parts: Members leave rather than merge, and newcomers still avoid the church. The new budget is only fractionally higher than the combined budgets of the previous churches, and no less vulnerable to the deaths of important givers and inflationary costs in personnel and property maintenance. Within five to ten years, the merged church is in crisis.

It is better for a church to endure stress and pray hard than leap into a strategic planning process that it does not have the unity or strength to sustain. We can think of one formerly prestigious church on particularly hard times. The church struggled in every way, with aging members, declining numbers, financial deficits, factional disagreements, and pastoral-relations strife. It seemed like the breakdown of its air conditioning system was the last straw. Toxic fumes forced the city to condemn the sanctuary. Yet rather than succumb to a panic attack, the congregation moved to its gymnasium for worship and started to pray. Through endurance and perseverance, its prayers were eventually blessed by a bigger, bolder vision.

Unexpected Visions

2

God is bursting the boundaries of tradition and denomination,
location and culture, to revitalize the Christian Movement.

God's vision has always been *to thrive*, and not just *to survive*. We see in scripture than even when God's people were enslaved or exiled, they were never content with just being a righteous remnant that endured until the end of time. They took risks. They left Egypt and journeyed to the Promised Land. They abandoned the comforts of Babylon and rebuilt Jerusalem. They believed in God's promise to Abraham and Sarah to multiply their descendants. We see in history that even when the church was persecuted and in hiding, it never gave up on God's mission, and it continued multiplying disciples to transform the world. Jesus told the disciples that God did not give us talents in order to bury them in the bank to collect minimal interest, but to invest them in mission so that God's grace would multiply to bless others many times over.

It is helpful to understand God's vision organically rather than just institutionally. When a child is born, we want the infant to thrive. The ability of a child to thrive can be defined in many statistical ways (e.g., gaining weight and height, eating and sleeping well, moving eyes and limbs, interacting with mother and father, etc.) Yet it can also be measured in other, perhaps even more important, ways that are qualitative rather than quantitative. The child smiles and laughs; explores and enlarges his or her world; experiments with new things and generates new ideas; and gradually becomes accountable to the expectations of family life.

The urgency to merge grew exponentially in the latter half of the twentieth century as church attendance declined, charitable giving to churches plateaued, and overhead costs for property and personnel soared. The high-water mark for most churches and denominations was around 1965. Everything after that has been a struggle—and for many a losing battle. It seemed logical even then that smaller, declining churches should merge. Yet despite the best efforts of church leaders, most mergers failed. The whole was smaller than the sum of the parts, and after a few years of seeming stability, the merged institutions started declining again.

Many reasons have been proposed to explain this. However, the single, underlying reason for the failure of past mergers is that *their vision was too small*. Denominational loyalties were just not strong enough to break local traditions. Geographical proximities were just not strong enough to overcome institutional competitiveness. Quest for quality and the lure of larger resources were just not enough to motivate risk-taking and eliminate self-centeredness. The limitations imposed on the vision to merge were too small to be taken seriously.

Today God has revealed a bigger vision: God's churches *must* thrive so that God's mission can grow. Mergers are successful when they dare to cross the boundaries of waning Christendom.

The first boundary to be crossed is tradition. The old categories that used to divide churches matter less than ever before. It used to be that "mainstream" and "evangelical" Protestants, Eucharistic and non-Eucharistic churches, historic and Pentecostal traditions, or "denominational" and "independent" churches never mixed. Mergers might happen *within* groups, but never *between* groups.

God's vision is bursting these limitations. As more and more people drift farther and farther away from Christian faith and practice, the old distinctions become less and less meaningful. The key to a successful merger is no longer internally consistent duty and dogma, but externally effective relevance and immanence. In other words, churches are finding ways to collaborate in meaningful ways to change neighborhoods, cities, regions, and the world. They are determined to help people *experience* the power of God and the real presence of Jesus the Christ, rather than cajole people to *agree* with every nuance of polity, liturgy, and doctrine.

This does not mean that tradition is no longer important. Certainly it is, but it's just not everything. Mergers are based on the greater and deeper mystery of God that lies behind our polities and dogmas, that can never be fully contained or fully defined by human acts and minds, and that stretches our imaginations and judges our stereotypes. Christians can love, respect, and serve without always agreeing with each other or behaving exactly alike. Mergers are about diversity, not uniformity, and as such they are more credible to publics that value uniqueness more than conformity.

The second boundary to be crossed is denomination. The tribes, franchises, and organizations that once guarded their memberships and competed for attention also matter less than ever before. Some might say that the ecumenical movement stalled because declining denominations became more inward and protective in general. Yet in regard to mergers, the ecumenical movement stalled because it did not go far enough to ensure real success. Ecumenical cooperation tended to be focused in very rural or remote areas, or in urban core settings that were exceedingly poor and often dangerous. These mergers were more about rotating clergy than sustaining leadership credibility, dividing income proportionately among institutions rather than sharing money generously in the community, and sustaining a denominational "presence" in dire circumstances rather than transforming communities for justice and sustainable living.

God's vision is bursting denominational inwardness and expanding ecumenical expectations. As more and more people lose respect for top-down institutional demands and surrender tribal allegiances, the old ecclesiologies are less and less important. The key to a successful merger is not professional leadership and denominational subsidy, but lay empowerment and entrepreneurship. In other words, churches are finding ways to reduce overhead costs for personnel through volunteer training and team deployment. This sustains leadership credibility in the community over the long term, and focuses congregational life on day-to-day spiritual disciplines rather than occasional worship attendance. And this encourages merged churches to develop nonprofit organizations that can seek funds from multiple directions.

Again, this does not mean that denominations are unimportant. It means that denominations have a different role to play in successful church mergers. Denominations no longer tell local churches what to do with property, programs, and personnel; nor do they try to impose ideologies and policies that handcuff innovative leaders. Instead they define essential boundaries of faith and spiritual practice that must be honored, give permission for local innovation, and equip leaders with nonprofit training and technology upgrades for more effective social service and networking.

The third boundary to be crossed is culture. Most church mergers in the past were designed on the principle of ethnic homogeneity. In other words, the people involved in the mergers were all Caucasian, or all African American, or all Hispanic, or all from a particular country of origin and speaking a common first language. The mergers that succeed today, however, are designed on the principle of lifestyle compatibility. Church leaders recognize that there is diversity within *each* ethnic group; that some lifestyles within one group are more compatible with lifestyles of another group; and that people no longer bond around a common ancestry or first language, but around particular behavior patterns and ministry expectations.

And so God is bursting cultural homogeneity. At the time of this writing there are over seventy-one distinct lifestyle segments in North America.[1] This includes at least twelve distinct lifestyle segments with high proportions of Hispanic and Latino people, and at least ten distinct lifestyle segments with high proportions of African American people. People today connect around lifestyle habits and gravitate more and more to cultural diversity. They are willing to learn the basics of a second language, alter their worship preferences, adapt their learning methodologies, and gather around different small-group affinities because they behave in similar ways beyond age, race, language, national origin, family status, or even income brackets. Mergers succeed because the lifestyle segments represented by each partner are compatible with each other even though they may look different.

Once again, this does not mean that race, language, and national origins are unimportant. There is a unique dignity and identity for each culture that is precious and should be preserved. This simply means that these old demographic markers are no longer the *definitive* ways people gather together in a congregation. Publics are migrating more rapidly than ever before from one lifestyle to the next, and they expect their churches to keep up with them.

The last boundary to be crossed is about size and location. Mergers in the past focused on geographical proximity and proportionately small memberships. We assumed that the only congregations that would *want* to merge would be small, and that the only congregations that *could* merge would be physically close together. What we discovered more often than not was that small congregations liked to be small "families" rather than extended networks of relationships and that they really didn't want to merge if they could avoid it. Each "family" formed an impenetrable circle that worried more about losing one of its own than gaining new people. We also discovered that congregations that were geographically close couldn't merge anyway, because neighborhood rivalries and long-time prejudices couldn't be overcome. They would rather fight than unite.

God is bursting our assumptions about location and size. The migrations and transitions of people have extended the reach of most churches far beyond their former "parish" areas. Members remain quite active through social media and easy transportation, even though they live far away. And there are new tactics shaped by new technologies that help them sustain intimacy and shared ministries over long distances. The more churches recognize this new reality, the more they understand how mergers advance God's mission and grow their memberships. Large churches are merging with large churches, large churches are merging with small churches, and small churches are merging with several partners all at once.

This is all part of the emerging "multisite" and "microcommunity" strategies that are reshaping congregational mission regionally, nationally, and globally. There can be one church in many physical and even digital locations. The basic unit of mission is not the member but the team. The basic unit of fellowship is the small group and not the worship service. And the basic financial plan is not the unified budget but the designated cost center. The glue that binds the church together is not the tradition, denomination, ethnicity, or facility, but the shared and embedded DNA of core values, bedrock beliefs, motivating vision, and strategic *heartburst* (see chapter 3) to bless people other than themselves.

Get Moving! 3

The goal of a merger is to get stuck churches moving forward again!

The spiritual imperative for the church is: *Get Moving!* The first word of the Great Commission is: *Go!* This is why the outcome of the experience with Jesus that was described in the Gospels is not so much a Christian *church* as it is a Christian *movement*. The church is the vehicle (and perhaps, in the postmodern world, only one kind of vehicle) in which disciples of Christ travel.

The question to be asked of a church is: *What will it take to get this church moving?* If the church is moving but too slowly and not far, then the question to be asked is: *What will it take to move faster and get farther?* The questions are always about movement. The worries are all about slowing down and losing traction or veering off course and losing direction.

Since for better or worse America's primary mode of travel is the automobile, the analogy that addresses the key questions about Christian movement is most clearly explained with an automotive metaphor in mind. There are two kinds of mechanic today: mechanics who *restore* cars and mechanics who *repair* cars.

The former are hobbyists. They love icons, originals, or antiques. They restore cars to their original condition, with original parts, so that the cars can be admired in shows, win awards, and preserve memories. Yes, the motor runs and the car operates, but it will only be driven short distances, slowly and carefully, so that the owners and their friends can enjoy the ride without much risk. Mainly, the vehicle is parked in the garage and waxed every week.

The latter are really *drivers*. They love speed, utility, and function. They really don't just repair cars; they improve cars. They tune them up, upgrade with better and more durable parts, install new safety equipment and GPS, replace the tires, and return them to the open road. They may not care much about how the cars look. Their ambition is to get somewhere. They want their vehicles to travel fast, far, and safely. Mainly, they want to *move on down the road,* and pick up as many hitchhikers as they can on the way.

Mergers are about movement, not maintenance; and purposefulness rather than preservation. The purpose of a merger is to repair and repurpose the spiritual vehicle of a church in order to return it to functionality for its journey on the road to mission. Churches may get spare parts from other churches of the same make and model, but they may also incorporate or customize new parts from completely different sources and organizational sectors. When the merged church returns to the open road, it may not look the same. It may be a hybrid of several churches. It may have the chassis of a Methodist church and the wheels of a Baptist church. It may have the fuel pump of a Presbyterian church and the power steering of an Episcopal church. It may have the capacity of a megachurch and the intimacy of a house church. It may have the upholstery of a cathedral, but the accountability and fuel efficiency of a faith-based nonprofit.

The point is that the church is not for show, but for travel. Churches merge because they are not getting anywhere, or not going very far, or not moving very fast . . . and they desperately want to get going, and go as far as they can as fast as they can get there.

In order to start any journey, you don't have to know every mechanical detail or predict every bump in the highway. You really only have to know three things:

- Who is driving?
- Where are we going?
- Will the passengers behave themselves?

The moment merger is considered, many churches immediately immerse themselves in the details of polities, personnel, property, money, programs, liturgies, and other assorted tactics. All these need to be addressed along the way, but they do not need to be resolved in order to start the trip. Indeed, the tactics are often blown out of proportion and take on an importance they do not deserve; and the essentials about who is leading and where we are going are overlooked altogether. Churches are so busy grieving about the past, or preserving the harmony of the present, that they forget what is really sacred for the future.

This, of course, is what mechanics who aim to *restore* cars also do. Their hobby is preservation. They must worry about the details. They must be obsessed about vintage seating and upholstery, accurate paint dyes, archaic technologies, and all the minutia of restoration, because they know some fellow hobbyist (oldest member, history buff, academic, or denominational agent) will quickly spy the smallest detail that seems out of place or politically incorrect. The fact that the restored vehicle cannot sustain hard use, or travel fast or far, is not important. What is important is the collective sigh of fellow hobbyists that see the church as a living memory.

Who Is Driving?

The right answer, of course, is that God *is driving*. Language varies. Leaders might say that "Christ is the guide" or that "the Holy Spirit is in control." The point is that this is not just a theological abstraction. It must be the practical truth. There is often a great deal of confusion about who is driving in a church merger. Is it the pastor of church A or the pastor of church B . . . or another pastor altogether? Is it the board of church A or perhaps the trustees of church B? Is it the bishop or the church development committee of the middle judicatory? Very often it is an ad hoc committee that includes everyone from the president of the women's society to the representative of the youth group. They are all intent on protecting their special interests.

Fundamentally, however, it must be God who is driving. All leaders must surrender their special interests to the single purpose of Christ. It is the mission that matters and not the agendas of individual leaders. The "driver" of the church merger must be the most "sold-out" servant of Christ. This is the one who stakes the most, risks the most, and surrenders the most for the sake of God's realm. Over the years I have found myself repeating the same question whenever leadership for a church merger is being selected: "With your first breath in the morning and your last penny at night, will it be 'me first' or 'God's mission'?" The leader of a merger needs to be the person who is most prepared to sacrifice personal preference and membership privileges for the sake of blessing strangers to grace.

In theory, the best person to lead the merger process is the person or group who will have to live with the merger results. This means that mergers are best managed *locally* rather than *denominationally*. The diversity of the post-Christendom present that has replaced the uniformity of Christendom past means that it is almost impossible to legislate a merger "from above" or impose a merger by remote control. What "makes sense" at the head office often makes no sense whatever in context. The best mergers are led from within. The leaders who step up to organize the merger are the same leaders who will eventually direct the new organization in mission.

In practice, however, even the best local leaders often need help from outside. Local churches are often so enmeshed in corporate addictions—so enslaved by "sacred cows" that include sacred objects, sacred properties, sacred relationships, and sacred processes—that no one can break the addictions from within. It's not just that prophets are often unacceptable in their own hometowns, but that even the most well-meaning leader is entangled in past politics. Only someone from outside can challenge the power of membership privilege and turn hearts back to the original purpose of Christ.

There was a time when denominational officers or staff—or neighboring pastors—could do this, but that day is largely over. Many middle judicatories can no longer afford the staff. More importantly, denominational officers are often preoccupied by their own worries about organizational survival and unable to challenge churches and take risks for Christ's mission. They tend to be more worried about losing financial support than reaching out to include seekers and mature new Christians. Denominationally led mergers are often timid and slow because they are more concerned about appeasement than opportunity.

Similarly, neighboring pastors are often handicapped in helping local churches pursue mergers. Competition between churches and among clergy has grown exponentially as the church declines in North America. Even the most well-meaning pastors can have difficulty setting aside self-interest when they offer advice or guidance to a neighboring congregation. Moreover, neighboring clergy often have the same blind spots when it comes to interpreting demographic trends and mission opportunities.

The best help for local leadership today comes from independent consultants or from the pastor and staff of a megachurch or multisite church. They are more likely to have the clarity to focus on essentials, the expertise to challenge corporate addictions, and the objectivity to see emerging demographic trends and mission opportunities. They help the participating churches shed membership privilege and manage risk. Local leadership, aided by outside help, can ensure a smooth transition from "conception" to "implementation."

The most essential characteristic of leadership in a merger, however, is that the leaders have the credibility and courage to ask the question

Jesus posed to St. Peter: *Do you love me more than these?* Remember how the resurrected Christ confronted the disciples when they had returned to old habits in the familiar surroundings of their hometown. Jesus pointedly referred to familiar surroundings, comfortable routines, and long-time friendships—and then asked the disciples if they loved him *more* than those things. Are you willing to stake everything on Christ? Are you prepared to risk life and lifestyle for Christ's mission?

When churches talk about merger, among the first questions will be who will "drive" the conversation and who will eventually lead the merged church? If that decision is based on seniority or personality, the merger conversation will quickly break down. A faithful, mission-driven merger cannot be achieved if the priority is to honor denominational status or individual charisma. Even if that decision is based on skills for organization, communication, fundraising, or conflict resolution, the success of the merger will ultimately be in jeopardy.

The key requirements of leadership are *credibility* and *courage*. The credibility comes from the depth and discipline of spiritual life, and the transparency of the leader to reveal Jesus Christ. The courage comes from the readiness of the leader (and his or her family) to stake life and lifestyle on achieving God's purpose over institutional survival. Innovation must always trump tradition, even as tradition must always inform innovation. The credibility of the leader to balance innovation and tradition is important. But the courage of the leader to prioritize innovation *over* tradition is crucial.

The inescapable truth in any merger is that there will be losses and gains in membership. The radical courage of the leader is that he or she must choose *who* will be lost and *who* will be gained. This is driven by the 20-60-20 rule of churches and change. At any given time, 20% of the people will resist any change and threaten to leave if it occurs. Another 20% of the people will insist on change and threaten to leave if it does not occur. And 60% of the people are content with the church as it is, but are willing to follow a credible and courageous leader wherever they choose to go. Therefore, the stress in a merger is caused by the contest between the two minorities who try to persuade the silent majority. The leader is the critical difference in that stress.

Most mergers fail because the leader worries more about who will be lost than about who will be gained. The leader worries more about losing a handful of good givers or active members whom he or she knows by name—but does not worry enough about hundreds of potentially generous volunteers and active seekers that are not yet part of the church and whose names are as yet unknown. It sounds logical, and perhaps even easy, to lose a few in order to reach many. But in fact that approach is counterintuitive and very difficult for most churches. It requires enormous credibility and courage for a leader to persuade merging churches to act.

Those mergers that succeed are willing to lose a few old friends in order to make many new friends. They prefer to honor the 20% who are restless for growth and want to move forward, rather than honor the 20% who are resistant to growth and want to preserve the past. There are always people among the 60% who are compassionate toward all and ask if the church cannot do both. It takes courage for the leader to state the hard truth that you cannot do both.

Why can't you honor both the restless and the resistant so that everybody is happy? The first reason this is impossible is that there is no compromise that will satisfy both parties. Any compromise based on fundamental dissatisfaction with a merger will eventually lead to the departure of old friends anyway. You are simply postponing the inevitable. The second reason this is impossible is that the more time you waste seeking a compromise, the more likely the restless 20% will leave the church in frustration. Resistant people never have to win the argument. They only have to draw out the discussion as long as possible. Eventually the restless ones will give up and leave. The 60% who are content anyway will continue to submit to those who resist change. The merger will never happen, and the individual church will likely close by virtue of irrelevance.

The mergers that succeed choose leaders with the credibility to allow tradition to inform innovation, but with the courage to prioritize innovation over tradition. These may not be the people with the greatest seniority or status in the denomination. They may not be the people with the most charisma and popular appeal. They are people of profound spiritual life and discipline and a life history of staking everything for the sake of the Gospel. In an ideal world, the same leaders who lead the conversation about merger are the leaders who lead the merged church. They may be the leaders that select the new pastor. Credibility and courage define the leader.

Where Are We Going?

The right answer, of course, is that *we are going to the New Jerusalem.* If there is a city, region, or state of being in mind, it is summed up by that metaphor. The church is moving toward the Realm of God, where Christ is fully with the people, the sun never sets, and people will weep no more. Again, this is not just a theological abstraction, but a practical aspiration.

The goal of the church is more than keeping a community alive or a neighborhood healthy. It is more than an agent of socialization and assimilation, and more than a nonprofit for social action and health care.

Like vehicle headlights illuminating the road ahead, the vision cast by the leaders of a merger is bigger than institutional survival and social compact. It must be a big, inclusive, audacious, inspiring vision that elicits incredible sacrifice from anyone riding on the bus, and captures the imagination of anyone watching the bus go by.

If the issue of merger *leadership* turns on surrender to Christ, then the issue of merger *vision* depends on the church's unique experience of Christ. The merger forces the congregation to ask and answer this question: *What specifically is it about our wondrous experience with Christ that we urgently need to share with other people in our neighborhood, postal code, or city?*

Elsewhere Tom has described seven distinct experiences of Christ that not only characterize a faith community's identity and purpose, but which also draw the attention of specific lifestyle segments in any given mission field.[1] Churches usually emphasize in worship and outreach one or two of these experiences:

- Christ as Promise Keeper, blessing people with inspiration and hope for tomorrow
- Christ as Higher Power, blessing people with transformation and a fresh start
- Christ as Spiritual Guide, blessing people to cope with daily struggles and navigate life's ambiguities
- Christ as Teacher, blessing people with insight into eternal truths and authentic relationships
- Christ as Healer, blessing people with physical, emotional, relational, and spiritual wholeness and health
- Christ as Vindicator, blessing people with justice and raising their self-esteem
- Christ as Shepherd, blessing people with acceptance, belonging, and companionship

The vision that is cast for any church, and especially necessary for any merger, is a combination of its inward joy and its outward compassion. It is the precious gift that the church wants to give away with no institutional strings attached. It's a gift! It will change lives! And it is free!

We call this illumination a *heartburst*. The church cannot move forward unless its heart bursts for someone other than itself. The trouble with most declining churches is that their hearts burst only for themselves. Outreach is more about attracting new members who can pay bills, sustain traditional programs, and keep the infrastructure standing, than blessing strangers to grace with hope for tomorrow. A vision for survival, however, is not a heartburst but an ego trip, and God will not honor it. Even if the merger succeeds, the whole will always be less than the sum of the parts; and institutional decline will only plateau for a time and then accelerate again.

It really is true that the first shall be last, and the last must be first. Jesus was right when he said that only those who lose themselves will find themselves. Most mergers are fundamentally selfish. They cast a vision of self-importance. People are motivated by self-preservation. They are so eager to save themselves that they lose themselves. Successful mergers are just the opposite. They are fundamentally selfless. They cast a vision of blessing. People are motivated by generosity.

The question that must be answered by any church—and early on in any conversation about church merger—is about "heartburst." Exactly who are we called to bless? Who are they? Where are they? What are they searching to find? What hope are they yearning to experience?

The primary mission field of a church is defined by the average distance people in that region travel to work or shop. People will travel about the same distance to arrive at the spiritual destination that meets their needs. The real compatibility of churches considering merger is not based on the preferences of people who are already members, but the yearnings of people who are outside the church and are the object of urgent compassion by members of the church. Churches merge because they have compatible *mission fields*, not just because they have compatible *memberships*.

This is reflected in their mission statements and measurable outcomes. Churches considering a merger must compare both. A great mission statement is not a vague desire to love the world, nor is it a short list of program priorities and stylistic preferences. It is a clear articulation of *whom* the church wants to bless, and *what blessing* it hopes to communicate.

The litmus test of a mission statement is the summary of measurable outcomes. If a mission statement is too vague, there are no outcomes to measure. This usually suggests that the church actually exists to preserve the harmony of a club, rather than sustain a genuine mission to bless strangers to grace. If a mission statement is merely a summary of program and preference, the measurable outcomes merely articulate the status quo. This usually suggests that the church exists as a support group for dysfunctional clients, rather than a launching pad for healthy outreach. Both ways, these churches see themselves as "righteous remnants" in the midst of a godless society; and the real measurable outcome is decline itself. Statistics that demonstrate decline, stories of lamentation, and negative feedback from the community are actually all *verifications* that the church is fulfilling its destiny!

Healthy mergers are based on healthy mission statements; and outcomes that measure statistical growth, stories of joy and victory, and positive feedback from the community. The churches are clear about *whom* they want to bless and serious about measuring statistics of success. They are clear about *what blessings* they want to share and serious about measuring stories of success and feedback that tests credibility. Two or more churches want to consider a merger because they see that *they are clearly going in the same direction and to a common destination.*

Will the Passengers Behave Themselves?

This may seem like an odd question, but it is crucial to complete the journey. The church in transition is best compared to a school bus rather than a private automobile. It is not driven by a patriarch or matriarch, but by the spiritual leaders (usually the pastor and board) of the diverse congregation. The bus is traveling down the road to the Promised Land. But will the passengers behave like Christians or pagans? Will their comportment be sacred or secular? Will they fight with one another, yell at each other, bully the weak, tease the shy, throw garbage out the window, harass the bus driver, and generally behave like selfish brats? Or will the passengers honor each other, listen to each other, defend the weak, encourage the shy, smile at the pedestrians on the sidewalk, respect the driver, and generally behave like Christians?

Mergers are most successful in high trust environments. These are churches that practice a high standard of accountability for core values and bedrock beliefs. They intentionally behave like Christians, exercising the *fruits of the Spirit* (love, joy, peace, patience, kindness, generosity, faithfulness, gentleness, self-control). They intervene if any church member behaves contrarily. Since we are all human and mergers are stressful, people will make mistakes. But when they do, and they are reminded how Christians behave, they sincerely repent, seek forgiveness, and try harder.

Mergers often bring out the worst in a church, rather than the best in the church. This, of course, largely depends on the attitude of the church members when they board the bus. If their attitude is shaped by panic, and their goals are guided by self-interest, then they tend to behave competitively, confrontationally, and rudely. This is how members in any organization often behave in the world. Christians, however, are supposed to not behave like the world, but like Christ. If their attitude in boarding the bus is shaped by opportunity, and their goals are guided by the higher purpose of God's mission to redeem and bless the world, then they tend to behave respectfully and collaboratively.

Imagine a school bus with unruly passengers who are unable to hold themselves accountable to a higher standard. The chaos and backbiting gets so bad that the driver is distracted, misses the right turn, and gets lost. Even worse, the driver become so frustrated that he or she stops the bus, gets out, and gives up, which forces the church to hire a new bus driver who will have the same problems with the same results. Unfortunately, that is how many churches behave and why many church mergers fail. Church mergers will only succeed if the members of the participating churches *intentionally hold one another accountable to behave like Christians!*

The good news is that the merger journey will probably be successful if all three elements are present: If the spiritual leaders are driving, the higher purpose of God's call to bless the world is enthusiastically embraced, and the participants behave like Christians, then the merger will eventually succeed. Yes, there will be many unexpected bumps in the road and surprises in the future. The people will have a lot to learn and a lot to discuss, but all that is secondary.

Most mergers begin with a consensus to follow Christ no matter what the cost. Their spiritual leaders are empowered to explore the possibility of merger strategically, prayerfully, and purposefully. The members are expected to participate in the quest sensitively, generously, and faithfully. The drivers take their seats, the passengers climb on board, and all sing songs of hope and joy as they move forward into the unknown.

Steps on the Journey 4
Four Churches Finding
Their Way into the Future

Every merger process is unique, but not necessarily for the reasons you might think. They are unique because the context and calling of every church are special. The demographic and lifestyle mix in every community (even in rural and remote contexts) is complex and nuanced in ways that shape congregational culture and ministry practices differently even among churches belonging to the same denomination. Therefore, the call to mission for each congregation must be more sharply focused than ever before, and it is harder to find two or more congregations that are truly prepared to travel the same path.

On the other hand, the merger process can be more standardized than you might think. First of all, denominational identities and polities are less important than ever before. Most denominations recognize this and have become far more flexible in facilitating mergers between previously unlikely partners. Collaborations between denominations are increasingly common. Second, the mix of systemic dysfunctions and healthful principles is remarkably similar in every congregation. Regardless of context or denomination, the stories of decline and the leverage points for renewal are remarkably parallel.

Many leaders assume that the decision to merge is made in a single, scary, radical leap. That only happens when churches have let things go for too long and didn't have time to look before they leapt. In fact, mergers unfold in four distinct steps, each step marked by a decision to move forward.

- Merger *in Principle:* The first decision is to support the decision in principle, that is, as a real possibility for effective, sustainable ministry.

Potentially merging churches form a "vision team" (see chapter 7) to build trust, discern vision, do the research, and explore the options.

- Merger *in Practice:* The second decision is to merge into one church by choosing a new board and a new name, worshipping together, and developing an asset management strategy.
- Merger *in Fact:* The third decision is to merge assets, choose a location, and develop a staffing or leadership strategy.
- Merger *in Ministry:* The fourth decision is to keep, call, or appoint new leadership for both program development and administrative support. Then develop a basic strategic plan to improve programs, initiate new ideas, and terminate ineffective tactics.

It sounds simpler than it really is. There are many nuances and challenges to the process of moving people from grief to hope, and many surprises unique to churches and their contextual realities that will reshape the process along the way.

Here we introduce two stories involving two pairs of churches in conversations about merger. These are "true stories" in the sense that they are composites of our experiences in guiding mergers. Both illustrate the successful merge process.

Merger 1: Urbanization and the Shift to the Suburbs

The story of two churches caught up in the migration from the city to the suburbs

Wesley and Asbury are United Methodist churches in the urban sprawl of a major city. Their city is typical of many fast-growing areas like Philadelphia, Chicago, Omaha, Charlotte, Nashville, and San Diego. These cities reflect new urban realities in which population growth has outgrown transportation infrastructure and diversified far beyond the old stereotypes of race, age, and education.

Wesley is a historic, white, middle-class church of senior matriarchs and aging boomers educated in the old liberal arts tradition. It was once the prestige church of a satellite suburb with 1000 members and 750 in worship. Now it is an invisible church hidden behind high-rise apartments with 200 members (mostly relocated miles away or in nursing homes) and an average of 75 in worship. It has a strong sense of sacred space, but also provides space for several nonprofit organizations for day care and food distribution. The pastor has announced his retirement next year, and it is unclear whether the church can afford full-time ministry.

Asbury was established in the glory days of the 1960s. It's a black church with a mix of families and singles, with a large representation of upwardly mobile African American professionals. The congregation once had a reputation for social action, but it struggles to find identity as the neighborhood becomes more multicultural and dominated by young singles. Ten years ago it had 500 members (mostly active) and 300 in worship. Now it has 150 members and 100 in worship on a good day in between amateur sports seasons. It believes in youth ministry, but has a relatively small youth group, and it hosts addiction intervention programs. The church has experienced the tragic death of one pastor and a scandal with another. Its young pastor is the fourth pastor in six years.

Merger 2: Urban Renewal and the Transformation of the City

The story of two churches in
the multicultural mix of the urban core

Faith Temple and Pine Street Presbyterian belong to two different traditions, but they are located in the same urban core of a major city. Their city is typical of many economically depressed and multicultural urban core environments like Newark, Cleveland, St. Louis, Jacksonville, New Orleans, and Los Angeles. These cities reflect the urban realities of changing economies that have created housing crises and left legacies of pollution, underemployment, and poor education.

Faith Temple is an independent evangelical church with a long local history, and is loosely connected with a Baptist association. The congregation's formal membership is scattered across the city, and its average worship attendance numbers about sixty and is quite ethnically diverse. The church building needs major upgrades, and parking is limited; but the education wing has been updated to house a K–8 Christian charter school. The church sustains itself through rental income to the school, but the school needs more capital investment.

Pine Street Presbyterian Church is also a formerly prestigious church that has experienced a significant congregational split over a public-policy position by the denomination. The pastor and a large part of the congregation left the denomination. The remaining congregation is led by an interim minister and pursuing a visioning process. It rents space to several small ethnic churches, but is struggling to make ends meet and debating how to cut staff. The church is not known for any particular outreach ministry, but it has an excellent choir and historic pipe organ. They currently have an interim minister. She has served the church for about eighteen months.

The leaders and boards of each pair of churches have decided to merge *in principle* and begin their respective merger conversations. The conversation has been given some urgency for Wesley and Asbury because the bishop wants to model bi-racial ministry—and cut back on denominational subsidies. The conversation for Faith Temple and Pine Street has been given some urgency because the mayor and neighborhood constituencies need healthy churches that can sustain healthy neighborhoods.

There are two "partners" that will emerge from time to time in these churches' conversations about merger. The first is an independent consultant. This consultant is independent either because he or she is experienced in multiple denominational traditions and politics, and is not biased in one way or another, or he or she comes from beyond the politics of church and community and brings a larger perspective of ministry effectiveness and relevance. Consultants bring an objectivity that helps churches overcome control, reduce stress, and deepen their understanding.

The second partner is a multisite megachurch. Such churches are springing up around most major urban centers and have a strategy of acquiring congregations that are well below critical mass for survival, infusing them with a new attitude and resources, and creating what is essentially a clone to the mother church in a new location. Their strategy may or may not be helpful, but their experience and their passion for mission are very helpful. And their leaders are almost always ready to offer advice on innovative ministries, nonprofit outreach, lay empowerment, and staff development. In our story, this church is called "Harvest Community Church."

The True Cost of Discipleship   5
Anticipating the Real Price of Success

Successful mergers rarely begin with top-down directions from the head office of a denomination. They almost always begin bottom-up from the urgent, candid, conversations of pastors and other church leaders.

Merger 1: Wesley and Asbury

It was mid-January when the idea of merger was seriously considered. Both Methodist congregations had had their annual Charge Conference in late November. Advent and Christmas were behind them, and they were anticipating annual leadership retreats. These pastors normally met for lunch every Monday, and this time the district superintendent joined them to follow up on the merger proposal.

The best one can say is that the pastors were each cautiously excited. They each wanted their churches to be relevant to their changing communities, but they realized how stressful the merger idea might be for their congregations.

After the initial enthusiasm, the group began to discuss the inevitable objections. One problem was unexpected and unique to their denominational context. The district superintendent told them that there was no blueprint, and it was up to them to find a way. The bishop only promised to leave future pastoral appointments open-ended, but (contrary to past experience) there was to be no top-down imposition of a strategic plan. Mergers based on top-down decisions had all failed. Successful mergers required bottom-up ownership.

However, the district superintendent recommended a number of books for background reading, and referred the pastors to the websites of a number of outside consultants who could offer good advice about the real "cost" of a merger.

Merger 2: Faith Temple and Pine Street

It was the first Monday in February that the idea of merger was first raised seriously. The pastors of these two churches had been meeting regularly for prayer and mutual support. They often collaborated with each other in ministry. They shared outreach projects. They covered for one another during illness or vacation. They shared similar challenges in the church and in the community. Most importantly they encouraged each other in spiritual life, in the struggles to sustain the church and bless the community. On this first Monday in February, both pastors had just completed their annual meetings. The intersection of prayer and reality prompted the discussion.

The idea of merger sounded wonderful. It seemed but a further step in a collaboration that had been unfolding between these churches for years. Why not merge? It actually made perfect sense to merge. Together they could go deeper in faith and go further to bless the community. They could pool their volunteer and financial resources. They could downsize bureaucracy and reduce financial overhead. They could worship in inspiring numbers and impact the community with more energy.

After the initial enthusiasm, the pastors began to discuss the inevitable objections. One problem was unique to their urban context: They each represented very different traditions. Their theologies were alike, but different. Their spiritual practices were familiar, yet foreign. Their organizations had parallel committees, but their decision-making habits were different. The Presbyterian pastor had strong obligations to a middle judicatory, and worried about her career. The other pastor was suspicious of denominations and worried about his reputation.

Given their hopes and anxieties, they initiated additional conversation with the senior pastor of Harvest Community Church, the megachurch at the edge of the city. That pastor was able to share his experience of the struggles and joys of church growth.

Beyond these unique problems, both sets of pastors faced similar objections. The first common objection was that each church tended to define itself by what it was *not* rather than by what it was. Unclear about their own identity and purpose, the one thing each church did believe was that it was not like the other. Each church had a distinct culture. While many members among the churches got along, others did not. Each church included elements of the community that were not present—and perhaps unwelcome—in the other churches.

The next objection was that both pastors felt a duty to support their own program and support staff. Moreover, each church had a core group of volunteer leaders. There just wouldn't be room in a merged church for all the staff to have a job. A staff leader might lose his or her job; a volunteer leader might lose authority.

Then, of course, there would be objections about property. Each church would expect everyone would come to *its* building. Each church would assume everyone would sit in its pews, enjoy its stained glass windows, and hold its hymnbooks. Emotional ties to properties and technologies were huge. Just imagine the upset, turmoil, and grief! Not to mention the competition, jealousy, and anger!

And finally there was the money. True, each of the four churches was in difficult financial shape. Each annual meeting had just passed deficit budgets. Capital savings were rapidly being used up. Even if they sold property to raise capital, heaven only knew where the money would come from to merge a church, build or renovate new space, and hire or redeploy and train staff. Members were aging, and money was tight.

The amazing thing, however, is that neither pair of pastors were discouraged. Indeed, each surprised the other by remaining so enthusiastic. Why? They recognized in each other a clarity about identity and calling. Each pastor had a deep faith in the real presence of Christ in their lives and in the life of the community; each knew that, although they had their disagreements, they all lived by the same code of respect and love. Each one had a deep aversion to letting *the* church die and a readiness to make whatever sacrifice needed to be made in order for *the* church to thrive. And each one shared a deep compassion for the diverse and sometimes desperate community in which they lived.

And here was the best news of all for both sets of pastors: they knew several leaders in each of their churches who shared that vision. They were not alone. So despite all the objections, it was time to get serious.

Church mergers inevitably bring significant changes. The correct process can minimize the stress. Church members begin to realize that not only will some leaders, programs, and assets change, but some may disappear; and new ideas may take church members further out of their comfort zones. No matter how honestly churches reality-test their situations, or how enthusiastically they embrace the bigger vision to multiply disciples and bless the world, there are still many sacred cows, assumed privileges, and personal and factional agendas that lurk in the background.

Churches must intentionally count the cost of discipleship and plan how to address inevitable stress. Many mergers fail because planners think their job is done once they have an action plan. They are unprepared for the backlash. Misunderstandings and conflicts emerge that take leaders by surprise, and there is no clear way forward to overcome the stress.

The true cost of any change in leadership, program, property, or technology is actually divided among seven distinct cost centers:

- Tradition
- Attitude
- Leadership
- Organization
- Property
- Technology
- Finance

The best way to reduce stress is to count the cost for every change or new idea in that order. Begin counting the cost in changing tradition, proceed through the next cost centers in order, and end by counting the financial cost.

Most churches count the cost backward—and cause so much stress debating finances and assets that they can't even talk rationally or civilly about the other cost centers. In our story, church members immediately objected to many elements of their respective strategic plans: *There's not enough money for it! Individual and family donors of various properties and technologies will never stand for it!* However, the leadership teams had the good sense to patiently start by identifying the cost of change in the proper order. By the time they were done, members in both pairs of merging churches were willing and able to commit to their plans.

Tradition, Attitude, and the Stress of Change

The first set of costs are often hidden and subtle, but the most difficult. They must be considered first. Even when churches think they are willing to pay these costs, they will revisit this stress several times in the merger process.

Tradition

There are three possible costs to tradition that churches must to be willing to pay to enter a merger. The flexibility of churches here varies considerably from context to context and depends on three factors, in order of importance: (1) the spiritual credibility of the pastors and board leaders; (2) the clarity around accountability to core values (behavioral expectations), beliefs (bedrock convictions), spiritual practices (prayerful habits); and (3) Gospel mandates (Great Commandment, Great Commission). This is why the first steps in a merger conversation involve building clarity and consensus about these things.

HISTORIC TRADITION. There are still huge gaps between the four great historic traditions of the Christian movement (Roman Catholic, Eastern Orthodox, Protestant, and Pentecostal). These traditions do have very different theologies and polities, and it is unlikely that churches will merge across these historic divides easily. However, the collapse of the ecumenical movement in the last decades of the twentieth century revealed that these barriers are less about theologies and more about political differences and cultural influences. The more mass migrations and global communications transform the twenty-first century, the more these divisions will be tested—perhaps not by the theologians and authorized hierarchies, but by the laity. In the 2010s, however, mergers are unlikely between these traditions.

DENOMINATIONAL TRADITION. The most recent estimate is that there are about thirty-three thousand or more Christian denominations worldwide—and still fracturing! The fact that denominations are now multiplying, rather than declining, means that the potential for merger across the traditional denominational lines drawn even twenty-five years ago is increasing. Even within the Roman Catholic and Eastern Orthodox traditions, respectively, openness to congregational collaborations and mergers varies from country to country and diocese to diocese—or from cultural heritage to cultural heritage.

If local churches are uncomfortable compromising their historic traditions too much, they are much more open to crossing denominational boundaries. Their sense of integrity no longer depends on loyalty to any given polity or franchise. Local pastors and laity are taking a more pragmatic view of denominational loyalty. In the last twenty years, denominational authority to dictate curricula, program, and public policy has weakened considerably. The only denominational "hold" on congregations is authority over property and clergy personnel. Litigation across North America has dramatically loosened denominational control of property, and the growing shortage of clergy is shifting power to lay leadership.

The openness of denominational leaders to congregational mergers within and between denominations has grown exponentially in just the last twenty years. This is true both in national and regional offices. This is being driven by awareness that denominations have essentially been top-down organizations as in the modern corporate world—and if they are to survive in the emerging bottom-up postmodern world, they need to adapt. They are recognizing that if the gaps between *historic* traditions are real enough, the gaps between *denominational traditions* are mainly due to mis-understanding, politics, power, and prejudice. Part of the denominational cost of discipleship is that such selfishness must be jettisoned.

LOCAL TRADITION. Far and away, the biggest cost of discipleship for a congregational merger has to do with adjusting local tradition. You will often hear local "controllers" claim to be defending the "ethos of our denomination." That is almost always code for: *Denominational tradition is what I say it is.* All kinds of sacred cows, odd liturgical practices, quirky theological convictions, and culturally conditioned moral and religious as-sumptions are preserved in the fog of vague claims about denominational loyalty.

The demand that church people step out of their comfort zones and away from their claims to personal privileges imposes the biggest cost on tradition. In any merger, there is usually a laundry list of local or factional sacred cows that church members don't want to give up. Think of an ice-berg lying in wait for the merger conversation as it steams along. The list of privileges is only partially visible above water. Most of it is hidden, and it is on that jagged edge that many a ship founders. Suddenly and unexpect-edly passions flare about which hymnbooks will be used, whose pews will be preserved, how the elements of Holy Communion will be distributed, when Sunday school must happen, which rooms are available for whose use, and on and on.

Local tradition is the *real* cost of discipleship. Historic and denomina-tional traditions do matter, but it is often surprising just how peaceful the conversation is and how flexible leaders can be about those two cost factors. Yes, expectations about word, sacrament, and pastoral care can be honored between historic and denominational traditions. Yes, arrangements can be made about property ownership and clergy personnel appointments. The real heat, however, comes from quarrels over local tradition.

Attitude

The conversation over the cost center of tradition almost always leads to the next conversation, which is over attitude. Mergers inevitably reveal the positive or negative attitudes church members have toward other churches (even in their own denomination), and toward lifestyle segments that are currently over- or underrepresented in their memberships. In other words, talk about merger reveals favoritism and judgmentalism, prejudice, and bigotry. It challenges church claims to respect, include, honor, and love others.

Church people at some level are all hypocrites, no different from anyone else in our society. It really doesn't matter if the organizational merger involves school boards, hospitals, voting districts, or churches. Mergers reveal hidden hypocrisies, and these are always stressful.

It is remarkable how overtly condescending or critical church people can be toward other church people. Countless sermons contain direct or oblique jibes at other historic or denominational traditions. Funny little jokes and stereotypical anecdotes are always told about "those people." For example, there are two churches of the same denomination in Washington DC that cannot even share a civil potluck supper between them because each endorses a different political party. And their buildings are literally across the street from one another.

It is perhaps less surprising, but equally tragic, how dismissive, snobbish, disrespectful, and even hateful people in one lifestyle segment can be toward another. Thematic mapping can often vividly demonstrate how two completely different lifestyle groups can be divided by a single road or street. On either side the housing, retail shops, restaurants, and city services can be entirely different, even though both sides of the street are in the same zip code. In poor areas, each side of the street has different gangs; in wealthy areas, each side of the street has different service clubs. More to the point, each side of the street has different churches with distinctly different lifestyle representations.

This was once an issue of simple demographics. The dividing lines of prejudice and privilege were basic and visible. In the early twenty-first century there is enormous lifestyle variation within races, between ages, and among occupations, and little connection between education and income. As diversity increases, prejudices increase even among people of the same race, age, occupation, income, education, and so on. It is often this obstacle more than any other that blocks church mergers. Established churches have all grown along the lines of homogeneity, and church members can find it very hard "to let *those* people have control over *my* stuff."

Stress Management over Changes in Tradition and Attitude

Wise leaders anticipate inevitable stress over changes in tradition and attitude. They can identify and/or uncover the sacred cows of local traditions, the regional resistance within denominations, and even the deeper anxieties to preserve the integrity of historic allegiances. They can do this through personal observation, but it is better to broaden the analysis in more objective ways. Focus groups, intentional interviews with denominational leaders, and even a book or course on the ups and downs of the ecumenical movement will all be useful to them.

Since the greatest stress in a merger involves *local* traditions and *lifestyle* biases, however, the fundamental strategy for stress management involves *personal growth.* Leaders overcome stress by encouraging adult members to grow intellectually, emotionally, relationally, and spiritually. An emphasis on adult education and faith formation is crucial.

This is not accomplished simply by reading a few books and preaching a few sermons. It usually involves educating church boards, program *and* support staff, ministry area leaders, trustees, and especially teams associated with worship (choirs!), Sunday school (teachers!), fellowship (executive committees for women, men, and youth groups) over a period of months. Reading and preaching must be supplemented by dialogue and interaction. They must bring together, in any number of groupings, leaders from all churches in the merger conversation. Only dialogue and interaction can move education and insight from "head" to "heart"—and ultimately to open minds and open hands.

Intentionally draw into personal growth any of the "key influencers" of a congregation. These may or not be people currently holding an office or leadership role. In the church, one "influencer" can directly shape the attitudes and decisions of about fifteen to twenty people. Chances are that in a church of about 125 active members, 35 active adherents, 100 inactive members by reasons of health or mobility, and a variety of "friends of the church" who donate money and time to various outreach ministries, there are about 20 key "influencers." Those are the people to target and involve in specific programs and projects for personal growth.

In addition, intentionally draw into personal growth any of the "bridge builders" between generations, genders, long-standing Sunday school classes or small groups, and semiautonomous groups related to the church. They are people who may or may not overlap with the "influencers." They are also people who "get along" with a diverse group of friends who don't necessarily "get along" with each other. Certain people have a reputation for peacemaking, communication, and credibility. Chances are that in the same size church as above, there may be an additional five to ten bridge builders. Target and involve them, also.

Leadership, Organization, and the Stress of Change

The next set of costs are clearer and often the most pressing for churches in a merger. Beloved staff (ordained, program, or support staff) may be moved, retrained, and/or redeployed. Veteran lay leaders may need to step back and new leaders step up. Local habits of governance may need to adapt.

Leadership

This cost center usually becomes clear once stress over changes to tradition and attitude is addressed. There is a price to be paid for leadership. Every church has a number of paid (full- or part-time) and volunteer leaders. Some leaders may continue in job descriptions that are relatively unchanged, others may be redeployed in the same church; others may be moved to other churches; and still others may be terminated. This is not only stressful for the leaders; every church leader tends to have a group of personal supporters who will be anxious on their behalf.

CLERGY. Many merger conversations begin when a clergy leader is retiring or moving, or during an interim ministry. Nevertheless, there is no guarantee that clergy (senior or associate pastors) will continue until the process of prioritization and strategic planning is completed. The church is being re-missioned, so to speak, which means that the future merged church may be a different kind of church from any of the original churches that once called or appointed clergy. The pastor who was relevant and effective in the past may or may not be the pastor who will be relevant and effective in the future.

Let's be clear: Merger is not a method to preserve the jobs of clergy. It is a method to more effectively multiply disciples and bless the community. One of the strengths of denominational policy is that there are clear personnel guidelines to acquire or dismiss pastoral leadership. These must be followed carefully, along with other state or federal guidelines protecting employees. Follow the proper procedures, but be clear that the mission is more important than any individual clergy leader.

PROGRAM AND SUPPORT STAFF. The same things can be said about full- or part-time staff. Merger conversations are often times when program staff (e.g., music directors, Sunday school superintendents, parish nurses, and others) may choose to look for other opportunities. Neither the staff person nor the church should feel guilty about that. Program staff leadership in particular is not a job, but a vocation. Leaders know that their calling and the emerging church calling may or may not coincide.

There can be more stress regarding change in support staff (secretaries, custodians, part-time bookkeepers, paid soloists, etc.). They often do not see their work as a vocation, but simply as a job. And now their jobs are at risk. Church members often feel very guilty about this. It is important in a merger to emphasize that a staff person *cannot be the focus of mission!* Staff are hired *to facilitate mission to others!* The future merged church cannot simply "grandfather in" former staff who may or may not be effective in helping the new church accomplish mission.

Churches should follow the fair practice of most nonprofit organizations. Once the policies and plans for the new church are clear and job descriptions are modified, candidates for the job can uniformly be evaluated or interviewed based on the consistent criteria of mission attitude (wholehearted commitment to the mission of the church); high integrity (sincere commitment to honor the core values and beliefs of the church); competence (appropriate skills to achieve the goals of the church); and teamwork (collaboration to work harmoniously with other staff and volunteers). Whether the applicant is an existing staff person or a new person, each is uniformly evaluated using the same criteria. Existing staff are usually given clear guidance and a reasonable timeline to live up to the new standards of attitude, integrity, skills, and teamwork. Regardless, decisions about support staff cannot be personal or political, but objectively based on the new expectations of the new organization.

VOLUNTEER LEADERS. Perhaps the *most* stressful cost of discipleship is change regarding volunteer-ministry-area leaders. This is because churches do not usually follow the same guidelines for volunteer accountability as their nonprofit (social service and health care) mission partners. Churches tend to assume that volunteers *cannot* be dismissed, whereas effective nonprofits know that volunteers *must be dismissed* if they are unable to commit to the mission attitude, model its high integrity, work to its standard of competency, and collaborate with generosity. A hospital, for example, cannot afford to compromise community trust by allowing a volunteer to breach any of those four expectations for long. The same is true for a church.

Nonetheless, this is very stressful for a church. In a merger, volunteer leaders often assume that they *deserve* to remain in leadership. Since many similar programs are managed by volunteers with similar job descriptions, this can lead to competition and conflict. The same principle is applied to volunteer leadership choices as to salaried personnel choices. The decision cannot be personal or political. It is based on universally applied expectations for attitude, integrity, competency, and teamwork. If this principle is uniformly applied, much conflict and hurt can be avoided.

Organization

A merger is often an opportunity to change and streamline organizational structure. Declining churches usually experience expanding bureaucracies. As the church grows smaller, committees actually multiply. The situation becomes so confusing that the most common complaint in a small church (paradoxically) is that people don't know what is happening. The church becomes smaller, but members spend more time in meetings.

The basic model of governance often changes as churches merge. Small churches frequently operate using a consensus or council model of governance. Even the smallest decisions require near majority of support, and only a single objection can delay decisions forever. The council strategy tries to compensate, bringing representatives from every task area to the table. But task areas keep multiplying, committee representation at the table is rotated, and eventually anyone and everyone is invited to participate— returning the church to a consensus model.

The merged church cannot function this way. The congregation is larger and more diverse than before. There is no shared history between different members, so that decisions always feel more risky. Inevitably, some former leaders lose authority; and authority is delegated to former strangers.

In a merged church, boards can no longer govern by task management. There is simply too much to do, and the community is changing too fast for drawn-out decision-making. Committees need to learn to function as teams. The difference is that a "committee" has lots of responsibility, but little authority. It has power to implement but not to initiate or even evaluate. A "team" has both responsibility *and* authority. It has power to discern, design, implement, and evaluate ministries without having to defer back to the board.

This shift can be frightening, particularly among churches with lifestyle representation in which people tend to be "followers" rather than "leaders." They fear making mistakes. They prefer to be told what to do. The temptation in a merger is to depend too much on the pastor and paid staff to make decisions, stifling volunteer empowerment. Churches can go from one extreme to another: Formerly *everybody* was involved in administration, and suddenly *nobody* is involved in administration.

This is why board training becomes especially important in a merger. It is often provided by denominational leaders or outside consultants. Churches learn how to develop high trust organizations and how to delegate initiative to teams without losing control of the church.

Stress Management over Changes in Leadership and Organization

The ultimate goal to manage stress related to changes in leadership and organization is to create a culture of accountability. This culture pervades the entire church: all the staff, all the volunteers, and all the members. Visitors and newcomers recognize a culture of accountability because they feel *safe* as well as *welcomed*. Safety is assured because the core values and beliefs of the church are immediately visible. A school posts its core values in the vestibule at the entrance. A church re-presents its core values and beliefs in any room where people gather (entrances, fellowship halls, and worship centers) either as static images or data streams across video screens.

A culture of accountability makes sure that doors are secure (especially near children), parking lots and exits are illuminated, and dark hallways are eliminated. Children are never left alone, teens are never unsupervised, women never leave the building alone, and strangers cannot roam about freely.

The most important thing, of course, is that everyone behaves well. Ushers and greeters are sensitive to diverse cultures and speak, touch, and make eye contact appropriately. Receptionists and secretaries are patient, generous, and, well, *human*. Pastor and program staff *care* about volunteers and don't just *use* volunteers. Inevitably there will be breakdowns in behavior because we are all sinners. The difference in a culture of accountability is that these do not go unnoticed and unaddressed. An angry word, derogatory joke, hurtful remark, or mistaken behavior is quickly addressed with a gentle but firm reminder about *how we behave here*.

The four basic keys to accountability are: mission attitude, high integrity, skills, and teamwork. These expectations pervade every activity.

Visitors can see it among the custodians mowing the grass, the servers working in the kitchen, the choir practicing music, and the staff leading ministries. It is universal. No one, paid or unpaid, veteran or newcomer, is treated with greater or lesser accountability. That spontaneous deed or unrehearsed word that contradicts core values and beliefs can be addressed *by anyone*. A twelve-year-old can readily and respectfully remind a senior, "That's not how we behave here."

This culture of accountability is important in all churches, but particularly in the high stress environment of a merger when the church family now includes lots of people hitherto unknown. One can start, of course, by creating safe environments and training staff and volunteers. There are four places to start:

- The program and support staff
- The board
- The hospitality team
- The music team

These groups are the "face" of the congregation. Their behavior is immediately visible to newcomers as well as to the members who see them all the time. They model accountability for everyone else. If they do it, the people will do it. If they don't do it, the people will never do it. And if visitors don't see it, they may never return.

Property, Technology, and the Stress of Change

Paradoxically, these cost centers are less stressful than many churches think, but only if they have already committed themselves to pay the price in tradition and attitude, and leadership and organization. This is because the value of things is subjective. Even the most sacred of objects can be deconsecrated if leaders and organizations choose to do so.

Property

It should have become apparent why churches should postpone counting the cost of change regarding property, technology, and money until *after* the previous cost centers have been addressed. These hot topics in a merger can now be discussed more calmly and objectively.

Mergers almost inevitably mean property change. Many churches toy with the idea of keeping *all* the properties to preserve heritage and perhaps gain income through property rentals. This is almost always a big mistake. As long as the merged church holds onto redundant properties, the new congregation will never be united. You have to bring closure to grief before starting a new life. Preserving unused properties for rental income is also a mistake; it sidetracks the attention and energy of leadership at a crucial moment in the church's evolution. Leaders become landlords instead of missionaries.

Remember that the order of strategic planning is always as follows: foundation, function, and then form. First, focus mission and build leadership; next, prioritize goals and develop programs; and only then decide what properties and technologies will best achieve the outcomes defined by the board and resource the strategies designed by the leadership team.

The same four keys to accountability used with personnel can be adapted to property. First, the property needs to communicate by its internal and external architecture and symbolism the vision and mission of the church. Second, the property must protect the safety and confidentiality of property users, facilitate the relational and spiritual growth of the lifestyle segments targeted by the church, and help the church address the physical and emotional needs of the community. Some lifestyle segments gravitate toward ecclesiastical-looking buildings, with traditional Christendom symbols inside and out. Other lifestyle segments gravitate toward utilitarian-looking buildings, with nontraditional symbols of spirituality. Decisions about property may honor the expectations of each church partner, but it is even more important to honor the expectations of visitors, seekers, and publics who are underrepresented in the church. Members make sacrifices to make the church more relevant, and God more accessible, to those who may be strangers to grace.

This is one reason why mergers often sell *all* the buildings and start anew. It brings closure to the past, frees the energy of leaders for the mission of the future, and provides the most relevant resource to guarantee future success achieving the right outcomes. Many mergers use the sale of property to generate revenue. Some mergers sell property at a loss or give it away to other, poorer churches or to social service agencies. The "profit" does not lie in money, but in higher visibility and respect in the community.

Technology

Strictly speaking, property is a form of technology. Mergers, however, usually treat all the furnishings, furniture, symbols, equipment, electronics, ecclesiastical accoutrements, memorials, and other resources as "technologies." These are things that communicate identity and the tools that get things done.

In some traditions (e.g., Roman Catholic, Anglican, Episcopalian, some Lutheran, Eastern Orthodox), some technologies are considered sacred and have been consecrated and set aside for sacred use. These technologies (e.g., chalices, vestments, etc.) are usually preserved in a merger, given to other churches that will similarly cherish them, or deconsecrated and sent to an archive or museum.

In Protestant and Pentecostal traditions, no technology is sacred . . . period. The pews may be nostalgic, but they are not sacred. The pulpit Bible may be historic, but it is not sacred. The only thing that is sacred is God's purpose. Technologies, therefore, are just tactics. Church mergers force leaders to make some hard choices about what to keep, what to improve, and what to discard, but the decisions are always based on *what will be most effective to accomplish God's purpose for this church in this context.*

It is usually only when a church has counted the cost in changing traditions, attitudes, leadership, and organization that its leaders have the peace of mind, clarity of purpose, and depth of trust to make hard decisions about these technologies. Some of the hardest decisions are about:

- Pews, pulpits, and chancel furniture
- Organs, pianos, and hymnbooks
- Windows and memorials
- Historic artifacts and record books

Most mergers make it a priority to archive historic records and dedicate space in a new building or location for a museum. The larger furnishings are more difficult. Choices about larger and often more nostalgic items should be based on relevance to the lifestyle-segment expectations of the community rather than on historical preservation. Different lifestyle segments value different things. The tools and resources they prefer fit their attitudes, learning methodologies, and unique tastes. Some lifestyle segments prefer to sit in pews, surround themselves in hardwood, and hold printed books. Others prefer to sit in movable chairs, surround themselves in plastic, and view video monitors. God doesn't really care what you use, only that whatever you use blesses even the least of Christ's brothers and sisters.

Stress Management over Changes in Property and Technology

The best way to resolve stress over changes in property and technology is to increase mission sensitivity. Whenever a debate over property and technology looms, always begin the conversation by referencing the mission of the church, and always end the conversation by referencing the people you are called to bless. Let mission and people frame the conversation that lies in between.

Leaders should recognize that debates over property and technology are not really what they seem. The issue is never about pews, windows, steeples, hymnbooks, and *things*. It is about *what these things represent*. They are powerful symbols. They represent an appreciation for the past and a celebration of identity. Hard decisions about property and technology can only be made once appreciation for the past and identity in the present are clearly better expressed in some other way. Then people can replace or dispose of property and technology without feeling guilty or lost.

Properties and technologies are also symbols of power. They represent a time when the church was more influential in the community than it is now. The towering steeple that once towered over the neighborhood is now dwarfed by office and apartment buildings. The stained glass windows and pipe organ that were once the talk of the town, treasured by the arts community, and coveted by other churches are now ignored or disused. Hard decisions about property and technology can only be made once a church has regained self-esteem and sees a way to once again be influential in the community.

The discussion, then, is really about effectiveness for mission. Who is out there? How does God want us to bless them?

Financial Management, Fundraising, and the Stress of Change

Surprisingly, the *first* cost center most churches think about in a merger is the *least important*. There are few contexts in North America in which money is the real obstacle. If the mission is clear, and the members are motivated by a heartburst for other people than themselves; if the leaders are willing, and the organizations adapt; and if the property can be surrendered, and the technologies can be updated; then there is almost always money that can be found, raised, or reprioritized.

Financial Management

Churches manage money in different ways, which often makes it difficult to compare resources and liabilities, and giving patterns. Some churches use line budgets, and some use narrative budgets. In a merger discussion, it is most helpful for all the churches to use a narrative budget to begin comparisons. This helps leaders see the "big picture" of how each church spends money proportionately among various ministries. They can then refer to line budgets to answer more detailed questions about how money is managed.

There are always concerns about confidentiality, especially if one or more of the churches shares more publicly the actual giving of members and others do not. There is no value judgment here. Each strategy has its pros and cons. In a merger discussion, it is best to preserve confidentiality (at least in the beginning). All that is really needed is a breakdown in levels of giving. This helps church leaders understand the real depth and breadth of financial support in each church. Clearly, churches in which only a handful of "good givers" underwrite the budget are in a more precarious position than churches in which there is a higher expectation of percentage of giving for all the members.

Often, established churches that own property, support a denomination, or invest in mission partnerships manage reserve funds that are separate from the general budget. In order to preserve trust, there must be full disclosure of the amounts in these reserve funds. All assets must be included in the merger conversation, and nothing can be withheld by a small group or committee. Limitations on the use of memorial funds must also be disclosed—and verified—since the "oral tradition" that limits the use of dedicated funds may be different than actual legal obligations.

Full disclosure is also necessary regarding debts and other liabilities. This includes financial obligations to banks and denominations and any private loans or personal debentures by members that supported past capital campaigns. In particular, it is helpful for each participating church to calculate the percentage of its annual budget that is dedicated to debt reduction. Churches that dedicate more than 15 to 18% of their budget to debt relief are in a much more vulnerable position.

Finally, each church must clarify where authority to manage money lies. In some churches this is fairly simple, but in others it is more complex. As the process unfolds, and assets and liabilities are merged, authority to manage money will also be consolidated in a new system of accountability.

Fundraising

Most congregations raise money in four distinct ways, and some methods may be more important than others.

The first two sources, subsidies and rentals, may be the most vulnerable in a merger. Struggling churches are often too dependent on denominational subsidies to keep the doors open or pay personnel. Since most denominations are struggling financially also, they are likely to see a merger as an opportunity to cease subsidies altogether. Churches can also be too dependent on rental income from outside groups with no connection to the church. This income may also be lost if the church sells the building, or if the larger merged congregation requires more space.

The second pair of sources will be much more important to a successful merger: stewardship campaigns and nonprofit income. The trouble is that too many churches have grown lazy about stewardship campaigns. The merged church will need a year-round strategy that is more aggressive. Fortunately, church leaders can use a resource like www.missioninsite .com to objectively define the true giving potential of any given church membership or mission field. Some churches support their own nonprofit organization as a part of their mission but separately incorporated in order to receive donations and grants. This will become even more important in a future merger.

Stress Management over Changes in Financial Management and Fundraising

The truth is that in North America, finances are rarely the issue. If a church is prepared to pay the cost of discipleship to change tradition, attitude, leadership, organization, property, and technology, there will *always* be money. There are some exceptions in contexts of extreme poverty, but in North America at least, these are rare compared to the rest of the world.

In order to address stress over financial change (usually due to raised financial expectations), leaders must focus the conversation on lifestyle adjustments. It is not poverty but the mentality of poverty that is the root of the problem for most churches. Members claim to be poor when it comes to church support, but many of them still take vacations, buy new cars, and enjoy many luxuries.

Fundraisers confirm what Jesus observed. The poorest people are often the most generous givers; and the richest people are often the stingiest givers. The financial challenge of the church, therefore, is not really addressed by fundraising per se, but by persuading and coaching church members to reprioritize their lifestyles. Stewardship has never been about *how much* you give. It has always been about *what percentage* you give. The average giving in many established, declining churches is less than 2% of income. The priority of God's mission through the church is simply too far down the list of personal and family lifestyle priorities.

Now we come to the most important tactic for addressing the financial stress of change. Leaders have to lead. The members will only reprioritize their lifestyles if the leaders visibly show them the way. People won't give more unless leaders give more. As a general rule of thumb, members will not increase their percentage giving to 4% if the leaders don't publicly commit to raising their percentage giving to at least 6%. Just do that, and stress over financial change is dramatically reduced.

There was a time in Christendom when money was readily available to churches in the form of grants and low interest loans, or legacies left behind by faithful members. That era is ending. Denominations, banks, and families seeking to honor their dead will only advance funds if the leaders and members of the church demonstrate that they are prepared to alter their lifestyles to raise money themselves.

Obviously, financial management is the locus of control in many churches. This is why conversation about cost centers inevitably leads to a discussion about trust. Trust will be revealed through the spiritual practices of leaders—especially financial leaders. Financial leaders must be held accountable for their daily, weekly, and annual spiritual habits in order to have credibility with each other and the constituencies they represent. These habits usually include regular worship attendance, commitment to Bible study or theological reflection, daily prayer, personal service, and other factors.

Preach It!

There are four Gospel texts that launch and guide the merger conversation. Preachers build their sermons around them. Bible study classes build their discussions around them. Individual leaders and members build their daily prayers around them.

- *Matthew 7:24–27*: "Everyone then who hears these words of mine and acts on them will be like a wise man who built his house on rock. The rain fell, the floods came, and the winds blew and beat on that house, but it did not fall, because it had been founded on rock. And everyone who hears these words of mine and does not act on them will be like a foolish man who built his house on sand. The rain fell, and the floods came, and the winds blew and beat against that house, and it fell—and great was its fall!"

- *Mark 8:34–37*: He called the crowd with his disciples, and said to them, "If any want to become my followers, let them deny themselves and take up their cross and follow me. For those who want to save their life will lose it, and those who lose their life for my sake, and for the sake of the gospel, will save it. For what will it profit them to gain the whole world and forfeit their life? Indeed, what can they give in return for their life?"
- *Luke 14:28–34*: "For which of you, intending to build a tower, does not first sit down and estimate the cost, to see whether he has enough to complete it? Otherwise, when he has laid a foundation and is not able to finish, all who see it will begin to ridicule him, saying, 'This fellow began to build and was not able to finish.' Or what king, going out to wage war against another king, will not sit down first and consider whether he is able with ten thousand to oppose the one who comes against him with twenty thousand? If he cannot, then, while the other is still far away, he sends a delegation and asks for the terms of peace. So therefore, none of you can become my disciple if you do not give up all your possessions. Salt is good; but if salt has lost its taste, how can its saltiness be restored?"
- *John 15:1–8*: "I am the true vine, and my Father is the vine grower. He removes every branch in me that bears no fruit. Every branch that bears fruit he prunes to make it bear more fruit. You have already been cleansed by the word that I have spoken to you. Abide in me as I abide in you. Just as the branch cannot bear fruit by itself unless it abides in the vine, neither can you unless you abide in me. I am the vine, you are the branches. Those who abide in me and I in them bear much fruit, because apart from me you can do nothing. Whoever does not abide in me is thrown away like a branch and withers; such branches are gathered, thrown into the fire, and burned. If you abide in me, and my words abide in you, ask for whatever you wish, and it will be done for you. My Father is glorified by this, that you bear much fruit and become my disciples."

The preachers in both sets of merging churches decided to collaborate, each pair developing a sermon series and Bible study program for their own merger. Each pair together prepared basic outlines for their sermons; then the members of each pair individually nuanced each sermon for the liturgy, character, and terminology familiar to his or her own congregation.

Trust   6

The Foundation for
Candid and Faithful Conversation

When the boards of each pair of churches decided, in principle, to commit to merger conversations and word of it spread among their respective constituencies, the reaction was predictable. Initially there was great enthusiasm for the idea. Both sets of churches had been cooperating with each other for years, faced similar challenges, and had similar opportunities but not the resources to seize them.

It wasn't long, however, before all the objections were raised. Calm consideration soon broke down into a chaos of worry. "Controllers" from each church took advantage of the chaos and tried to stop the conversation before it even began. "Controllers" are what we call influential members of a church who subtly or overtly try to shape the church around their own preferences and priorities, and impose on others their personal tastes and values, as the boundaries beyond which a church cannot go. They function best when organizational trust is low, vision is foggy, and mission is vague.

Merger 1: Wesley and Asbury

Controllers from Wesley gathered a group of middle-class retirees who were chronically anxious about debt and wanted to preserve large reserve funds against rainy days, and a group of well-educated, senior-management professionals who were nervous about surrendering authority over assets to blue-collar or middle-management people who didn't know how to budget.

.Meanwhile, controllers from Asbury gathered a group of protective parents who were worried about the future of the youth and wanted to preserve the innovation of the children's ministries, and a group of choir members and lay pastors who were passionately concerned that their style of worship would be subsumed by an elitist understanding of hymnology and liturgy.

The undercurrent of anxiety, of course, was the hidden racism that thrived on stereotypes entrenched in each congregation. Many members from both churches simply didn't believe a truly bi-racial church could thrive.

Merger 2: Faith Temple and Pine Street

Controllers from Pine Street rallied a group of theological purists, denominational exclusivists, and multicultural enthusiasts. They were afraid that the purity of "Reformed Theology" might be lost, and that the merged church would behave more "Baptist" than "Presbyterian." Moreover, although rental income to other churches never paid the bills and never resulted in any real cooperation between cultures, they felt that the church couldn't abandon the ecumenical initiative of housing other fledgling congregations.

Meanwhile, controllers from Faith Temple rallied some of the matriarchs and patriarchs who were top givers, a large group of inactive and nonresident members with family roots in the historic church, and a few teachers committed to the preservation of historic buildings. They feared the loss of their historic building as a visible symbol of faith, and argued that the church would dishonor the memory of past church members.

The undercurrent of anxiety, of course, was the not-so-hidden suspicion among many members of each church that people in that other church were not really saved or sufficiently Christian.

The vision team, and the pastors and boards from each of the churches, realized that they did not have a solid foundation for honest conversation. They couldn't calmly discuss the costs of discipleship without knowing—and respecting—one another's deepest convictions, behavioral expectations, and organizational aspirations. They did not share a common language. They did not have comparable assumptions. The "corporate cultures" of each church were surprisingly different.

- **Wesley** often referred to "Wesleyan" tradition and theology and defined community by weekly celebration of Holy Communion.
- **Asbury** often referred to "black" history and experience and defined community by "spirit-filled" worship and social service.

Interactions between the two churches were always polite and politically correct, but rarely profound and humble.

- **Faith Temple** often referred to the Bible, and defined community by assent to a specific set of doctrines.
- **Pine Street** often referred to "Reformed Theology," and defined community by participation in committees and task groups.

Interactions always reflected long-standing rivalries. They all told jokes at the others' expense. They all had stereotypes of the others that were caricatures of reality.

None of the churches had really worked to define in everyday language the bedrock beliefs it actually turned to for strength in times of trouble; nor were the churches very clear about positive behavior patterns in which their members would be trained, and for which their members would be held accountable; nor were they daring enough to admit negative behavior patterns that consistently sabotaged their best-laid plans. Each church needed to build its own consensus around shared values and beliefs, in order for the churches to build productive conversations with each other.

Each pair of pastors jointly developed a plan for their respective churches to build clarity and consensus about their own identities (core values and bedrock beliefs) and trajectories (history and vision). This took some time and required a combination of large and small groups to involve as many people as possible. Once each congregation became clearer about values, beliefs, vision, and mission, the conversation was then expanded to include both churches at once. They were able to establish and celebrate deeply held faith convictions that they turned to for strength in times of trouble. They were all willing to hold one another accountable to positive behaviors epitomized by the *fruits of the Spirit*.

Of course, education and preaching were not enough. The most heated debate that arose was really about power and self-interest. Each pair of pastors and boards arranged for a multitude of intentional conversations between controllers and individual people or families in their groups, and specific people who were their friends and also supportive of the mergers. In other words, they got friends talking to friends, and in the midst of caring persuasion, many people calmed down, felt reassured, and became supportive. The process was also helped along by denominational leaders who were related to each of the merger conversations and who supported the plans, and guest speakers from churches that had undergone similar mergers and succeeded.

Each pair of pastors wisely understood that neither reason nor relationship would quell the opposition of a few. They individually warned their churches that some members would leave in a merger, and there could be short-term financial loss. They also explained to their churches that many new people would be attracted to the larger merged churches, and that there would be long-term financial growth.

Churches all have a unique culture, but they are rarely able to describe it. The first step on the journey toward merger, therefore, is to help each church in the conversation to be able to clearly articulate its identity and purpose. Only then can two churches explore the question of compatibility: *Are we enough alike to merge?*

There is a mystique around corporate culture. We like to think that it is only intuitive and can never be analyzed, that it is a mystery that can never be fully understood. It is often surrounded by a congregational mythology that vaguely recalls a glorious past of wonderful harmony, effective ministry, working technology, and enormous community influence. These are always exaggerations. The beginning of serious dialogue about merger calls each church to "demythologize" its past and "demystify" its communal life.

To do so, churches must acknowledge the checkered history of their past and face the realities of the present. It is a kind of corporate confession. It is the repentance that is the prelude to all recovenanting in scripture. Churches not only admit their failures and shortcomings, but go deeper to identify their "corporate addictions": self-destructive habits that they chronically deny. Now they must face them openly and, hopefully, in the spirit of community in which each partner in the merger dialogue acknowledges that they all have similar issues. Honesty within each church is necessary before there can be honesty between churches. And when church leaders and members discover that they share many of the same negative habits, they also discover they share many more positive habits. Trust is the first and essential step toward vision.

Sadly, some churches cannot even get this far. Honesty is beyond them. That means that the merger conversation is over before it really started. The arrogance of any one church or the judgmental attitude of any one church over another dooms the conversation. Other churches will follow their lead, turn away from honesty, and retrench mythology. One reason merger conversations are often so interminable—going round and round, consuming time, and burning out one leader after another—is that they are fundamentally devoid of honesty. Posturing leads to more posturing. Those members with the highest integrity will not only drop out of the merger conversation, but may also step away from their own church because they cannot abide the hypocrisy. Once churches trust one another's motives, they can begin to trust one another's actions.

It sounds harsh, but the unsettling truth is that this kind of dithering is exactly what some influential members of each church in a merger prefer. Trust has been compared to a clear day on the open sea, and distrust to a foggy day in the harbor.[1] Churches that are unclear about their core values and bedrock beliefs live in a fog. Fog encourages foghorns. Controllers are intimidating or influential people in a church that behave like foghorns. They control what committees can or can't do the way foghorns control ships in the harbor. They like the fog because it gives them power. They will do anything to avoid clarity because they will lose control.

Controllers are often mythmakers. They weave complex mythologies about the history of their church. They claim to see hidden significance in ancient artifacts and broken technologies. They ascribe enormous importance to relatively insignificant events. They explain away failures with complex conspiracy theories involving the denomination, former clergy, supposedly dysfunctional families, and imagine success based on little or no evidence of actual mission outcomes. Most importantly, they exaggerate broad harmony in the church, friendliness toward outsiders, inspiration in worship, depth of faith, passion for mission, and generosity in money and service that doesn't really exist. It is all a pretext to claim that everything is okay and the church doesn't really need to merge, or that everything will be fine if the other churches just allow their church to tell them what to do.

Most churches considering a merger receive well-intentioned but poor advice from their denominational leaders or theological colleges. They are advised to start by celebrating and comparing their strengths. This sounds like good advice. It feeds their need for appreciation. It reinforces their emphasis on caregiving. It helps church leaders believe that decline was never their fault. And there is a great deal of truth in that: Decline is the result of many forces beyond their control, and they probably have tried hard to renew the church.

Nevertheless, starting a merger conversation with a celebration of the past is the wrong place to start. The right place to start is with radical humility. Only when churches are honest with themselves can they really begin to be honest with each other. The essence of repentance is really not blame. It is humility. It is a complete surrender of ego and arrogance, and a wholehearted appeal to God for deliverance and hope. It is a sincere acceptance of one's own shortcomings as a community of faith, and a complete reliance on God's grace for the future. It is, after all, God's church and not our church. We are but stewards of the church, and even our best efforts are tainted by self-interest. First we "come clean" with God, and then the future will be full of potential.

Trust in a congregation (and any organization) is a clearly transparent, highly accountable consensus around core values and bedrock beliefs. It is "transparent" in that positive behavioral habits are consistently visible among all the members, all the time, everywhere. You see them happen before your eyes again and again. The church claims to behave in certain ways. Perhaps, like the earliest church, they claim to be peaceful, patient, gentle, loving, compassionate, generous, self-controlled, and forgiving. However, trust is not based on words but actions. Insiders and outsiders, people visiting the church for the first time, and veterans who have lived in the church all their lives readily see that behavior. Or if they do *not* see that behavior, they *do see* an intervention that apologizes for misbehavior, corrects the mistake, and ensures it will not happen again. That's trust.

Churches mistakenly think that core values are all about agreements around public policy. They presume that a merger can only happen when churches agree on specific ethical positions or moral principles. In fact, ideological agreement does little to shape corporate culture. Corporate culture is not based on the rehearsed word and the strategic plan, but on the unrehearsed word and the spontaneous deed. One church can claim to be open and inclusive, yet behave with condescension and privilege. Another church may be stereotyped as closed and exclusive, yet behave with extravagant generosity and humility.

In fact, churches with compatible corporate cultures may actually disagree about public policies and ideological agendas. They may successfully merge because of their shared values—and intentional practices of accountability—to be respectful, open minded, humble, and so on. They know that ethical issues are complicated and social policies evolve. They are united by common assumptions about how Christians in their faith community ought to treat one another and the world at large.

Churches also mistakenly think that bedrock beliefs are all about theologies and dogmas. They presume that a merger can only happen when churches agree about theories, propositions, creeds, and the nuances of their many doctrines. In fact, theological agreement does little to shape corporate culture. It is not based on intellectual assent, but on those profoundly existential faith convictions that give people strength in times of trouble, help them endure persecutions and tragedies, and rescue them from despair. These are often not carefully rationalized theories, but impulsive actions. These are not the beliefs that make sense of the world, but the convictions that give courage to face the future.

One of the problems of the post-Christendom church, of course, is that churches have a lot of doctrines and Christians espouse various theologies, but when a crisis occurs and lives are at stake, everybody is suddenly a skeptic. Churches are often notorious for their many beliefs and their complete lack of *belief*. How can churches merge if each of the partners really doesn't believe in anything? In an emergency, Christians become tongue-tied and confused. They are unable to rally around each other with confidence or encourage one another with words of life. They can't stare death in the eye and stake their lives on the eternal.

Accountability and confidence are the essence of trust. The best core values are verbs, not nouns. They describe actions that can be evaluated and found true. They are outcomes, not processes. They describe realities, not wishful thinking. Church mergers are not founded on high ideals but on consistently positive, predictable patterns of behavior that are normative for their daily behavior and earn respect in the surrounding community. In the same way, the best bedrock beliefs are stories, not theories. They demonstrate from the contemporary history of the church the convictions on which their members are ready to stake their lives and lifestyles. They reveal the steel that remains true in adversity. Church mergers are not founded on theologies of this or that, but on deeply held convictions about God, life, and hope that are more likely contained in songs and pictures than mere words.

The foundation of trust may be *influenced* by denominational identity and tradition, but it is not *determined* by it. Trust is deeper than denominationalism and bigger than institutionalism. This is why it is indeed possible for churches from different denominations and traditions to successfully merge. The partnership may result in some remarkably creative tactics in worship, for example, but everyone can function happily together despite their differences. They can even argue and debate ideologies and theologies with one another without breaking their unity.

This point about denominational identity deserves more attention. In the modern world, most mergers were achieved (if they were achieved at all) within the same denomination or tradition. In those days, denominational identity formed a common bond. Worship styles, educational resources, local and regional outreach, and even facility design were standardized. You could travel anywhere, visit a church of the same denomination, and feel like it was "just like home." The feeling was reinforced by the strength of gender- and age-based denominational groups with similar organizational purposes and programs (women's and men's groups, seniors and youth groups, etc.) In the postmodern world that standardization has largely disappeared. Churches of the same denomination can literally be across the street from each other, yet be so different they could not possibly merge, and they barely cooperate. The same churches can partner with a congregation from another denominational tradition easily and productively.

This is another reason why all churches participating in a merger must bring to the conversation real clarity and consensus about their core values and bedrock beliefs. Only then can they explore the compatibility of their individual corporate cultures. This reflects the bottom-up nature of organizations in the postmodern world. Mergers can no longer be imposed top-down by a denominational hierarchy. This is not necessarily because the hierarchy lacks credibility (although too often that is also the case). It is because the church constituency is far more diverse. The variations in worship style, educational methodology, small-group design, outreach priorities, and technologies belie deeper differences in core values and bedrock beliefs.

The most important point to remember is that clarity about core values and beliefs demystifies corporate culture. Churches can objectively compare the different behavioral expectations and faith convictions that define their unique identities. They can share paradigmatic stories that typify or encapsulate who they are. Imagine a group of church leaders talking informally over coffee at some local or regional ecumenical gathering. One asks another: *What exactly do you mean by this core value?* In reply, the other leader tells a recent story of a member whose behavior perfectly models the value in question. Another leader overhears the response and shudders: *We would never behave like that!* And yet another leader exclaims: *That's exactly what we do—and here's another illustration from our church!* Some can talk seriously about merger, and others not.

There are many techniques with which to build clarity and consensus about core values and bedrock beliefs. Churches use a mix of large gatherings with table groups (which generally attract regular members); small groups in homes (which often attract irregular members and adherents); and focus groups and listening teams (which reality-test self-perceptions against those of the general public). The process usually gathers both positive core values and true bedrock beliefs, and along the way reveals negative corporate addictions that must be resisted.

One church happened to have blank walls on either side of the sanctuary. They ended their discernment process by painting each wall. On one side was a mural of the Tree of Life, with each leaf naming a positive core value and each fruit naming a bedrock belief. On the other side was a mural of a raging fire, with each spark naming a negative addictive habit and each puff of smoke a common fear or doubt. In subsequent merger talks, they only had to bring their conversation partners into the sanctuary and say (with the right balance of confidence and humility): *This is who we are!*

The difficulty is that a church's final list of core values and bedrock beliefs is often too abstract. Abstractions don't fully capture corporate culture. It is interesting that biblical churches faced a similar dilemma. When Paul lists the *fruits of the Spirit* in Galatians 5, the single words can easily be interpreted in different ways. When he creates a similar list of core values in Romans 12, each word is qualified by adjectives or adverbs that bring out the nuances of each behavior pattern. Similarly, bedrock beliefs in the New Testament are rarely expressed as abstract doctrines. They are shared as a quotation from a hymn, as the point of a parable, or as a shout of acclamation.

This is why each core value and bedrock belief should be accompanied by a paradigm story. The story should come from within the *current* membership, preferably within the last year, and perfectly illustrate the behavior or conviction being shared. The first meetings in a merger process are not about listing abstractions, but about telling stories that define who we are. These stories may not always describe how all of us behave all the time, for after all, we are sinners. Some of our stories may illustrate hidden addictions or a negative behavior pattern that blocks or hinders us from living up to all God wants us to be. Therefore, there will also be real-time stories of accountability for each value and belief. Core values and bedrock beliefs are not just about how we behave, but how we *really want to* behave. When we fail to behave this way, we feel real guilt, accept criticism, learn from our mistakes, try all the harder, and support one another in the process.

Corporate culture is often a mix of local customs and convictions, and denominational traditions and doctrines. However, as churches move into the postmodern world the proportion of that mix is changing. In the 1950s and 1960s, the mix was heavily weighted toward denominational traditions and doctrines; but by the 1990s and the first decade of the new millennium the mix became weighted more toward local customs and convictions. The era of institutional standardization is ebbing, and the era of community uniqueness is growing.

The traditional wisdom about mergers is that the first step is to find a common vision. We don't think that is true anymore. Vision is important, but it will emerge later in the process as participating churches explore their primary mission field, merge assets, and begin strategic planning. No, it is not vision that is crucial at the beginning of a merger. It is trust. Most churches don't trust one another (even if they are in the same denomination or judicatory), and until they build clarity and consensus around core values and bedrock beliefs, they will never generate a deeper conversation and prayerful process to discern vision. Start with trust.

Vision Team   7
Trusted Leadership to Discern the Future

It was time to fish or cut bait for both mergers under consideration. Both pairs of churches understood that each congregation's board working separately could never develop a recommended strategic plan for merger. Therefore, each pair of churches held a congregational vote supporting, in principle, their respective mergers and appointing representatives to ad hoc committees that would develop strategic plans.

Each pair of churches called these committees their vision teams. In each potential merger scenario, the team would eventually bring a plan back to the congregations for final approval. Depending on the plan, it might also require approvals from parent denominational judicatories.

At the very beginning, it was important for all church members from both churches to understand the real mandate of a given vision team. It was not just representing the interests of each congregation. It was developing a plan to grow God's mission in the city from the combined spiritual lives and institutional assets of two churches.

The mandate of the vision team can be described using the metaphor of the Seeds and the Sower (Matthew 13:1–9). The "soil" was the mission field: all the lifestyle segments represented in a given pair of churches' particular neighborhoods. The "seeds" were those two churches: all of the human and physical resources that are dedicated to Christ. And the "sower," in this case, was the vision team itself in imitation of Jesus. The responsibility of the vision team was not to preserve each seed in a little bag for the sake of posterity, but to sow those seeds in particularly fertile ground so that they could bring forth a harvest "a hundredfold" more than the original church members.

In both merger scenarios, both churches assumed that their pastors would be a part of the vision team. There were some special circumstances in each merger process:

Merger 1: Wesley and Asbury

The pastor of Wesley initially wanted to decline. He felt that since he would be retiring soon, he should not have influence over the future of the church. His board, district superintendent, and other church partners persuaded him that his lack of participation would be a mistake. He was widely respected, and his experience was extraordinarily valuable to the planning process.

It was helpful for both pastors to talk with a church consultant. The consultant's experience helped the pastors understand how important their mission attitude and leadership credibility were to a merger conversation. Many people might have doubts and anxieties, but they will still commit to the conversation because they trust the leader. Where the leaders go, so goes the church.

Merger 2: Faith Temple and Pine Street Presbyterian

Similarly, the interim pastor at Pine Street wanted to decline, thinking that an interim ministry was more about pastoral care and healing divisions rather than future planning. A number of church members encouraged her decision. Again, her board, executive presbyter, and interim ministry colleagues persuaded her otherwise. The most important role of an interim pastor is to help the church live into God's future.

It was helpful for these pastors to talk with the senior minister of Harvest Community Church. He helped them see that the real issue in a merger is not ecclesiology, but missiology. Healing divisions in a church is a waste of time unless a mission heart is instilled in the people. Otherwise, the church will continue to be internally focused and a new set of divisions will emerge next year.

The tricky question for both merger processes, of course, was determining who else would be on the vision team! Everyone involved understood that for trust to be firm, the same criteria for nominations must apply to both churches participating in the merger. The criteria were simple, but crucial:

- Broad credibility as a leader across the diversity of each congregation
- Experience in long-range planning and organizational development
- Strong spiritual disciplines including prayer, Bible study, and regular worship attendance

The vision team for each merger process would include current pastors. Team members might or might not already hold offices in their home church.

In addition to these criteria, each pair of churches agreed that all team members would be held accountable by their home church to the four basic categories of credibility.

- Each needed to have a "mission attitude" that placed the greater good of the Realm of God above the needs of its own institution, and needed to wholeheartedly endorse the vision (theme song, inspiring image, and mission statement) of its congregation. This was a bit of a problem at Pine Street, as controllers there resisted the visioning process and wanted to lobby for their candidates for the committee. They were blocked. The authority to appoint representatives to the vision team lay with the Session.
- All promised to live up to the integrity of core values and bedrock beliefs that was the consensus of their congregation. This caused a stir at Faith Temple, because (unfortunately) some of the best strategic planners among the members were in fact undisciplined in spiritual practices. One appointee courageously took on a steep learning curve regarding biblical literacy and church doctrine.
- All promised to use or acquire whatever skills were necessary to create strategic plans that were relevant, realistic, and missional. This challenged people at Asbury, which had few members with senior-management experience. A continuing-education plan was developed to help appointees learn about demographic and lifestyle-segment research and to read up on organizational theory. Wesley actually gave money to Asbury to facilitate the necessary continuing education.
- All promised to work patiently, productively, and respectfully with colleagues on their respective committees. This proved to be the most challenging for leaders at Faith Temple. These leaders were not used to the collegiality of true teams. They had always worked in top-down "program silos" that rarely communicated or coordinated with other leaders. They needed to overcome habits of conflict avoidance and learn new skills for conflict reconciliation.

Both vision teams began their work with weekend retreats at a neutral site within their mission fields, but outside of their church facilities. Each team elected its own chairperson and secretary and promised to update each home church board (and relevant judicatories) on the progress of its work.

In both cases, it was generally assumed that the future board of any future merger would probably be based on the members of the vision team, but that issue would become clearer only through subsequent events.

The term "vision team" may not provide an accurate idea of exactly what such a team is about. This is because the noun "vision" and the gerund "visioning" are used in so many different ways. Vision is sometimes a metaphor to describe an inspirational goal, sometimes it is a pathway to get to a Promised Land, and sometimes it is a prophecy for the true cost of discipleship. The vision team inspires, guides, and challenges—and more. It may be more accurate to describe it as a "futuring team," because its real goal is to develop a new vehicle of relevance for the church to bless the mission field.

One of the most useful tools for the vision team is MissionInsite, www .missioninsite.com. This is the most sophisticated demographic and life-style search engine available to churches today, and many denominations subscribe to it and provide free access to their congregations. MissionInsite allows churches to not only investigate their communities in great detail, but it also enables them to plot their memberships and compare proportionate representations of lifestyle segments between their memberships and the community. This tool will be used in several ways in the merger conversation.

There are some basic challenges that will be faced by any vision team. The smallest challenge is to balance tradition and innovation. Every church tradition has a legacy of mission and adaptability, just as every tradition displays integrity about Christian values and bedrock beliefs. Once the legacy is uncovered and integrity is clarified, the power of controllers is lessened and churches can become much more flexible and open to consider future possibilities. It is somewhat more challenging, however, to balance future mission with the personal selfishness that lies at the heart of even the best of church members. Members of an established church almost inevitably assume that seniority matters, and often think of their church as a club for the privileged few. This is because stewardship campaigns are always so inwardly focused. The priority is always to *first* pay the bills of institutional salary, maintenance, and program, and *then* give whatever is extra to the mission. Even in the healthiest times, the stewardship ratio is about 70/30, but once churches have declined to the point of merger, that ratio is about 90% inwardly focused resources, and 10% outwardly focused resources. That mindset of what is "first mile" generosity and what is "second mile" generosity is deeply ingrained in church members of all traditions. It encourages an innate selfishness because it makes a subtle distinction between "what is ours" and "what is God's." It is hard to convince people that *it is all God's*. None of it is ours. Therefore, church resources must *serve the mission field, and not the membership*.

The two Methodist churches and Pine Street had access to www .missioninsite.com through their respective judicatories. They were able to use it to compare and contrast ministry expectations among the membership with ministry expectations in the community. They could see how their current programs in hospitality, worship, Christian education, and small groups were designed to bless the people they already had in membership; how their facilities and technologies, financial management and stewardship, and advertising and communication strategies were designed to be relevant to the people they currently reached. They could contrast these findings with how their programs and strategies would need to change to bless people in the community who were not represented or were underrepresented in the churches. These insights helped them see the "hidden selfishness" that shaped their churches.

These challenges are best addressed by the pastors from each church, and it is the real reason why they need to be on the team. Their preaching and, even more importantly, their role-modeling and individual mentoring will free the vision team to understand the mission field and reimagine the church.

The final and, perhaps, biggest challenge is to balance the possible and the impossible. Call this the "doable, stretchable continuum." Somehow the team must develop a way forward that is doable. It cannot be so expensive, complicated, or challenging that no matter how enthusiastic church leaders become, there is literally no realistic hope of achieving the outcome. Vision teams can get carried away. They use exalted rhetoric, cast grandiose visions, and imagine heroic results.

This was true of the vision teams in our story. During both retreats, to varying degrees, excitement was high. They all imagined new buildings with state-of-the-art technologies and social service alliances blanketing their mission fields; they had big hopes to convert large numbers of people to faith and rescue large numbers from suffering. It all sounded good, but it was simply not realistic.

The team also must develop a way forward that is stretchable. The way cannot be so cheap, simplistic, or easy that church members accomplish it without any extra financial generosity, additional commitment to learn and serve, or added incentive for spiritual growth. It has to tap the *real potential of generosity* of the people, and not just the *self-perception of poverty* of the people. Vision teams are tempted to simply accept staff reductions, diminishing programs, and maintenance of a status quo as inevitable. They use defeatist rhetoric, chase mundane visions, and imagine only limited results.

This was also true of the vision teams in our story. After additional retreats, they found their excitement dashed with the cold reality of high debts, aging memberships, and limited imagination. They went to the opposite extreme. They imagined relocating into warehouses, burying their dead with honor, baptizing the children of their remaining faithful families, and welcoming a handful of newcomers with bad coffee. It all sounded readily achievable, but was simply not hopeful.

Again, MissionInsite was helpful because it allowed the vision teams to objectively compare the financial potential of their church memberships against the financial potential for charitable giving in the community. The leaders in each vision team were astonished to discover just how much financial potential lay untapped among their members. They discovered that some members were not as poor as they thought. If membership giving were just motivated by the right vision, an increase in average giving from 2% of income to 4% of income could open a wide range of exciting possibilities.

These challenges are best addressed by the laity on a vision team, and those members should be chosen not just for their broad respect in the congregation, but for their experience in organizational and long-range planning, and their spiritual disciplines, which give them strength in adversity. They discern a way into the future that may *stretch* the commitment and resources of the congregations, but which *can be accomplished* if the people really want to do it.

This is why the four keys to accountability (see chapter 5) are so important and must be rigorously applied to the vision team.[1] Without such accountability, the vision team will not be able to help the churches balance tradition and innovation, generosity and selfishness, or the doable and stretchable. Team members may deliver a good plan, but people will either not believe them or refuse to do it.

Every vision team struggles with a different key to accountability at different times. Typically, initial struggles with accountability involve skills and teamwork.

Most vision teams feel immediately overwhelmed and inadequate. That's normal, because vision team members *are* inadequate! They have much to learn. They have new skills in analysis and synthesis to acquire. They have to master certain skills that may be common in other business or government sectors, but which are less developed among church and nonprofit leaders (e.g., how to develop focus groups, evaluate the safety and structural integrity of properties, empathize with the challenges of staff, understand new technologies and fundraising strategies, etc.). They may have to develop new disciplines for reflection and mission that may be common among educators and theologians but less developed among church members without liberal arts or other advanced training (e.g., understanding different learning methods, theological traditions, missiological principles, demographic research, etc.)

When skills are inadequate, the team must develop a continuing-education plan. Team members may need to read books, talk to experts, do online research, take a course, or visit another merger project in a similar context. The vision team needs to have a budget to accomplish such things.

Teamwork is usually the next early challenge. Even though the mandate is clearly defined, even the best leaders enter a vision team with a measure of defensiveness. They often feel overly protective of their pastor, people, or tradition. They may harbor condescension or judgment toward other traditions. And there are always anxieties over potential personality conflicts. Vision team conversations (like those of most small groups) progress through several levels of intimacy and trust—from cautious curiosity, to comparing expertise, to articulating deeper questions and insecurities. At that point there are clashes of egos and inevitable personality conflicts.

When team-building staggers, the team must take time for listening and relationship-building. It may need to have another retreat, invite a coach or mediator into its midst, involve expertise from its denominational program staff, develop shared disciplines of prayer and worship, or temporarily pair team members for more confidential conversation. This may not involve budget, but it does involve a spirit of goodwill and forgiveness.

As the vision team bonds around its larger purpose, conversation deepens and work progresses. There is greater trust and appreciation for the diverse skills, personalities, and perspectives that team members bring to the table. However, stress levels will also increase. Some of that stress will be about leaders and agencies *beyond* the churches, because the team will likely discover a level of suspicion, mistrust, or even hostility that it had not dreamed possible from city officials, social service agencies, banks, schools, and even other churches. Some of that stress will come from the staff, committees, and members *within* one or both churches as concern grows about future change.

At this point, accountability around attitude and integrity becomes urgent. It is tempting for individual team members, when they are alone in different contexts outside or inside the church, to subtly misrepresent the mission of the merger or compromise the values and beliefs shared by the team. Occasionally this can happen quite intentionally as team members try to overcome obstinacy or objection, thinking that "the end justifies the means." But usually this happens unintentionally and unconsciously as team members simply try to avoid conflict and smooth over problems. Either way, it is easy for the unity of the attitude and integrity to begin to fracture, so that there are multiple assumptions about the merger process and its anticipated outcomes, and therefore multiple opportunities for mis-understanding and feelings of betrayal.

Therefore, the vision team must be rigorous about regularly defining, refining, and celebrating the mission of the church and the team. And it must be consistent about reviewing the core values and beliefs that have been hammered out by the consensus of the congregations at the start of the process. This review and celebration should be a significant part of *every* team meeting without fail, no matter how urgent other practical matters seem to be. That is the only way team members can protect themselves and the team from somehow forgetting, subverting, or contradicting the purpose and integrity of the merger project.

The vision teams in our study soon discovered that the most funda-mental demand of leadership was courage. They needed to model for each congregational constituency the courage to take risks for the sake of the Gospel. They had to have the courage to endure inevitable stress and anxiety from the membership, and to be patient with inevitable doubt and suspicion from the community.

Quite aside from the details of any emerging future plan, the practice of vision team accountability helps ensure the long-term success of the ven-ture. As a general rule, accountability decreases as churches decline. There-fore, the practice of establishing the vision team as an effective model for all leaders in all participating churches is crucial. It helps church members to understand the importance of attitude, integrity, skills, and teamwork, and to "step up" to a higher standard of collaboration, continuous learning, behavior, and faith. That bodes well for the future merged church.

Facing Reality   8
Critical Mass and Critical Momentum

Both merger conversations started because both pairs of churches were in spirals of decline and/or financial trouble. The pastors recognized, however, that decline and financial struggle were only symptoms of deeper issues as the churches failed to thrive. The dialogue about trust identified *positive* shared values and faith convictions. Facing the reality of their situations, however, forced them to dialogue about *negative* behavior patterns or "corporate addictions."

For example, Wesley, Faith Temple, and Pine Street all had to own up to the "sacred cows" of their buildings, memorial objects, and other outdated technologies that cost money to carefully preserve. These did nothing to encourage church growth, especially among younger generations, and they dominated the agendas of many meetings that should have focused on other programs. Any change to property caused enormous conflict. Some sacred cows actually discouraged participation by younger generations, multiethnic groups, and other publics that were growing in the mission field.

A second reality to be faced by all the churches was the extraordinarily low participation of adults in any structured midweek program of faith formation. Lack of accountable adult spiritual disciplines not only hurt giving, but it reduced volunteerism and undermined evangelism. This was especially hard to face for the leaders of Faith Temple and Pine Street because the Baptist and Presbyterian traditions had always stressed adult spiritual growth. The current lack of participation might be explained by the wide disbursement of members across the city, but how the situation originated was unclear.

There were some especially difficult "reality checks" in store for some churches in each merger conversation.

Merger 1: Wesley and Asbury

These churches had very different practices regarding worship, stewardship, and outreach. Wesley emphasized classical music and the visual arts in educational worship; Asbury emphasized gospel music and dance in more inspirational worship. Wesley raised money by pledge, and invested in outreach through financial grants and board leadership. Asbury raised money by tithe, and invested in outreach through hands-on service and nonprofit partnerships.

At this point, its vision team had another very instructive conversation with a consultant. She taught them how to do a comprehensive systemic analysis of the life and work of a church. They were able to see beyond programs to the processes and habits that were unique in every church.

Merger 2: Faith Temple and Pine Street

Both these churches had to face the "revolving door" problem that leaders had allowed to persist in their churches: Visitors would come but not return; new people would join by confession or transfer and fail to attend; weddings and funerals yielded little interest in the church. Their bad habits of poor follow-up to create opportunities for new and renewing Christians translated into chronic volunteer burnout (Faith Temple) and chronic financial deficits (Pine Street).

Although it was not the most important factor, the age of regular participants in worship and church programs strongly influenced critical mass (see below and chapter 22). Wesley and Pine Street had the higher median age in each of their merger pairings. In the '90s this meant that they had the most bequests, but that income stream dried up in the new millennium. Asbury and Faith Temple had younger median ages in each pairing, but their more ethnically diverse participants had less disposable income that was eroded even further in the new millennium.

In both cases, the pastors and home boards generally conceded that their churches should have begun their conversations about merger a decade earlier. Now there was a serious question whether even merger would provide sufficient resources to either pair of churches to sustain critical mass. And certainly they would have to face the deeper issues that brought them to this impasse in the first place.

In order to face reality, outside perspective and advice is helpful.

Faith Temple and Pine Street once again talked with the leaders of Harvest Community Church. Whatever its points of agreement or disagreement were about the theory and practice of ministry, the one thing at which Harvest

Community excelled was the ability to sustain critical momentum. It had mastered the art of both organizational and missional growth and was able to offer invaluable coaching around the processes of seeker sensitivity, adult faith formation, volunteer deployment, and risk management.

Wesley and Asbury once again talked with a church consultant. Whatever her points of agreement or disagreement were about public policies or alternative theologies, the one thing the consultant understood well was critical mass. She helped the church understand that the ability of a church to thrive did not just depend on sustainable "bricks and mortar," but also on a critical mass of visitors, membership diversity, small group participation, and focused outreach.

Their insights from these outside voices helped the vision teams see their strengths and weaknesses in a whole new way. They began to see how mergers could help them address their weaknesses and build on their strengths. The vision teams saw the advantages of working with an outside consultant who knew how to adapt the learnings from one church and apply them to the polities and practices of others.

Churches that seriously consider merger most often rely on an outside expert. This is usually an experienced leader who is familiar with many different traditions and polities or who has led or guided church transformation. This expert is *within* the Christian tradition, active in faith, and acquainted with the idiosyncrasies and organizational peculiarities that set churches apart from other nonprofit services. On the other hand, this expert is independent from any one congregation or denomination. He or she can stand apart from the politics, prejudices, and hidden assumptions that inevitably involve church insiders.

The vision teams of both church pairs invited experts to lead workshops for them on critical mass and critical momentum. Most churches have no real idea about either process, and individual members tend to project their assumptions and biases on the merger conversation. Doing so immediately skews the conversation, sidetracks debate, and sabotages future strategic plans. Large corporations use consultants in their mergers; and the truth is that even small churches are actually more complicated and change is more emotionally charged than in large corporations.

Critical Mass

The first thing to assess in reality-testing is *critical mass*. This is a frank evaluation of the organization to achieve the minimal requirements to sustain community life and mission. In other words, there are certain measurable outcomes required simply to *survive*, if not *thrive*. These benchmarks vary from sector to sector and organization to organization. Sustaining critical mass is the primary responsibility of the board.

In a church, critical mass may vary among Christian traditions, denominations, and groups. However, if by "church" we mean what most people think of when they refer to a "church," it is not that difficult to define critical mass at this point in Christendom. Most people think of a "church" as a Christian community with a clear identity and purpose, led by spiritual leaders, worshipping weekly in a designated and often recognizable space that stands apart in the community. This "church" is an institution led by certified priests or pastors, with specific rules and sustained by generous members. It supports programs to educate people in the polities and purposes of the institution. It holds leaders and members accountable to certain norms of behavior and belief, and for the accomplishment of uniquely Christian goals.

It is possible to define benchmarks for such a "church" to sustain itself in the post-Christendom world. Different traditions and contexts might certainly modify the measurements, but they will still be fairly consistent across the spectrum of institutional churches today. (For an in-depth treatment of critical mass, see chapter 22.) Here are the criteria for critical mass for an institutional church in the mid-2010s, in North America, in a nutshell:

- Clarity and consensus around the vision/mission, core values, and bedrock beliefs of the congregation
- 4–7 board members, respected as "spiritual leaders" of the church, mentoring emerging leaders and modeling core values
- 125–150 members (resident or active at least 9 months of the year in congregational programs)
- 100–125 weekly average worship attendance
- 100–200 first- or second-time connections to worship each year
- 1 worship service that is highly motivational and culturally relevant to 1 or more major lifestyle segments in the community
- 1 strong hospitality team, trained in seeker sensitivity and regularly in prayer for the community
- 60% adult worshippers active in a midweek small group (fellowship plus accountable spiritual growth)
- 33% adult members regularly volunteering in hands-on outreach specifically sponsored by the congregation
- 1 major, year-round, outreach focus or signature outreach ministry for which the church has a public reputation

- Pledging by church leaders that is at least 3 to 5% *higher* than the average or median congregational pledge (whichever is higher)
- An intentional, year-round stewardship plan with multiple choices in giving, and optional coaching for personal and family Christian financial planning
- 1 regular, affordable, accessible location at which to gather

The same criteria can be used in church planting and multisite ministry. Harvest Community Church, for example, used a similar template in its development of additional church sites. Once a new site of ministry achieved critical mass, this larger church could "turn them loose" and re-direct assets to start another church.

Most churches find the summary of critical mass daunting. Today, in fact, as many as 80% of the churches in North America fall below critical mass using the criteria here. But this does not necessarily mean that they must explore merger immediately. There are extenuating circumstances:

- Membership and participation may fluctuate seasonally as people migrate south or north.
- Education and fellowship may still be strong in traditional large women's and men's groups.
- Outreach ministry may be anchored by a separately incorporated nonprofit that receives significant grants.
- Denominations may significantly subsidize small churches that are crucial to their regional plans.
- Church members may be expected or required to tithe.
- The overhead costs of location and facility may be maintained by another agency.

Even with these extenuating circumstances, however, churches that fail to sustain critical mass will likely need to consider merger or some other "drastic action" in ten to fifteen years. The trend is to sustain critical mass in a central place and then radiate small groups that are led by laity and located in borrowed or rented facilities as different sites of the same church. In other words, congregations and denominations are becoming more urgent about healthy and faithful mergers in the post-Christendom world.

Church plants, of course, start small and are usually below critical mass. If they are subsidized by a denomination, they are expected to become sustainably independent within about five years. In our story, Asbury started small and then grew to about two hundred members. Along the

way, it achieved other marks of critical mass. It practiced strong accountability to values, beliefs, and mission, and chose board members widely
respected for spiritual maturity. They welcomed well over two hundred
visitors in a year, invested in strong hospitality, and enjoyed 80% member
participation in midweek small groups. Although average giving to the
church was low due to the target public reached, giving by leaders was
very sacrificial. They had a city-wide reputation for youth ministry and
addiction intervention.

The decline of Asbury and Pine Street offers lessons that are instructive
for any board seeking to sustain critical mass. The vulnerability of Asbury
lay in its dependency on a single pastor. When the church experienced the
tragic death of an early founder and then a scandal involving a later pastor,
worship attendance plummeted. The vulnerability of Pine Street lay in its
uncritical allegiance to denominational public policies. When the denomination committed itself to a controversial policy, respect for the pastor
and board plummeted, and the church split into two factions that were
incapable of respectful dialogue or calm negotiation. In both churches,
volunteers disappeared and small groups declined. Reputation suffered and
giving went down.

This is instructive, because it reveals that money is not the primary reason churches fall below critical mass. Poverty, poor locations, inadequate
parking, and dilapidated facilities do not, by themselves, drive a church to
that point. A downward spiral actually begins with diminished leadership
credibility, decreasing commitment to adult faith formation, decreasing
relevance of Sunday worship, and a splintered relationship in which the
faith community and social outreach go in different directions.

Critical Momentum

The second step in facing reality is to assess *critical momentum*. This is a
frank evaluation of the ability of an organization to take raw materials
(physical or human resources), shape them in an effective and repeatable
fashion (programs or technologies), and ultimately deliver a quality product (programs or people) that is relevant and effective to continually grow
the church and maximize mission impact on the community. Sustaining
critical momentum is the primary responsibility of a core leadership team.

In a church context, *critical momentum* is the process through which a
church includes new people and welcomes seekers; brings them into a life-
shaping experience of God; matures them to understand faith; calls them to
take their place in God's mission; equips them with whatever tools, teams,

and resources necessary to do mission well; and finally deploys them to bless the world in the name of Christ—thereby drawing new seekers into the life of the church where the process is repeated over and over again. The "product" of a church is the multiplication of disciples and the maximization of positive social change.

Six basic subsystems combine to grow a church in spirituality, membership, and resources, and maximize its mission impact on the community and the world:

- **Radical Hospitality**—How a church communicates a message, welcomes and accepts people, builds new relationships, listens to their needs, and invites them to meet Jesus
- **Targeted Worship**—How a church designs the method and content of worship so that people experience Christ in relevant ways and are motivated for further spiritual growth and mission service
- **Mature Discipleship**—How a church assimilates and educates members, shapes profound spiritual life, and networks Christians in lifelong spiritual growth
- **Volunteer Empowerment**—How a church mentors callings, trains leaders, preserves integrity, encourages creativity, and sustains accountability
- **Intentional Stewardship**—How a church raises money, manages debt, maintains property, upgrades technology, and uses the resources of the church to equip servants
- **Relevant Outreach**—How the church prioritizes mission, deploys mission teams, develops action plans, measures success, and networks with other organizations

These subsystems are all linked together. Each one forwards people to the next system. Seekers that know little about God and God's mission are moved through a process that eventually deploys disciples to bless the world. These disciples invite new seekers to participate in the system with them, and the process—critical momentum—goes on and on. (For an in-depth treatment of critical momentum, see chapter 21.)

Critical momentum breaks down when any subsystem fails to forward people to the next subsystem. The explanation above is very tidy but, of course, life is very messy. People today can enter disciple-making at any point in the process, and continue to grow in faith and participate in mission in different and counterintuitive ways.

For example, newcomers who became involved at Wesley usually did so in the traditional way. They came to worship on Sunday morning. Based on their experience of radical hospitality and current options for Christian education, they might choose to return. This traditional means of entering the disciple-making system, however, is not the only way (and today is not even the most popular way).

People entered the life of Pine Street Presbyterian Church primarily through small midweek groups or special affinity groups like choirs. Then they attended special services at Christmas and Easter (or other holidays); and only after a year or more would they even consider attending Sunday worship regularly.

People entered the life of Faith Temple and Asbury in yet another way. They first connected with the church through outreach ministries. Some individuals and families first participated in the charter school before they attended worship at Faith Temple. Other individuals first participated in addiction intervention programs and support groups before they ever came to worship.

The very "messiness" of the disciple-making process makes it even more important for church leaders to understand, monitor, and intentionally move people into the next step to maturity and service. The trouble is that most churches are declining precisely because leaders don't understand how to monitor people's progress or move them forward.

A church board can even "score" each subsystem on a scale of one to ten. A "one" means that the subsystem is completely failing to achieve desired outcomes; and a "ten" means that the church is perfect in achieving desired outcomes. This is admittedly a subjective process, but if church leaders encourage different groups (e.g., youth groups, women's groups, members under five years, members over five years, first-time visitors, etc.) to score the church from their perspective, the average score will provide a pretty good assessment of the real success of a church. The exercise is even more helpful if it includes a perspective from denominational staff or an independent consultant.

As a rule of thumb, an average score in any of the six subsystems that is between "seven" and "ten" suggests that the ministry area is highly effective and just needs a few "tweaks." A score that is from "four" to "six" suggests that a ministry area is inconsistent at best and requires leadership training or shifts in strategy. A score that is between "one" and "three" suggests that a ministry area is critically failing and needs drastic change.

In the postmodern world of diminishing resources and reduced time, any church that is *struggling* in two or more ministry areas (i.e., scoring 4–6) is in serious need of church renewal. And any church that is *failing* in two or more ministry areas (i.e., 1–3) needs to consider drastic action (merger or even closure). Consider the "scorecards" for each of the four churches (table 8.1):

Table 8.1.   Case Study Examples for Rating Church Systems

Average Scores from Focus Groups and Independent Consultant	Wesley	Asbury	Faith Temple	Pine Street
Radical Hospitality	4	8	5	2
Targeted Worship	4	8	4	3
Mature Discipleship	4	3	3	4
Volunteer Empowerment	2	1	2	2
Intentional Stewardship	3	2	2	4
Relevant Outreach	3	5	7	5
Total	**20**	**27**	**23**	**20**

Note that there were some widely contrasting perspectives among focus groups in each church. These prompted important discussions between younger and older members, veterans and newcomers, singles and families, and so on.

The goal of a merger is to create a synergy of personal growth that transforms seekers into disciples—and sends disciples to bless seekers. Therefore, it is helpful to understand where individual churches are strong or weak. Chapter 21 addresses the fact that churches considering merger are usually dysfunctional in at least three of the six subsystems. This is why their best efforts for church renewal fail, even though their leaders are sincere and their programs are correct. Even at their best, these declining churches only take people so far in the disciple-making process; the churches lose them somewhere along the way.

Remember that nothing is "sacred" except the disciple-making process. No member in any church can claim authority over any step in the disciple-making process as his or her "turf." No program in any church can claim to be untouchable or unchangeable. Christ called us to make disciples who would bless the world in his name. He did not call us to preserve a Sunday school, preserve old hymnals, endorse hereditary board members, rescue pews and stained glass, or maintain unsuccessful mission projects.

Church boards (especially *declining* church boards) often allow them-selves to be drawn down into micromanagement, and lose the big picture of critical momentum. This bad habit is carried over into merger conver-sations. They leap to discuss tactics regarding staff deployment, worship format and specific programs, specific property and technology dilemmas, and fundraising and debt management. Instead, they must focus on the systemic dysfunctions that have led to decline in the first place and which must be corrected if any future merger is to be successful.

That said, it is vital for churches in a merger conversation to avoid *hasty* decisions about staff, worship, and property. Too many churches leap to argue about staff configurations, worship practices, and property use with-out first understanding the strengths and weaknesses of the disciple-making process. Hasty decisions about staff, worship, and property only accentuate and accelerate loss in critical momentum.

Wesley and Pine Street Presbyterian, for example, were both in clergy transitions. It was tempting for them to reap short-term benefits in budget planning by cutting back on full-time ministry or postponing merger con-versation until there was a clergy vacancy. This would have been a major error. The merger discussion is precisely the time when a church needs full-time professional leadership. Moreover, this pastoral leadership must model the positive values and beliefs of the church and contribute to the assessment of critical momentum. The leaders not only have expertise and experience, but the Holy Spirit works through their leadership.

Meanwhile, Faith Temple was tempted to discontinue what it de-scribed as its "contemporary" worship service early in its merger conversa-tion. It considered combining its two services into a single blended service in order to gather more people in the room. The goals to improve fel-lowship and communication were good ones; but this would have been a major mistake. Blended worship *always* favors tradition over creativity, no matter how hard worship designers try to avoid it. There will inevitably be complaints, but those from older, traditional members who are more likely to be good givers *always* outweigh those from younger, less traditional members who are often poor givers. The younger adults and families and some ethnic groups would have dropped out rather than attend a so-called blended worship service. Their voices would have been lost in the merger conversation. Fortunately, Faith Temple continued both worship options, and even added funding to the "contemporary" service, knowing how im-portant it was to have younger and culturally diverse voices in the merger conversation. The church expanded the refreshment time *between* services to mingle the two congregations and improve communication.

Finally, all four churches, in both merger conversations, were tempted to maintain financial stability by renting out all of their available space to other church, nonprofit, or for-profit organizations, rather than raising expectations for generosity among members They wanted to pretend that "rental" meant "mission," but it was really just a fundraising plan. A premature decision in this vein would have caused more conflict down the road. First, it would have complicated future conversations about sale or renovation of property and facility. Other organizations would now have a vested interest in that conversation, and the churches would artificially limit their options. Second, the churches would have restricted the available space for their *own* ministries, undermining efforts to increase hospitality, expand education, and/or multiply small groups, because outside groups claimed space. Finally, controllers within each congregation would have been tempted to use contracts or commitments as a means to pursue personal, rather than congregational, agendas.

Thus, the director of music at Pine Street wanted to protect sanctuary space because the city symphony preferred it. The memorial committee of Wesley wanted to protect parlor space because the civic museum displayed artifacts in it. The youth group of Asbury wanted to protect the gymnasium because the "Upward Sports" program played basketball in it. Fortunately, the leaders of all the churches managed to resist these temptations. They found other ways to raise money, and indicated their readiness to *listen* to community organizations but maintain independence in strategic planning.

Mergers not only regain critical mass, but they also renew critical momentum. The factors that cause decline (leadership credibility, adult faith formation, relevant worship, and outreach that is simultaneously social service and evangelism) are the same factors that start renewal. Healthy mergers build on the *foundations* of church life (trust, vision, leadership); expand the *functions* of church life (programs, ministries); and only then focus the *forms* of church life (facilities, stewardship). The goal of a merger is to achieve and sustain critical mass and critical momentum for the life and mission of the church.

Breaking Control

Surrendering Privileges

9

The first crisis in both merger conversations caught the pastors and vision teams by surprise. Both pairs celebrated the growing self-esteem, seeker sensitivity, and mutual respect that they were building. Each congregation began to put into practice clear expectations for positive behavior patterns and clarify bedrock beliefs. Yet this was precisely what some individuals and families in each church actually feared and resented. "Controllers," the influential personalities that want to shape the church around their personal preferences, tastes, lifestyles, convictions, and opinions lost power once the church focused on God's vision.

Control can be unconscious or intentional, subtle or overt, but it usually emerges in predictable stages. As each stage of control is addressed, controllers often escalate stress to the next stage. Control begins with denial; continues through turf protection, inflexibility, and dithering; and can eventually lead to denigration, hostage-taking, and king-making.

The crisis of control unfolded in a predictable pattern, although each church experienced peaks of stress in different ways.

Merger 1: Wesley and Asbury

Wesley struggled most with "denial" and "turf protection" (the first and second stages of control). Two key families and strong financial givers simply would not admit that the church was in trouble, that the neighborhood was changing, and that the church should adapt in order to bless strangers to grace. They felt a strong sense of denominational superiority and feared that merger would undermine their control of the remaining trust funds of the church.

Perhaps ironically, Asbury also struggled with "denial" and "turf protection" for opposite reasons. Two or three of the founding members refused to recognize that their church was in trouble, that African American publics were diversifying, and the church should adapt to more complex multiculturalism. They feared that what they perceived as a grass-roots movement would be taken over by wealthy power brokers in the historic church. They felt that their authority to interpret the spirit and influence tactics might be diminished.

Wide participation and personal diligence in the trust-building and vision discernment processes went a long way to break the churches out of denial and turf protection. The pastors wisely enlisted the help of strong supporters of the merger conversation who were also friends with the controllers. They were able to speak faithfully and reasonably with the controllers about keeping eyes open toward the mission field and hearts open to other churches.

Merger 2: Faith Temple and Pine Street

Pine Street Presbyterian and Faith Temple struggled most with "inflexibility" and "dithering" (the third and fourth stages of control). Two trustees at Faith Temple wanted to delay the merger conversation and insist that even small decisions be made by consensus of the entire congregation, knowing full well that they could always sway a minority for a negative decision. Meanwhile, two members of the Pine Street board who were active in denominational committees interpreted denominational polity as narrowly as possible and insisted on judicatory approval to even allow merger talks. They were motivated by fear that a merger would give too much power to the local congregation and undermine denominational public policies.

The leaders of each church got into the habit of sharing inspiring stories of externally focused churches and successful mergers in worship, newsletters, and fellowship gatherings. These inspiring stories motivated participants to insist that the churches "get on with it" and develop a serious strategic plan despite the objections of a minority. The more people became results-oriented rather than process-obsessed, the less they dithered. Fortunately, regional denominational leaders who were more aware of the challenges of the postmodern world and more open to creative thinking in organizational development, cautiously encouraged the congregations to continue the conversation.

The power of control did not cease, however. Each church suffered "denigration" and "hostage-taking," the fifth and sixth stages of control, in greater or lesser degrees. Two families decided to withhold their financial contributions while continuing to attend. Several controllers announced their intention to leave the church (and take their financial contribution, the choir, their Sunday school class, etc., with them) if the eventual merger strategies did not meet with their approval. The pastors of Wesley and Faith Temple were safe from denigration owing to their long tenures and great respect, but individual board members unexpectedly faced criticism about both faithful leadership and personal lifestyle.

The young new pastor of Asbury and the interim pastor of Pine Street felt more pressure. The office of the clergy in both these churches had lost credibility through past conflicts and embarrassments. Each church had unconsciously empowered powerful personalities to evaluate clergy with narrow "litmus tests" of ideological agreement or dogmatic purity.

Control issues did delay and sidetrack merger conversations for a time. However, the momentum for trust and vision was hard to stop. A clear majority of members and adherents from each church saw the potential to become a real blessing in the name of Christ in the community. The leaders were encouraged to keep talking and develop a serious proposal for the future.

The very first thing a ship must do to get under way is to remove the heavy cables that tie it to the dock. The ship can have the very best officers and a well-disciplined crew, and an accurate map and a clear destination; it can even feel the winds of the Spirit billowing the sails; but unless the cables tying the ship to the pier are removed, it will never get anywhere. Yet that is precisely what happens to many churches in a merger.

The truth is that churches may be clear about values and beliefs, but frightened by accountability. They may be hopeful to participate in God's mission to bless the world, but frightened by the sacrifices. They can have meeting after meeting, revisit and fine-tune the mission statement, and enjoy countless potluck suppers that bring congregations together, but lack the courage to remove the cables and get going.

In every church merger there are a few individuals or families from each church that seize on this lack of courage to undermine the process. If they can just keep the church tied to the dock long enough, the adventurous folk in favor of merger will eventually become discouraged and give up.

After all, no matter what the strategic plan might be, there are always three kinds of reactions. About 20% of the people urgently want change, another 20% of the people urgently do *not* want change, and about 60% of the people are reasonably content, open-minded, and will follow wherever the leaders lead. This means that change of any sort is a struggle between two minorities to influence a sleeping majority.

By the time the merger conversation has laid a foundation of trust and hope, those proportions have been dramatically altered. By this time there is a much larger group of people pushing for change and a much smaller group of people resisting change. This smaller group of "controllers" may only be three or four individuals, couples, or families, but they usually influence a larger circle of faithful but anxious individuals. Their influence is usually behind-the-scenes—in the kitchen or Sunday school room rather than in the sanctuary or the board room—and they play on the fears of disharmony that change inevitably implies.

"Controllers" are people who want to shape the church around themselves. They want the church to shape programs around privilege. The church must honor their aesthetic tastes, their tactical preferences, their personal needs, their ideological points of view, and their theological idiosyncrasies. They are unwilling to sacrifice their personal desires for the good of God's mission. The merger process that builds trust and accountability and that focuses mission and hope is a direct challenge to their ability to control what happens. The more the church celebrates trust and enthuses about mission, the more worried, anxious, and desperate this diminishing group of controllers becomes.

The difficulty in dealing with controllers is that they do not need to win any argument. They only need to delay decision-making. This is why they dislike clarity over values, beliefs, vision, and mission. They thrive best in confusion, ambiguity, and uncertainty. They can then impose their own preferences and opinions as the boundaries beyond which the church cannot go—and call that "tradition."

Controllers emerge in a vacuum of leadership. Small churches cannot fill all the offices and leadership positions that the denomination requires (or that the church believes to be necessary). Therefore, they lower the criteria for leadership, making it possible for those with the least credibility and greatest need for authority to lead the church. They are often micromanagers, can be highly efficient, and become the dominant force in the daily affairs of the church. They become so enmeshed in the infrastructure of the church that the mere thought of losing them terrifies the members. The church cannot afford to offend them, saying, *What would we ever do if so-and-so weren't around?*

Controllers often function as a "shadow board." Young adults know that the *real* party is the one *after* the party. Controllers know that the *real* decisions are made in a restaurant or living room *after* the board meeting. They gather the people most susceptible to their influence and revisit every report, recommendation, and decision. They strategize on how to undermine decisions they don't like and accelerate decisions they do like.

The result of micromanagement and second-guessing is that everything becomes a negotiation in the merger. Trust is undermined, and every decision large or small must be endlessly discussed and approved by a near majority. Most church polities entrust important decisions to a cadre of credible leaders (i.e., those with a mission attitude, high integrity, relevant competencies, and sense of teamwork). Controllers advocate congregational consensus, knowing that in the resulting confusion and turmoil they can delay decisions forever and emerge as the saviors of the congregation once the more adventurous members and leaders leave.

The great fear in a merger is disharmony. Some family might be forgotten. Some member might be disappointed. Someone might leave. Controllers play upon this fear. They always focus the merger conversation on appeasing members who are already there, rather than blessing the publics that are not there. The fear of losing a few always overshadows the joy of blessing many. Controllers always claim to be speaking on behalf of a large group of people; they shrug off demands to identify those people as a breach of confidentiality. This leaves the silent majority of contented but open-minded members worrying about hurting beloved personalities and unrealistically searching for guarantees of success.

The final stage of control, king-making, is often the most insidious. By this time, many controllers have left, but the few that remain use their influence to bargain for leadership. They make the vision team or pastor a tempting offer. They agree to support the merger process completely, and restore harmony to the church, in exchange for having ultimate power to approve or veto the choice of pastoral leadership in the newly merged church. In essence, they become the chamberlain who guards access to the king.

The only way this last gasp of control can be defeated is by returning again to the big, bold, faithful vision that drives the merger process itself. The more the vision of multiplying disciples to bless the community in the name of Christ dominates the hearts and minds of the church, the easier it will be to resist the temptation of harmony at any cost. Everything and everyone should align with the vision, and not with compromise.

As we followed the stories of the two pairs of churches, we saw that control was exercised in different ways (denial, turf protection, inflexibility, dithering, denigration, hostage-taking, and king-making). Two of the seven control strategies are the most common and deserve elaboration.

Dithering is by far the most effective strategy to undermine a merger. Analysis of critical momentum and critical mass can overcome denial and turf-protection. Stories of success and urgency for local mission, often combined with support from regional denominational bodies, can overcome inflexibility. *Dithering* is the strategy that controllers exercise the most, and it has been remarkably more effective in blocking mergers (and eventually closing churches) than any other strategy. It ties up the energy of leaders with meetings, surveys, and negotiations; focuses on the *internal* wishful thinking of members rather than the *external* needs of the community; and frustrates leaders who are urgent about change.

The best way to counter the strategy of *dithering* is to raise expectations for leadership and use clearer values, beliefs, vision, and mission as vehicles for membership accountability and ministry planning. This takes away confusion (like blowing away fog from a harbor), and disempowers controllers (who function like foghorns in a fog). Values, beliefs, vision, and mission are intentionally included in every worship service and used in every nomination process from the lowliest to the highest volunteer position. They start every training and evaluation process. They help prioritize every strategic plan. And they are the bottom line for all merger conversations.

Trust replaces control. Leaders can be given both responsibility *and authority* to make decisions. Decisions are made with clear boundaries and goals that are supported by the majority of members. Self-centered members or dysfunctional leaders no longer have the freedom to disrupt proceedings at will, but faithful members and mission-minded leaders have more tools to evaluate the integrity of any decision. The merger can now be built on policy and purpose, rather than on personality and peer pressure.

King-making is the second most effective strategy to undermine a merger. This is not to say that other layers of control are not painful and difficult. Controllers often undermine the merger by denigrating leaders through gossip, slander, or condescension, but these can be overcome by the integrity, spiritual discipline, and expertise of staff and board. Controllers also undermine a merger by hostage-taking (withholding money, threatening splits, or even launching legal appeals); but these can be overcome by excellent communication and the solidarity of staff and board. In the end, king-making is the last resort of control.

King-makers are controllers who offer a "devil's bargain": *I will support the merger in every way, provided I have status and power in the new church.* This offer can be very subtle and surrounded by many promises of eternal friendship. Indeed, the king-making bargain is often more personal than professional. Leaders may be so hurt and bruised that gestures of personal support and promises for a final victory can be enticing. The pain suddenly goes away, and the path becomes smooth.

It is this kind of control that usually leads to some formula for power-sharing in the newly merged church. Administrative structure is now moved forward in the merger conversation, even before seeker sensitivity, program-planning, and staffing needs. In other words, before the ministries of the church have ever been evaluated and revised, prior agreements determine who will do the evaluation and revision. The new board is chosen to represent power brokers from each church. Controllers trade seniority and influence for status and power. The controller becomes the pastor's "best friend" and "right hand," and starts to function like a "chamberlain" that controls access to the "king."

Two things are noteworthy about the subtlety of king-making. First, controllers are not always mean or adversarial. Those controllers often leave the church, or step away from participation, once denigration and hostage-taking fail. King-makers have been holding back and lying in wait. They may well have been vocal supporters of the merger from the beginning. They have stood behind the pastor or supported the board, and celebrated the merger. Yet in the end, it is still about control rather than mission. It is really about power rather than blessing. Merger leaders who have overcome personal agendas to embrace a larger purpose are met with another set of personal agendas imposed in the *guise* of a larger purpose. In a very short time, negative behavior patterns return, mission to the community loses energy, the new congregation turns inward again, the fog blows back into the harbor, and another set of foghorns imposes boundaries of self-interest.

This is a primary reason why mergers fail. The whole fails to be more than the sum of the parts. The pastor of the newly merged church becomes short-term and is soon replaced. Even the name of the new church becomes just a hyphenated list of all of the congregations that were once separate.

The best way to counter such control is to focus attention on the overarching vision of mission to the community, rather than the individual pastor, priest, or patriarch. The merger is not embraced as a gesture of sympathy and support for the pastor, but as a renewed commitment to bless the world in more effective ways. Too often that pastor is given the credit, when in fact the Holy Spirit should be given the credit. Once again the consensus around values, beliefs, vision, and mission must be elevated higher than any individual leader.

The second noteworthy insight is that *there is a hidden controller inside every one of us!* We can become a controller without even realizing it. It is not that easy to separate personal desires from God's plans. Indeed, we confuse the two all the time. Our agendas and preferences can easily be mistaken for the only right path.

The best way to counter the hidden controller in all of us is through the disciplines of a spiritual life. Honesty and humility cannot be achieved without it. A merger is not just an administrative triumph. It is a spiritual breakthrough. The merged church goes deeper in faith formation and further in mission outreach. It reaches a new level of spiritual discernment and lifestyle surrender. The king-maker will always balk at going still deeper and further. The true leader never stops.

Hope

10

Opening to God's Grace

The conversations about merger were now gaining momentum in each pairing of churches. The staff and boards were now fully engaged. The members and stakeholders in each congregation were regularly updated and invited to comment. Every worship service in every church included earnest prayers for spiritual guidance and wisdom for the leaders. The stress level was going up, but so far this was a good thing. It meant that people were paying attention and thinking about the true cost of discipleship. The churches were weak, but God was strong. It was crucial to seek God's will for each church individually and collectively.

The trouble was that none of the churches had a clear vision or particularly memorable mission statement. Their statements were either generic denominational slogans or vague intentions to worship, educate, and serve. As a result, there was no overall goal with which to align all activities nor clearly defined measurable outcomes with which to evaluate success. This made the merger process vulnerable to control in the form of "king-making." And it was difficult to do strategic planning for either merger.

The vision teams led their respective churches through similar discernment processes. In addition to personal and corporate prayer, the discernment process included prayer walks through the surrounding neighborhoods, prayer triads lingering in public places to listen and observe, focus groups to understand the questions and needs of the diverse publics, and interviews with social service and health care agencies.

In each merger conversation, each church was asked to add three things to the conversations about merger: a theme song that powerfully expressed the motivation and *raison d'être* of the congregation, an inspirational image that captured the values and beliefs of the congregation, and a revised mission statement that was memorable and useful to measure success.

Merger 1: Wesley and Asbury

Wesley celebrated a traditional hymn by Charles Wesley ("Love Divine, All Loves Excelling") and chose a classic image of Jesus the Good Shepherd (based on a stained glass window above the altar). Then they reduced their long, pedantic mission statement to three simple, memorable words: "Community, Communion, Compassion."

Asbury celebrated a traditional hymn by Charles Tindley ("Stand by Me") and chose a contemporary painting of "Christ Healing the Sick" by Romeo Beardon (an African American painter and jazz musician). The church let the youth group write a new mission statement that was highly motivational and memorable: "Christ SO BIG he can embrace all your friends!"

Merger 2: Faith Temple and Pine Street

Faith Temple unhesitatingly chose a camp song that they sang after every children's story in worship: "This Little Light of Mine." A classic Sunday school image of "Jesus with the Little Children" accompanied it. Their revised mission statement revealed their educational emphasis and linked the church to their charter school: "Shaping Future Disciples of Jesus Christ."

The music director at Pine Street composed an original song for the congregation entitled "I've Seen the Light." The refrain was "Jesus knows your name / We can guarantee! / He commands, you obey / He'll set you free!" They also chose the well-known image of the "Laughing Jesus" as their inspiration (perhaps in reaction to the congregational split they had previously experienced). Their mission statement was still fairly intellectual: "Think . . . with the mind of Christ, Love . . . with the heart of Christ, Serve . . . with the might of Christ."

The spiritual discernment processes deepened the faith and raised self-esteem in each of the churches. In the weeks to come, the songs, images, and statements were shared and celebrated repeatedly in worship, Sunday schools, small groups, and board meetings of each participating church. This built mutual understanding and respect. Many questions about faith, strategy, structure, and leadership remained, but an intuitive and heartfelt bond began to be forged among the congregations.

As the listening strategies among the neighborhoods continued, members and leaders of each church began to see opportunities for outreach and witness. They began to think of others more than themselves, and to focus on community health and development more than just institutional survival.

Church mergers are not necessarily a means of survival; instead, they can offer a great means of hope and grace to churches that want to reach their community. Once a church faces the reality of its situation, it can be open to God's grace, which may be extended through a merger. A merger does not necessarily mean that one church is dying. A church may be growing and reaching its community but desiring a building that a church merger can provide. In the same way, a church that is dying may be able to add more people through a merger. In both scenarios, hope and grace are extended to both churches through the possibility of a merger.

Often when we lead organizational change, we ask people to dream for a moment. In this dreaming exercise, we ask them to dream about what God may want us to do. We place no limitations on what the dream may be; money, resources, and people are not issues! We simply ask, using a sanctified imagination, *What do our people believe God is leading us to do*? We ask them to let their hopes and dreams have life for a moment.

At this point in the merger process, it is often helpful for vision teams to step back and reflect upon a biblical theology of hope and how it integrates to the dreaming process. The essence of faith, so the writer of Hebrews tells us, is the substance of things hoped for and the evidence of things not seen (Hebrews 11:1). Hebrews 11 then goes on to tell us stories of persons who, only believing in the promises and faithfulness of God, take action based upon who they believe God is and what he has promised. The essence of faith brings about hope, and hope leads believers to action because they believe God is true to his promises and is faithful to keep them.

A great example of hope on which to focus is the life of Abraham from Hebrews 11. Abraham, only believing in the promises of God, moved his family and possessions to the land that God showed him. He did not look back, but looked forward, trusting that God had a plan to bless the family and use it for divine purposes. Abraham's object of faith was God alone: knowing that God had been faithful in the past and would be faithful in the future. God's character does not change, and so Abraham was able to act upon who God is and what God does. In this way, Abraham's faith led him to action because he hoped in God.

Churches considering mergers may draw upon this biblical theology of hope. For both a declining church and a growing church, God's promises to his church concerning victory and triumph still hold today. The declining church may hold its faith in God's promises and move toward action knowing that its legacy and faithfulness have not been in vain. The growing church may hold its faith in God's promises and move toward action knowing that God wants the church to grow in their ministry to a community. In either case, both churches can move forward in a merger knowing that God is faithful to keep his promises.

Why would a church want to consider a merger? Simple: There is hope. There is hope that God will do more with both churches in a merged scenario. There is hope that a church's ministry will expand in a community. There is hope that the legacy that has been lived by believers in either a declining church or a growing church will continue to deepen.

The following reasons for hope are based upon our experiences with mergers of various situations. As mentioned before, whatever a church's situation may be, a merger should be seen as an opportunity to both congregations for the following reasons. First, a merger brings the possibility of *more people* for both churches. For a declining church, the merger will naturally provide more people and will be an immediate boost to numbers. Even for the growing church, more people will be certainly a boost. Nevertheless, churches should not see people merely as a way to fill the pews. Instead, people should be seen as resources for ministry. Each person has been given a spiritual gift that can be used in ministry. Ephesians 4:11–12 provides insights concerning how the Spirit operates when dispensing spiritual gifts. The Spirit gives spiritual gifts so that churches may grow according to God's plan and purpose. People should be seen as resources that God is providing to help a merged church do ministry and outreach to a certain community. Yes, with more people come more numbers, money, and volunteers. But ultimately hope is grounded in the spiritual gifts God has given each Christian.

Second, because people bring spiritual gifts with them, people also multiply *more ministries*. Based upon Ephesians 4:11–12, when people are set free to work with their spiritual gifts, ministry naturally happens. As God brings together people in a church merger, the new church may find that new ministries may happen. Often in a declining church, those with what may be called "spiritual talent" often leave for various reasons. The members left are usually the ones that will "hold down the fort." They become focused on maintenance and the sustainment of the church rather than on ministries that may grow the church. A church merger may provide ministries with new people who provide for both the inward growth of those already in the church and for outreach ministries to the community.

Third, church mergers may bring *more resources*. Resources can be classified as anything or anyone that will help to further the ministry of the church: money, volunteers, buildings, energy, time, or even motivation. One may think of resources as material and nonmaterial resources. Material resources can include buildings, money, chairs, or musical instruments. While a church may be growing, it may not have a building. A merger may allow a church to expand its ministries in a certain community due to the presence of a building. As nonmaterial resources, more people may bring renewed energy, excitement, and motivation to a merged church. In the examples of material or nonmaterial resources, people or buildings, one should never view people as merely resources or even buildings as merely physical assets. One must view these things as resources that are gifts from God to bless the world, not merely assets to be used to sustain the institution.

Let us say a special word about physical and monetary resources that may come available during a church merger. Many times mergers may happen between a church plant that has no building and an established church that has been around for, say, more than a century. Both parties need to be honest. A church building can provide a more central location in which to do ministry in a community. Church ministry can certainly happen without a building, and indeed the church is *not* the building, but rather the people. However, many times when church mergers happen, the parties dance around the issue of buildings and monetary resources because they do not want to appear greedy. Hiding the issue is immature and creates unrealistic expectations. Both parties should be up front concerning the real physical and monetary resources a church merger may bring to the table. God's leadership, a love for each party, a deepening trust, and above all a mission for the community must also be present in a merger. Nevertheless, property and money can make the mission happen.

Fourth, a merged church scenario often means *more community connections* through which to do ministry. We define "connections" as those relationships in the community that provide opportunities for ministry. Connections may include relationships with other churches, nonprofit organizations, community neighborhood societies, and businesses. It is often through these connections that ministry opportunities occur, allowing church members to be in the community to form relationships and create more ministry opportunities. A declining church may have a long-standing presence in a community yet, because of decline, many of the people who were part of the church and lived in the community may have left. A church merger with a growing, vibrant church may often lead to connections in the community that the declining church may not have. On the other hand, because a declining church may have been established in an area for a long period of time, a merger may allow the new church to have access to relationships that often take longer to form in the community.

Fifth, a church merger can bring about *a missional focus*. The word "missional" has come into use in the early twenty-first century to describe churches or ministries being focused on reaching and engaging the culture with the Gospel. As a church goes into decline, a vicious cycle can begin as the church wants to reach out but must place all its energy and motivation in maintaining the status quo. A merger may bring, along with more talent, gifts, and resources, a renewed focus on reaching the community. Based upon their talents and gifts, people may generate new ideas about how they may be able to minister to the community.

All of this means that church mergers bring about *more hope*. Many declining churches have served for decades as faithful witnesses and points of ministry in their community. Many growing churches have ministered for many years in a community without being able to have a physical presence (such as a building) there. These churches go through the long years of wanting and praying for growth and community transformation, only to have disappointment after disappointment. If God is truly leading in a merger scenario, hope can spring up from the opportunities of a merger.

Hope occurs in a situation when God's people exercise their faith to walk blindly into a given situation and, though perhaps not seeing any material signs of success, believe in God's promises. Churches in merger situations may be able to see the merger as a way of God being faithful to his promises toward the church, both universal and local. Remember Romans 5:3–5 where Paul writes about how faith brings about a perseverance that carries believers through trials. The trials produce character, and eventually the character provides hope. Hope does not disappoint, because as Paul reminds us, it is given to believers by God through the Holy Spirit who is at work in the heart of those who believe.

Such a hope lies at the core of a merger process. Because of their faith, a remnant of church members often chooses to stay in difficult community contexts, with hard ministry situations only to have little fruit. Yet God rewards them for their faithfulness and perseverance. It may possibly be that just at the right time, God brings about a merger between two church bodies that possess the giftedness that God intends to use to have a greater impact on a community. Remember, hope *is* hope because it rests on the promises of God and the confidence that God will fulfill those promises.

The role of the vision team is to make God's promises more concrete. In this way there is not just unfocused hope, but hope that motivates people to take risks for concrete action. Although modern churches relied on statements and words to make hope concrete, postmodern churches are recovering ancient and more biblical methods. When Moses led the people out of Egypt in a risky venture of freedom and faithfulness, he used the metaphor of a "Promised Land flowing with milk and honey." His sister Miriam, his partner in the venture, led the people out of Egypt with song and dance.

Note especially the *order* in which vision emerges. Hope emerges from trust. Biblical visions emerge from a renewed sense of covenant. Only when people renew profound trust in God's promises, and hold one another accountable to core values and bedrock beliefs, does vision become clear.

Compatibility
Demographic Research, Lifestyles, and Mirroring the Mission Field

11

The vision teams in both merger conversations managed to avoid one of the most common mistakes in merger conversations. They did *not* plunge into strategic planning and start comparing the internal programs and assets of each church to the other. Instead, they started by comparing the proportionate representation of lifestyle segments in each church to the real proportionate representation of lifestyle segments in the mission field.

Thus, from the very beginning, each team declared its intention to fashion a merger that was externally focused. Future program-planning would be based on relevance to the mission field and not on accommodation to the previous habits of individual churches. This was clearly a bold move on the part of each team, and it made each congregation nervous. At the same time, it encouraged the congregations to believe that the merger would try to preserve *their best and most effective* ministries.

The teams used the best demographic and lifestyle-segment search engines to do their research into the urban environment. They were able to identify ten-year trends, predict the migrations of lifestyle segments across neighborhoods, anticipate the kinds of ministries that would be most relevant, and also anticipate the kinds of spiritual leaders that would be most helpful. They reality-tested their research by interviewing social service and health care personnel, police, municipal planners, board of education planners, businesses, and other key players that shaped the neighborhoods surrounding the churches.

In order to do comparative research effectively, each vision team needed to redraw the boundaries of what would become the new mission field of the new church. This was more difficult than either expected. In both cases, neither church could define the new mission field for the merged church based on current locations of members—but for different reasons.

Merger 1: Wesley and Asbury

These two churches were caught up in a vast flow of urbanization that covered a large area. Their memberships were actually scattered over multiple zip codes and even several counties; but the overwhelmed transportation infrastructure blocked active participation in the church. Therefore, the vision team members drew the new boundaries for the mission field based on a twenty-minute drive time to get to the church. This roughly paralleled the maximum time people were willing to travel to schools, hospitals, and recreational centers.

They further refined the boundaries of their new mission field by scanning for population density of distinct lifestyle segments. They heeded their consultant's advice, realizing that the merged church would only thrive if they focused on the seekers within their reach, rather than the members beyond their reach. Even then, diversity was a daunting challenge.

Merger 2: Faith Temple and Pine Street

These two churches were situated in an urban core that had a high population density, but which was limited to a small area proscribed by beltway highways, canals, railroads, and industrial areas. Church *participation* tended to draw people within a ten-minute walk of the church; church *membership* tended to include people who commuted to work for as much as forty minutes and stayed connected to the church because of family roots or past activity. Neither a ten-minute walk time nor a forty-minute drive time defined the primary reach of the church.

Therefore, its vision team members used the beltway and bus routes to define an area that was primarily urban (not exurban or suburban) and included a larger variety of lifestyles. When they plotted membership and adherent locations, they realized that a large band of publics lay between their current local and regional database, and that untouched area represented the real potential for congregational growth.

One of the most interesting insights was that each church, in both merger conversations, tended to overrepresent and underrepresent different lifestyle segments. Despite the fact that all of them claimed to be welcoming, it became clear that each of them was exclusive in its own individual way. This was not really a theological issue, but a social bias. Each church unconsciously repeated the homogeneous habits of Christendom. They tended to attract only those seekers who already resembled the members.

Moreover, some lifestyle segments are less compatible with other lifestyle segments, and this tended to be mirrored in church participation. That meant that church development and community development needed to go hand in hand. The healthier the church, the healthier the community would be. The more peaceful and respectful the cross-cultural community, the more the church would grow in numbers and impact. The principle of homogeneity so strongly embedded into the life and work of each church needed to be replaced by the principle of heterogeneity: respect for cultural diversity.

A second interesting insight was that three of the churches (Wesley, Pine Street, and Faith Temple) tended to overrepresent a lifestyle segment of aging, white, economically stable, moderately well-educated, childless, married couples that was in fact *decreasing* in the surrounding neighborhoods. The fourth church (Asbury) tended to overrepresent only a few of the many African American microcultures in the community and failed to connect with emerging Hispanic and Asian populations that were growing in their midst. Despite their desires to reach different kinds of people, each church struggled to establish a credible bond with the publics currently living in their neighborhoods. Any merger would have to minister to both the declining core of veteran members and the emerging diversity of seekers currently alienated from the institutional church.

Despite the post-Christendom imperative for cultural diversity and inclusivity, the vision teams realized that no institutional church can be all things to all people overnight! Within their respective scenarios, they would need to make strategic choices to prioritize the lifestyle segments they most wanted to reach. The motivation, however, had to be clear.

If the motivation to reach the public was simply based on *attraction* and the desire to perpetuate a historic institution, then the conversation on merger was doomed to failure. Each church would only want to attract people on its own terms and to perpetuate its own traditions. On the other hand, if the motivation to reach the public was based more profoundly on an urgent desire to *bless* people, then the conversation about merger would gain momentum. Merger would not be based on institutional need, but divine calling. And this, they all agreed, was a mission purpose that transcended any single institution or tradition.

Healthy, faithful churches mirror the demographic and lifestyle-segment diversity of the mission field. The lifestyles in the community are proportionately matched by the lifestyles in the church. This is a radical shift in thinking.

In the Christendom world, when most people at least claimed to be Christians and attend church occasionally, churches grew based on the principle of *homogeneity*. Churches tried to attract new members who closely resembled the current members in age, family status, income, education, occupation, language, race, and so forth. This is still the hidden assumption of many churches, despite their claims to inclusiveness. One reason that churches are so unclear about core values, beliefs, vision, and mission is that they actually rely on lifestyle homogeneity to unify the church and focus its outreach.

In the post-Christendom world, however, churches grow based on the principle of *heterogeneity*. Our world is much more diverse—and diversifying faster and faster. Churches like Faith Temple and Pine Street, or Wesley and Asbury, still tend to operate on the principle of homogeneity; but the neighborhoods around them have dramatically diversified. One demographic statistic is particularly telling: length of residence. In many churches, the average length of time a member has lived at a particular address is often ten to fifteen years; but the average residency for the community as a whole is only six to eighteen months.

This shift in thinking from *homogeneity* to *heterogeneity* is particularly urgent because emerging generations only respect those organizations that are sincerely and effectively cross-cultural. If a church cannot or will not welcome and bless all races and cultures, the full spectrum of incomes and occupations, traditional and nontraditional families, educated and uneducated adults, active and disabled, older and younger, then the church is not really living up to the mandate to make disciples of all people and bless the entire world.

Churches were severely limited in their access to demographic and lifestyle data up until about the mid-2000s decade. Now there has been an explosion of accessible and detailed data on demographic trends and lifestyle segments in any given zip code, census tract, and neighborhood. In merger conversations of the past, the best we could do was gather opinions from church members and community leaders on what they *perceived* to be changing in the community. Opinions often clashed and were usually unreliable, since people who live in a place a long time become "blind" to the changes going on around them. In merger conversations today we can use demographic and lifestyle search engines like www.missioninsite .com, which uses data from a variety of government, business, education, and nonprofit sources to develop more accurate and objective insights.

The greatest leap in understanding has been the definition and description of *lifestyle groups* and *lifestyle segments*. This is a method used by all sectors that clusters people together by behavior patterns, attitudes, predictable social values, retail and recreational preferences, and other daily habits.[1] This allows a church to gain insight into lifestyle expectations for ministries (e.g., hospitality, worship, Christian education, midweek groups, outreach, facilities and technologies, financial management and giving, and communication). At the time of this publication, there are seventy-one lifestyle segments in the United States, organized into nineteen lifestyle groups. The segments in each group are related to each other by a number of demographic and psychographic factors.

The transition from homogeneity to heterogeneity is accomplished following lines of *compatibility*. Compatibility does not mean that lifestyle segments agree with each other or live exactly the same way, but that they empathize with one another and often mingle in various activities. They behave in similar ways.

- The most obvious compatibilities are between lifestyle *segments* that belong to the same lifestyle *group*. For example, the lifestyle segment called *Full Pockets, Empty Nests* lives in the mission field of three out of four of our case studies ("empty-nesting, upper-middle-class households with discretionary income living sophisticated lifestyles"). They are part of a lifestyle group called *Thriving Boomers* and related to several other groups that include boomers who are unique in many ways but still related to one another.
- Less obvious, but even more profound, is the fact that some lifestyle segments *prefer* to mingle with other lifestyle segments even if they are in different groups. For example, the same lifestyle segment *Full Pockets, Empty Nests* often lives near and mingles with lifestyle groups called *Young City Solos* and *Significant Singles*. These other groups contain segments that look to older boomers for mentoring and career advancement, even as these boomers look to these younger lifestyle groups for entertainment and technology.

The most important thing is that these different lifestyle networks often articulate similar religious questions and share similar preferences for various ministries of the church.

Determining compatibility is like playing a game of dominoes. There are two sets of dots on each domino. The player matches one end of a domino with another domino with the same number of dots; and the other domino with another number of dots. The middle domino is a bridge between the other two. The players keep connecting the various ends of the dominoes to create an intricate chain of relationships. In a similar way, merging churches can compare proportionate lifestyle representation in their membership or neighborhoods and discern the most opportune connections. Some connections help members from different churches relate to each other; other connections help church members connect with lifestyle segments currently outside of, or underrepresented in, the memberships of any church. In this way, we can discern how compatible churches in the merger conversation really are with each other.

The truth is that some churches are simply *incompatible* with each other. This doesn't mean that they are right or wrong or good or bad. It's just that they are so different in their lifestyles that they will never really empathize with one another. This is true despite the fact that the churches may be of the same theological tradition, the same denomination, the same race, or the same average age. Past mergers failed because we made assumptions about compatibility that were simply without foundation. Future mergers succeed because we can do the research to confirm actual compatibility between churches and neighborhoods.

It is important to understand that compatibility or incompatibility is based on *lifestyle differences* rather than age, race, gender, income, or other broad demographic categories. For example, among the current seventy-one lifestyle segments, there are many that include "seniors" because the general population is getting older. This does not mean that they will all be compatible with each other. In the same way, there are many different kinds of "youths" today, but some "youths" are compatible with one another and some simply do not get along. It is not uncommon for one senior or youth to look at another senior or youth in total bewilderment.

This is especially significant concerning race or ethnicity. There is far greater diversity among African Americans than just twenty years ago. Lifestyle segments like *Suburban Attainment* have more and more empathy with a cross-cultural middle class. Hispanic, Asian, Caribbean, and other ethnic groups are stepping away from ethnocentric communities. Churches with ethnic families in their second and third generations often feel more empathy with majority lifestyles unique to their city or region than with their country of origin. The bottom line is that the opportunities to merge churches that are truly bi-racial or multicultural are growing.

Today it is possible to plot the location of every member or adherent (or even first- and second-time visitors).[2] This allows each church to list in order of size the lifestyles currently represented *in the membership*, and compare this to a similar list in order of size of the lifestyle segments currently represented *in the community*. The comparisons can help you understand and anticipate potential strengths or stresses in a church merger. They also help you identify the lifestyle segments with which you are either most compatible, or for which you feel the most urgency to bless in the name of Christ.

Vision teams often work with a consultant or denominational leaders to interpret these data, and explore the implications for church compatibilities and future ministries. They chart lifestyle-segment representation across the churches. They also chart lifestyle representation in the community and whether that representation would grow, decline, or remain stable over the next ten years.

Why is this important? Every lifestyle segment has different expectations for church leadership and church programs, that's why. People in any given lifestyle segment tend to gravitate toward those churches with leaders and programs that address their particular anxieties and needs and best facilitate their quest for God and experience of grace.[3]

In the two merger conversations we are following, each vision team plotted the membership of each congregation. They could then compare lifestyle representation in each church *to the other church* and compare this diversity *to the surrounding community*. Of course, in urban contexts there is great complexity; but in church membership it doesn't take long to identify the top lifestyles represented in each church, and then compare these to the surrounding neighborhoods.[4]

It is important to understand that the culture of a neighborhood (or the culture of a church) is basically shaped around the largest lifestyle segments, which usually comprise about 50 to 60% of the total. In a community, most of the retail stores, school systems, health care and emergency services, social services, restaurants, and other agencies and organizations are chosen and developed to serve those top markets. It is much the same in a church. The dress and behavior of greeters, music and style of worship, quality and diversification of refreshments, Sunday school methodologies and curricula, small-group affinities, and even the facility design and technologies of the church building, are chosen and developed to serve those top membership representations.

Compare lifestyle compatibility for Merger 1 (Wesley and Asbury). In table 11.1, you can see that over 55% of Wesley is composed of three segments of baby-boomers: *Aging of Aquarius, Boomers and Boomerangs,* and *Silver Sophisticates.* This means that church programs are primarily designed for the comfort zones and ministry expectations of aging boomers, with significant wealth, retired or soon-to-be-retired, plus some of the university educated children who have been forced to return home while they look for meaningful employment. They tend to live a balanced lifestyle and prefer topical education, affinity-based small groups with rotated leadership, and outreach that emphasizes interpersonal relationships and developing human potential.

Table 11.1.   Proportionate Lifestyle Representation (Merger 1)

Merger #1	Neighborhood Regional Urbanization	Wesley	Asbury
Aging of Aquarius (C11)			
Upscale boomer-aged couples living in city and close-in suburbs	8.5% and declining	32.3%	8.2%
Boomers and Boomerangs (C14)			
Baby boomer adults and their teenage/ young adult children sharing suburban homes	5.8% and stable	12.0%	12.5%
Silver Sophisticates (C13)			
Mature, upscale couples and singles in suburban homes	6.7% and stable	10.4%	0%
Generational Soup (B07)			
Affluent couples and multigenerational families living a wide range of lifestyles in suburbia	6.1% and growing	6.2%	5%
Suburban Attainment (D18)			
Upper-middle-class African American couples and families living in the expanding suburbs	16.1% and stable	5.3%	25.8%
Urban Ambition (O52)			
Mainly Generation Y African American singles and single families established in midmarket cities	5.5% and growing	3.5%	12.6%
Striving Single Scene (O54)			
Young, multiethnic singles living in Midwestern and southern city centers	7.6% and growing	2.7%	7.5%
Dare to Dream (R66)			
Young singles, couples, and single parents with lower incomes starting out in city apartments	3.3% and stable	3.6%	5.4%
Gotham Blend (K38)			
Mix of middle-aged and middle-class singles and couples living eclectic lifestyles	3.0% and stable	2.0%	3.2%
Total	**62.6%**	**78.0%**	**80.2%**

Meanwhile, a little over 50% of the Asbury members belong to lifestyle segments with high proportions of African American households. The largest, at 25.8% is called *Suburban Attainment*, which is the rising African American middle class. The others include younger singles and childless couples who are upwardly mobile. These people tend to live harried lifestyles, but yearn for balance. Many prefer Bible-based education and small groups, with consistent designated leaders. Their outreach emphases are similar. Their membership also includes another 20% representing boomer segments that are majorities in Wesley. These include *Aging of Aquarius* and *Boomers and Boomerangs*, two boomer lifestyle segments that are often quite open to bi-racial churches. These can serve as "bridge-builders" when the two congregations merge.

The challenge here is that the expanding urban region is becoming more diverse, younger, more eccentric in its religious sensibilities, and more eclectic in its organized-religion choices. This region, like many urbanizing regions in America today, is less and less bi-racial and more and more multicultural. You can that the chart only lists the top 62.6% of the total population. The remaining 37.4% includes emerging Asian and Hispanic lifestyle segments that are projected to grow over the next ten years.

So the good news is that the majority of Caucasian and African American lifestyle segments represented in each congregation can empathize with and respect one another and can work together in the same church. The *Suburban Attainment* lifestyle segment that is well represented at Asbury is growing in Wesley. The challenging news is that the very concept of a bi-racial church is breaking down in the greater diversity of the urban mission field. Churches must become ever more multicultural.

Compare lifestyle compatibilities in Merger 2 (Faith Temple and Pine Street). In table 11.2 below, you can see that about 65% of the membership of Pine Street is composed of three lifestyle segments (in order of size): *Aging in Place*, *Town Elders*, and *Diapers and Debit Cards*. This means that church programs are primarily designed for the comfort zones and preferences of stable, established seniors with traditional attitudes and long-term residencies in the area. They tend to be low risk-takers, late adopters for technology, and traditionalists. The next largest group is called *Diapers and Debit Cards*. They live unstable lives with contemporary attitudes and will likely relocate in five years or less. They tend to be moderate risk-takers, early adopters, and innovators. Already Pine Street has experienced tensions over worship design and public policy because these two groups don't often agree; but the majority of *Town Elders* and *Aging in Place* dominate the board and generally get their way.

Table 11.2 also shows that Faith Temple has a similar congregation, but with an added fourth lifestyle segment, *Midscale Medley*, whose members tend to be single or divorced. These people may support viewpoints from different sides, but they also hate conflict and will withdraw from a church if factional infighting is too severe. Therefore, despite the larger representation, Faith Temple tends to behave the same way as Pine Street because of their similar lifestyle representation.

Table 11.2.   Proportionate Lifestyle Representation (Merger 2)

Merger # 2	Neighborhood Urban Core	Faith Temple	Pine Street
Town Elders (Q64)			
Stable, minimalist seniors living in older residences, leading sedentary lifestyles	7.8% and declining	12.3%	25.3%
Diapers and Debit Cards (M45)			
Young, working-class families & single-parent households living in small, established city residences	18.0% and growing	32.7%	15.0%
Aging in Place (J34)			
Middle-class seniors living solid, quiet lifestyles in the same homes where they raised their children	6.4% and declining	16.2%	25.7%
Midscale Medley (P56)			
Middle-aged, midscale income singles & divorced individuals	10.7% and stable	18.9%	5.3%
Striving Single Scene (O54)			
Young, multiethnic singles living in Midwestern and southern city centers	7.5% and growing	2.0%	2.8%
Dare to Dream (R66)			
Young singles, couples, and single parents with lower incomes starting out in city apartments	8.2% and growing	8.9%	3.0%
Boomers and Boomerangs (C14)			
Baby boomer adults and their teenage/ young adult children sharing suburban homes	6.0% and stable	5.8%	6.2%
Silver Sophisticates (C13)			
Mature, upscale couples and singles in suburban homes	5.7% and stable	2.3%	6.6%
Total	**70.3%**	**99.1%**	**89.9%**

So the good news for Faith Temple and Pine Street is that their congregational memberships are pretty compatible. The challenging news is that they need to take the church beyond the comfort zones of current memberships. That will require board restructuring, a different staffing strategy, and program changes.

You begin to see that there are three ways lifestyle data can be analyzed and applied to merger conversations. First, churches explore compatibility of *lifestyle segments between congregational memberships.* Second, churches explore compatibility *of lifestyle segments between their memberships and the wider community.* Third, churches compare the *motivations* for outreach to the *needs* for outreach in order to uncover the priorities for future mission.

Internal Compatibilities among Church Memberships

First, we explore the compatibilities of *lifestyle segments between congregational memberships.* A merger is more likely to be successful if the current memberships are likely to *get along with each other!* This means that their life anxieties and spiritual yearnings reinforce or connect with each other, making it more likely that current leadership and program expectations can be reasonably addressed. In our two merger stories, the major lifestyle segments in each church pairing have much to offer one another.

Wesley and Asbury (Merger 1) demonstrated great *internal complementarity* between lifestyle segments—both now and in the future. This suggested that the success of a merger involving these two congregations would depend on their ability to empathize with, and complement one another in practice. The strengths of one church would bless the other and vice versa.

Wesley includes a high number of more affluent boomers who are passionate about positive social change and experienced in managing nonprofits; and Asbury includes large segments of young entrepreneurs who have little expertise in managing organizations but are open to coaching. These two churches have an opportunity to match people with mentoring abilities with other people in great need of mentoring. Moreover, if these two churches merge, they would experience other opportunities for growth. Worship could become even more inspirational, and include more significant components of education for children and young families. The youth group would have more energy and resources. They would have more visibility across the spectrum of cultures in the mission field.

Of course, there will also be stresses, but these can be anticipated and managed. Education and small group ministries will need to become more diverse with options for both topical and Bible-based groups, openness to rotate leaders, but higher budgets to also train designated leaders. Staff and board would need to intentionally reflect the bi-racial or multicultural nature of the church.

Faith Temple and Pine Street (Merger 2) also demonstrated significant *internal consistency* between lifestyle segments represented in the church membership. This suggested that the success of a merger between these two congregations would depend on their ability to pool their resources.

Their major outreach ministries and reputations in the community for education and the arts indicate that they would likely be compatible. Faith Temple manages a charter school and has a larger proportion of young working-class families (*Diapers and Debit Cards*). Pine Street manages an excellent choir and classical music program and has a larger proportion of educated seniors (*Town Elders* and *Aging in Place*).

If these two churches were to merge, they could anticipate opportunities for ministries. Together they could enthusiastically support a larger, traditional Christian education program. The Sunday school would be more curricular and biblical, with classes based on age (rather than experiential, topical, and peer groups). The midweek program would support traditional gender-based women's and men's groups that were a mix of Bible studies and activities. The sanctuary would look and feel like a "church." It would use modern technologies (but no video screens or internet).[5]

On the other hand, the merger would raise stress levels in several ways, and leaders should prepare for this in advance. They will need to make hospitality more radical with trained greeters, a formal welcome center, and superior quality refreshments. Worship will be educational, but it will need to become more inspirational (energetic and motivational), and less merely caregiving (slow and meditative). Outreach will need to focus more on helping people discern human potential and build quality interpersonal relationships rather than on food pantries and clothing depots for the sake of sheer survival.[6]

The good news is that all of these lifestyle segments are generally compatible with each other. They can understand, accept, and empathize. Moreover, both churches appreciate the same kind of pastor (enabler and caregiver), although he or she will need to develop better administrative skills. The corporate culture of the merged church will not be too different from the former churches. On the other hand, there will be stress in reshaping hospitality and worship, and their outreach priorities will likely change.

In our two merger stories, the *internal* compatibilities are very strong. Different local identities or denominational affiliations do not need to become barriers to church growth.

External Compatibilities between Churches and Community

The second way to analyze and apply demographic and lifestyle data is to explore compatibility *between the lifestyles of the members and the lifestyles of nonmembers in the community.* A merger is more likely to be successful if there is strong empathy between the members of the church and the seekers in the community.

Wesley and Asbury have had significant success in reaching aging baby boomers, but also, and especially, a generation of "boomerangs" who, following college graduation, are living with their parents while they look for jobs. Their multigenerational openness bodes well for a potential bi-racial church. They also have reached significant numbers of middle-class African American households who are open to more formal ways of worship and interested in sustainable outreach ministries to youth. Already there is a growing edge for ministry among the growing number of *Generational Soup* households in the community.

Faith Temple and Pine Street have had significant success reaching a stable base of educated seniors whose continuing residence downtown indicates a commitment to the city. They have both connected with younger, more transient households with children (albeit to different degrees). Faith Temple has done better reaching a large population of single or divorced, younger, poorer, multicultural people; Pine Street has done better reaching older, wealthier boomers with senior-management experience who can shape the nonprofits that will bless them.

Note that when you compare congregations to neighborhoods, you see that the community looks different than the Faith Temple and Pine Street congregations. In addition to *Diapers and Debit Cards* people and *Midscale Medley* people (who are included in the Faith Temple mix), two other groups represent another 15% of the neighborhood population, and they are growing. *Striving Single Scene* and *Dare to Dream* represent different economic levels, but they are filled with young people—Gen X and Gen Y—representing many cultures. These creative, upwardly mobile people may be hard to reach, but they are the future of the church. Both the charter school and the music ministries of each church will attract their interest, but a merged church will need to significantly adjust its hospitality, worship, and small-group programs.

These snapshots of compatibility or complementarity are actually very common. Most established churches do not mirror the demographic and lifestyle diversity in the community or among neighborhoods in which they worship. This means that there are only two choices in a merger:

- One choice is to sell all the buildings and move to a new location that is central to the lifestyle segments that the church already supports. Alternatively, relocate to a highly accessible place (e.g., a major intersection on a beltway that surrounds the city), so that the lifestyle segments can readily come and go. The lifestyles proportionately represented in the church will then mirror the segments in the community.

- The other choice is to stay in, or close by, the original neighborhoods of the merging churches. However, church leaders need to understand that every new traffic light, pothole, one-way street, construction zone, increase in traffic congestion, or decrease in parking will deter today's members from coming to church. The church must change to connect with the people within its reach in order to mirror the diversity of the surrounding neighborhoods.

There is no right or wrong choice. Either choice may be God's plan for the church. The churches exploring a merger need to pray hard to discern God's will. The one thing that is *not* negotiable is that things must change. Either the church moves to be among the people it wants to bless; or the church takes bold steps to bless the people who are there. Adaptability is inevitable. The key is to make the changes *faithful* to the values, beliefs, vision, and mission shared by the combined churches.

Motivations and Needs for Outreach

The third and final way to analyze and apply demographic and lifestyle data is to compare the *motivations* for outreach to the *needs* for outreach. This helps churches uncover their sense of *urgency* to bless a particular public. That public may not be the largest lifestyle segment in the community, but it is the lifestyle segment for whom the hearts of church members "burst" with a desire to bless.

Note that this research is *externally* focused. The most successful church mergers follow the instructions of Jesus: The first shall be last, and the last shall be first. A vision team does not start by comparing the *needs of the members* to the *expertise of the clergy*. Successful mergers first unite congregations in mission and then unite congregations in caregiving. The first two levels of analysis (compatibilities of lifestyle segments *within congregational memberships*, and *between memberships and the wider community*) are ineffective unless you press on to the level of targeted mission.

The biblical model for this sense of urgency is found in Paul's mission to the gentiles. Paul and his team have a vision of a Macedonian saying, "Come over and help us!" (Acts 16). This vision is so compelling that Paul and his companions risk everything to go to the place where the

Macedonians live. They immerse themselves in the culture and customs of the Macedonians, discern their physical needs and spiritual yearnings, mentor lay leaders like Lydia, and customize a ministry to bless them in unique ways.

We consider this another example of a heartburst. The Macedonians are a definable, describable lifestyle segment in the community. Church members literally weep for them and are compelled to bless them. Every successful merger must have a heartburst that motivates the merging churches to make significant sacrifices for some person or persons *other than themselves*. It is this sense of heartburst that helps churches rise above self-interest and find new unity in a passion for mission.

Lifestyle segments look for different kinds of blessings, shared in readily accessible methods. There are at least seven distinct kinds of outreach: survival, addiction recovery, health, quality of life, human potential, interpersonal relationships, and human destiny. The kinds of outreach that people want *to receive* are sometimes different from the kinds of outreach people want *to share*.

For this analysis, it is often helpful to review *lifestyle groups*, which include several *segments* with similar needs and/or abilities, and then identify ten-year trends. This kind of research is what health care institutions, social services, boards of education, and other agencies do regularly. Churches often do part of this research online, but most of this research is done in direct conversation with nonprofit leaders in the community. Their research is often more detailed, specific, and up to date.

For example, the vision teams in our story identified the largest lifestyle segments in the community (listed earlier). However, they only represented about 60 to 70% of the mission field. So they expanded their research to include the remaining 30 to 40%. A good way to frame this research is to study the *entire* mission field using lifestyle *groups* rather than lifestyle *segments*. These are larger populations whose growth or decline can appear more statistically significant in complex urban mission fields when you look at ten-year trends.

At the time of their work, their research revealed the following for the Wesley and Asbury merger conversation (see table 11.3). Right now Wesley is very successful reaching several segments of baby boomers, and slowly building an effective ministry with *Flourishing Families*. Asbury is successful reaching several segments with African Americans, and slowly expanding ministry with young singles. When they merge, the outreach will need to be adjusted to focus less on holistic health and more specifically on addiction intervention. They will have to shift focus from Sunday

Table 11.3.   Lifestyle Representation Trends (Merger 1)

Merger 1 Community Context	Overall % of Growth or Decline
Booming with Confidence (C)	
Four segments including *Silver Sophisticates, Boomers and Boomerangs, Golf Carts and Gourmets,* and *Aging of Aquarius*	−2.0
Prosperous, established couples in their peak earning years: seek ministries about interpersonal relationships and health; and *share* ministries about quality of life and human potential.	
Suburban Style (D)	
Four segments including *Sports Utility Families, Settled in Suburbia, Cul de Sac Diversity,* and *Suburban Attainment*	+2.0
Middle-aged, ethnically mixed suburban families & couples earning upscale incomes: seek ministries about human potential; and *share* ministries about quality of life and interpersonal relationships.	
Singles and Starters (O)	
Six segments including *Full Steam Ahead, Digital Dependents, Urban Ambition, Colleges and Cafes, Striving Single Scene,* and *Family Troopers*	+6.0
Young and middle-aged singles and childless couples starting out in careers and temporary jobs: both *seek* and *share* ministries about interpersonal relationships, human potential, and recovery.	
Aspirational Fusion (R)	
Two segments including *Dare to Dream* and *Hope for Tomorrow*	+1.0
Multicultural, low-income singles and single parents living in urban locations and striving to make a better life: both *seek* and *share* ministries about interpersonal relationships, human potential, and recovery.	
Flourishing Families (B)	
Four segments including *Generational Soup, Babies and Bliss, Family Funtastic,* and *Cosmopolitan Achievers*	+3.0
Affluent, middle-aged families and couples earning prosperous incomes and living very comfortable, active lifestyles: seek ministries of human potential and human destiny, and *share* ministries about quality of life and health.	
Significant Singles (K)	
Four segments including *Wired for Success, Gotham Blend, Metro Fusion,* and *Bohemian Groove*	0 Stable
Middle-aged singles and some couples earning midscale incomes and supporting active city styles of living: seek ministries of interpersonal relationships, and *share* ministries about human potential and quality of life.	

school to midweek small groups, and from friendly fellowship to more serious adult faith formation.

At the time of their work, their research revealed the following for the Faith Temple and Pine Street merger conversation (see table 11.4). Faith Temple and Pine Street have a heartburst for lifestyle groups like *Golden Year Guardians, Families in Motion,* and *Autumn Years,* and Faith Temple in particular was reaching some of the emerging Hispanic and African American lifestyles included in *Cultural Connections.* But their education and fellowship ministries are better suited for declining lifestyle groups (*Golden Year Guardians* and *Autumn Years*). They emphasize curricula and classrooms and large men's and women's groups. If the churches really have a heartburst for *Families in Motion* and *Cultural Connections,* they need to shift toward more experiential and interactive learning modules and small, midweek affinity groups.

Perhaps the best way to reality-test compatibility between churches, and empathy between churches and mission field, is not to listen to sermons, but rather to listen to the "buzz" of conversation before and after worship.

- In Wesley and Asbury, the "buzz" of conversation is all about public policies and politics, race relations, health problems, and grandchildren. They will need to create a "buzz" about personal and spiritual growth, multiculturalism, interventions by a Higher Power, and opportunities for young adults.
- In Faith Temple and Pine Street, the "buzz" of conversation is all about theological and moral insights, family connections, generation gaps, and appreciation for the arts. They will need to create a "buzz" about day-to-day Christian living, urban environment, and meaningful employment.

Today the cohesion of churches depends more on quality relationships than abstract dogmas, and on positive behavior patterns rather than organizational polities. A successful church merger is not based on agreement with any particular public policy or creedal formula; it is based on common needs, similar behaviors, shared goals, and passions for outreach that together unite a body of Christ.

Table 11.4. Lifestyle Representation Trends (Merger 2)

Merger 2 Community Context	Overall % of Growth or Decline
Golden Year Guardians (Q)	
Three segments including *Town Elders, Reaping Rewards,* and *Footloose and Family Free*	−6.0
Retirees living in settled residences and communities: seek ministries about interpersonal relationships and health; and share ministries about survival, quality of life, and human destiny.	
Families in Motion (M)	
Two segments including *Diapers and Debit Cards* and *Red, White, and Bluegrass*	+5.0
Younger, working-class families living in moderate income communities: seek ministries about human potential and quality of life; and share ministries about health and interpersonal relationships.	
Autumn Years (J)	
Two segments including *Aging in Place* and *Rural Escape*	−2.0
Established, ethnically diverse, mature couples living contentedly in older homes: seek ministries about quality of life and interpersonal relationships; and share ministries about survival.	
Cultural Connections (P)	
Six segments including *Midscale Medley, Modest Metro Means, Heritage Heights, Expanding Horizons, Striving Forward,* and *Humble Beginnings*	+7.0
Diverse, mid- and low-income families in urban apartments and residences: both seek and share ministries about interpersonal relationships, human potential, and survival.	
Singles and Starters (O)	
Six segments including *Full Steam Ahead, Digital Dependents, Urban Ambition, Colleges and Cafes, Striving Single Scene,* and *Family Troopers*	+4.0
Young and middle-aged singles and childless couples starting out in careers and temporary jobs: both seek and share ministries about interpersonal relationships, human potential, and recovery.	
Aspirational Fusion (R)	
Two segments including *Dare to Dream* and *Hope for Tomorrow*	+2.0
Multicultural, low-income singles and single parents living in urban locations and striving to make a better life: both seek and share ministries about interpersonal relationships, human potential, and recovery.	
Booming with Confidence (C)	
Four segments including *Silver Sophisticates, Boomers and Boomerangs, Golf Carts and Gourmets,* and *Aging of Aquarius*	+1.0
Prosperous, established couples in their peak earning years: seek ministries about interpersonal relationships and health; and share ministries about quality of life and human potential.	

Setting Priorities
Measurable Outcomes

12

The vision teams were coming to the end of their mandates. Each had built a foundation of trust among the partners for its merger. They had assessed the effectiveness of their respective churches for *critical momentum*, and identified the challenges to *critical mass*. They had guided the churches to focus and find new hope by surrendering to God's purpose.

Now that the vision teams understood compatibilities between the churches and the wider community, and between the lifestyle segments that comprised each church, they turned their attention to the priorities for each church to accelerate church growth and positively impact the community.

Once again they had to carefully avoid being drawn into a premature discussion of specific programs and tactics. This was difficult because impatient members in all of the churches demanded answers about leadership deployment, program development, and (most of all) property-sharing. Yet this was not yet the time for strategic *planning*. This was the time to set strategic *priorities*. The vision teams needed to compare strengths and weaknesses in the organizational systems of each church—and to set some overarching goals or outcomes for any future merger.

Each vision team needed to answer more urgent questions. *Was the merger conversation itself worthwhile? Would any merger really matter? Would the merger really lead to growth in membership and participation, and would it really make a difference in the surrounding urban community?*

The biblical goals for all churches were clear enough. God required the church to multiply disciples and bless the world in the name of Christ. Exactly how this would define the measurable outcomes for a merged church in this community was an open question.

The vision teams used the simple image of a discipling process to guide their investigations. (Wesley and Asbury were helped by a webinar with a consultant; Faith Temple and Pine Street were helped by another conversation with the staff at Harvest Community Church.) The process was based on the subsystems of critical momentum they used when they initially faced the reality of current church life. Their next step would be to use a similar template to imagine a future church life.

Any successful church merger would need to connect seekers with believers, and people who are in need with people who can really help. To that end, the six basic subsystems for critical momentum were simplified. They would be led by a core team and be based on a clear consensus for values, beliefs, vision, and mission that would be the foundation of trust for the new merged church (see figure 12.1).

- Encounter Christ
- Experience God
- Grow in Faith
- Discern Call
- Equip Disciples
- Send Servants

The vision teams defined measurable outcomes for each of these six subsystems to sustain critical momentum. They wanted these outcomes to challenge the commitment of the church but still be achievable. They wanted these outcomes general enough to encourage lots of creativity, but clear enough to provide definite expectations. In other words, they wanted to guide the direction of their future strategic plans, but not tie the hands of the future ministry team leaders.

At first some vision team members balked at any conversation about measurable outcomes. It seemed like something a business might do, while a church would be much more tolerant of individual desires. Yet in their previous conversations with social service and nonprofit leaders about lifestyle expectations, they quickly learned that nonprofits must also define measurable outcomes in order to train leaders, refine programs, and get results. They also learned that churches and some other nonprofits had to define measurable outcomes somewhat differently from for-profit businesses. Outcomes were measured not only by statistics, but also by gathering stories from the mission field and intentionally gleaning feedback from mission partners.

Whatever outcomes were defined to measure the success of each merger would probably only be useful for about three years. After that, priorities would need to be revisited, and new measurable outcomes defined, on an annual basis. The new, merged churches would grow one lifestyle segment at a time (rather than one member at a time), as they multiplied and expanded their reach across their respective mission fields. And the lifestyle mix of the mission fields would be constantly in flux.

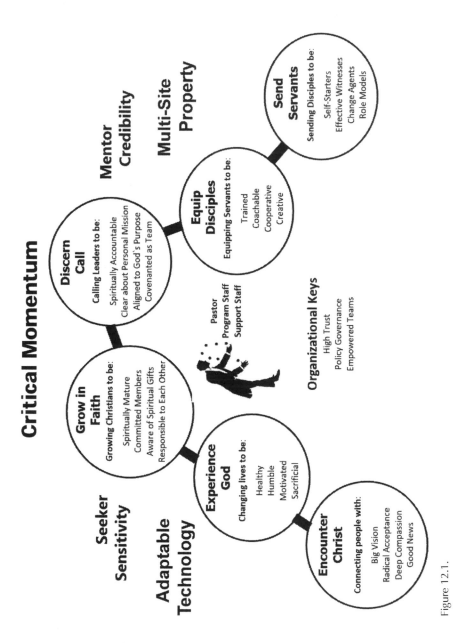

Figure 12.1.

Priorities are best understood as outcomes rather than goals. A "goal" suggests wishful thinking. An "outcome" implies a measurement of success. The measure of success has evolved over the years. In the 1970s the key measure of success was membership. In the 1980s the measure of success was worship attendance. In the 1990s it was small-group and mission team multiplication. These were often shaped by the tacit measurements of success for a denomination: financial giving, effective professionals, and overall harmony. None of these is particularly helpful today, especially in a church merger.

Outcomes are the measurable product of systems. Once the outcomes are defined, a church can then evaluate and choose whatever particular programs or tactics might best accomplish the outcome. For example, an early discussion about Christian education with Wesley and Asbury was initially bogged down by comparisons of Sunday school curricula and methodologies. They finally backed away from this quagmire of micromanagement and asked the more fundamental question about outcome. They said: *The outcome of Christian education in our unique mission context is that adult church members will model and mentor a courageous and mature spiritual life.* If that one crucial outcome was accomplished, faith formation for children and teens would follow automatically. This led them to see that midweek small-group ministry, rather than traditional Sunday morning classes, had to be the key program to deliver the outcome.

In another example, an early discussion about hospitality with Faith Temple and Pine Street was initially bogged down by debates about how to organize the ushers and what kind of refreshments to serve on Sunday morning. They finally backed away from this fight over personal preferences and asked the more fundamental question about outcome. They said: *The outcome of hospitality in our unique mission context is that meaningful conversations will multiply among strangers to grace and seekers of truth.* If that one crucial outcome was accomplished, the exclusive friendship cliques would break down, and everyone would feel part of a deeper dynamic of community. This led them to prioritize training for greeters, ushers, and servers to help them communicate.

Once the outcomes are defined, leaders can then list, compare, and evaluate various programs or tactics more objectively. They can avoid debate about personal preferences or privileges, or about traditions and habits, and focus on *what works.*

Outcomes may be expressed as statistics, stories, or feedback. They are *measurable* because data can be tracked, stories can be added up, and feedback can be summarized.

- Wesley and Asbury could *measure* success in achieving their goal in three ways. First, they could track statistics like *how many* adults were actually in covenanted mentoring relationships (either as mentor or mentee). Second, they could add up the number of stories they heard each month about milestones in adult faith formation and progress in spiritual growth. Third, they could quantify feedback about adult education into percentages of adults who found educational programs in the church to be unimportant, somewhat relevant, or immensely powerful.

- Faith Temple and Pine Street could *measure* success in achieving radical hospitality in three ways. First, they could deploy observers to literally count the number of significant conversations happening during post-worship coffee time each week, and over time track whether that statistic was going up or down. Second, they could add up the number of stories they heard from visitors about how welcoming their experience of Sunday morning was. Third, they could quantify feedback through focus groups of inactive members, active members, and the general public to discern their *perceptions* of hospitality in the church.

When churches are clear about outcomes, they no longer become obsessed with tactics, and they focus on results. The discussion is not about what curriculum to use, but whether adults are actually growing. The discussion is not about what kind of coffee to serve, but whether people are really feeling welcomed.

In chapter 8, we saw the six basic subsystems that combine to maximize a church's mission impact on the community and provide critical momentum for its growth: radical hospitality, targeted worship, mature disciples, empowered volunteers, intentional stewardship, and relevant outreach.

In the process of setting priorities, however, this terminology is too limiting. When church members from any given tradition hear these words, they immediately think of specific tactics. This limits their imagination as they develop measurable outcomes. Imagine the diverse interpretations of these terms in each of the four churches.

"Radical Hospitality": Wesley and Pine Street immediately thought about greeters, ushers, and basic coffee and cookies after worship. Faith Temple immediately thought about a central welcome center staffed by volunteers throughout Sunday morning, and multiple serving stations for adults and children. Asbury immediately thought about flexible seating, access to a refreshment center in the back of the room during worship, and lunch.

"Targeted Worship": Wesley and Pine Street assumed that worship meant responsive liturgy and the Christian Year; Faith Temple assumed worship meant thematic preaching to the issues of the day; all three assumed it would be presented from a stage to listening ears in the pews. Asbury assumed worship meant motivational singing and preaching, constant interaction between the congregation and preacher, and Bible study.

Similar differences emerge in the other subsystems as well. People simply associate these terms with specific tactics. Some people assume the maturing of disciples means Sunday schools and age-based curricula; and others assume this means midweek small groups and discussion. Some automatically empower teams via nominations and committees, and others by discernment of spiritual gifts, and entrepreneurship. Some raise money through canvassing and pledges, and others through coaching household financial management and designated giving. Outreach for many established churches automatically means survival ministries like homeless shelters and food banks, forgetting completely about other needs like recovery, quality of life, or vocational discernment.

The point is that conversation about church merger needs to unlock the faithful imaginations of leaders. They should not automatically presume that any particular strategy or tactic is the only way to accomplish a goal. Indeed, since many churches do not set priorities in the first place, they end up simply repeating the same old strategies and tactics that their parents and grandparents used. A merger is all about *relevance* as well as *faithfulness*, and should be a time to think outside the box.

This is why church leaders need to define the one (or perhaps two) key measurable outcomes, the achievement of which would cause the church to move people forward in maturity and mission. All programs are adjusted or initiated to achieve that. Any program that is functioning poorly to achieve the outcome needs to be perfected. Any program that diminishes or sidetracks the church from achieving the outcome must be modified or terminated. And any new idea that would enhance the success of each subsystem (without contradicting the core values, beliefs, vision, and mission that are the foundation of trust of the church) ought to be seriously considered.

It is helpful, then, to refer to the model of discipleship found in the Gospels, and shown in figure 12.1, that predates the institutionalized assumptions of the established church. There were six steps: The church would guide people through a process that started with meeting Jesus and ended by going into the world in his name. They would experience the mystery of Christ fully human and divine; learn how his life, teachings, death, and resurrection were significant; find their place in God's plan to redeem and bless the world; equip themselves for effective living and serving; and then share partnerships that bless others.

The conversation and work they shared in the community would then draw people back to the church to meet Jesus—and enter the same process of disciple-making. All of this would be founded on a trusting community accountable to shared values, beliefs, vision, and mission. Following the advice of Paul, they would do their best to become all things, to all people, so that by all means, they might rescue some (1 Corinthians 9:22).

Table 12.1 shows how the measurable outcomes looked in our pairs of churches. Of course, outcomes are customized for each church and context, and they provide examples of measuring statistics, stories, and feedback.[1] Each stage of disciple-making is oriented to a relevant scripture. This not only helps define the goal of each stage, but links the disciple-making process to the earliest church. Different stages in disciple-making lend themselves to different kinds of measurable outcomes (statistics, stories, and/or feedback).

In figure 12.1, it is clear that there is a pastor and leadership team at the center of the disciple-making process. They have operational authority to determine how each of the steps of discipleship will be put into practice. They have developed a detailed strategic plan. They routinely perfect programs, initiate new ideas, and terminate ineffective tactics. They do whatever it takes to get the results defined by the board and within the boundaries stated by a board. If the board manages critical momentum, then the core team manages critical mass.

The vision team in a merger must therefore focus on anticipated outcomes for successful pastoral leadership. This is not intended as a job description; outcomes are brief and pointed. They define what the future pastor and leadership team will be expected to deliver. In our example, each pairing of churches would need a distinctly different kind of leader (see table 12.2).

The vision team for Wesley and Asbury saw that those churches' heritage and context demanded a pastor who was more assertive, motivating, and extraordinarily empathic with the diversity of the neighborhoods. However, the vision team for Faith Temple and Pine Street realized that an effective pastor for that partnership would need to be a teacher, preacher, enabler, and facilitator—and to allow and encourage significant responsibility for volunteers.

Table 12.1. Church Systems and Measurable Outcomes

Encounter Christ.	*Now among those who went up to worship at the festival were some Greeks. They came to Philip, who was from Bethsaida in Galilee, and said to him, "Sir, we wish to see Jesus."* (John 12:20–21)
Wesley	At least 75% of worshippers will linger at least thirty minutes for conversation after worship.
Asbury	Fifteen "great stories of acceptance" will be received by the church each month.
	Health care agencies will readily know us and frequently refer people to our church for help.
Faith Temple	Ten new people will be added to the church database every week.
Pine Street	Images and stories of joyful fellowship and deep insight will be added to the website every month.
	Greeters will be deployed at every exit and in the Welcome Center, all Sunday morning.
Experience God.	*Jesus took with him Peter and James and his brother John and led them up a high mountain, by themselves. And he was transfigured before them, and his face shone like the sun, and his clothes became dazzling white.* (Matthew 17:1–2)
Wesley	We will offer at least two, distinct mission targeted worship services for inspiration and recovery.
Asbury	Stories of healing and personal transformation will be shared and celebrated weekly in worship.
	Five nonmembers will contact the church every week thanking God for our work.
Faith Temple	There will be a highly inspirational worship service with motivational preaching every week.
Pine Street	We will receive thirty requests each month from outsiders seeking our sermons and resources.
	Our community reputation will be for sound theology, biblical literacy, and ethical perspective.
Grow in Faith.	*Then beginning with Moses and all the prophets, he interpreted to them the things about himself in all the scriptures.* (Luke 24:27)
Wesley	Three new small groups will emerge every year; 50% of existing groups will continue.
Asbury	Small-group leaders will share stories of personal growth in every worship service.
	Survey respondents will prioritize small-group participation higher than seven on a scale of one to ten.
Faith Temple	45% of adults in worship will regularly participate in Bible study groups.
Pine Street	Parents of teenagers will frequently praise our membership classes and youth groups.
	15% of men's and women's groups will be nonmember adults under fifty-five.
Discern Call.	*He was praying in a certain place, and after he had finished, one of his disciples said to him, "Lord, teach us to pray, as John taught his disciples."* (Luke 11:1)

(continued)

Table 12.1. Church Systems and Measurable Outcomes

Wesley	Every board member and worship leader will mentor at least three young adults at any given time.
Asbury	Stories of 24/7 spiritual life will be told in the community about our members. Our reputation in the community will be for radical sacrifice in behalf of strangers to grace.
Faith Temple	Every board and ministry area leader will unhesitatingly define personal mission.
Pine Street	The church will turn down requests for money or volunteers that do not align with our mission. Church and service organizations look to our church to recruit board members.
Equip Disciples.	Then the righteous will answer him, "Lord, when was it that we saw you hungry and gave you food, or thirsty and gave you something to drink? 38 And when was it that we saw you a stranger and welcomed you, or naked and gave you clothing? 39 And when was it that we saw you sick or in prison and visited you?" 40 And the king will answer them, "Truly I tell you, just as you did it to one of the least of these who are members of my family, you did it to me." (Matthew 25:37–40)
Wesley	There will be 24/7 coaching in person and online for every volunteer leader of the church.
Asbury	Stewardship campaigns highlight spiritual disciplines (including standard of giving) of leaders. Our nursery will be consistently praised as the best equipped and organized in the community.
Faith Temple	Every church leader will receive at least three hours basic training every year.
Pine Street	The "buzz" in our community will praise the extraordinary competency of our volunteers. Other churches will ask our leaders to train their volunteers in worship, education, and outreach.
Send Servants.	After this the Lord appointed seventy others and sent them on ahead of him in pairs to every town and place where he himself intended to go. 2 He said to them, "The harvest is plentiful, but the laborers are few; therefore ask the Lord of the harvest to send out laborers into his harvest." (Luke 10:1–2)
Wesley	30% of our members will be active in young adult ministries every year.
Asbury	Church members will frequently be contacted by high school guidance counselors. Our reputation for high trust will be based on transparent practices of accountability.
Faith Temple	30% of our members will be active in educational and artistic outreach ministries every year.
Pine Street	Names of church members will appear in media news reports about service, year round. Service agencies will give awards to our church for community service.

Table 12.2.   Leadership Development and Measurable Outcomes

Pastoral Leadership	*Now the eleven disciples went to Galilee, to the mountain to which Jesus had directed them. . . . when they saw him, they worshiped him. . . . Jesus said to them, "All authority in heaven and on earth has been given to me. Go therefore and make disciples of all nations, baptizing them in the name of the Father and of the Son and of the Holy Spirit, and teaching them to obey everything that I have commanded you. And remember, I am with you always, to the end of the age." (Matthew 28:16–20)*
Wesley Asbury	The pastor will cast a bold vision and be the executive administrator of programs
	The pastor will be cross-culturally relevant in celebrating the sacraments and designing worship.
	The staff will design and manage programs that are extraordinarily seeker sensitive.
	The leadership team will reflect the generational and cultural diversity of the neighborhood.
Faith Temple Pine Street	The pastor will enable paid and unpaid leaders and committees for effective ministries.
	The pastor will be grounded in classic Christian faith, and open to fresh expressions of Spirit.
	The staff will equip laity to exercise their gifts and focus their callings.
	The leadership team model and mentor the values, beliefs, vision, and mission of the church.

Setting priorities requires leaders to focus on the essentials and delegate details to others. Outcomes are like leverage points. A vision team looks at the church in context like an enormous boulder sitting in a field. Somehow or other that inert boulder must become a rolling stone. A vision team walks around the boulder looking for angles, and examines the ground looking for pathways; it is looking for leverage points, which are the key areas where just the right pressure, in the right place, in the right direction, will make the boulder turn over and start to roll.

Outcomes are like leverage points. These are the few, crucial things that must be accomplished. If these few, crucial things are done, then everything else will fall into place. Leaders will be able to discern, design, resource, implement, and evaluate effective programs (critical mass) because the church will now be moving in the right direction (critical momentum).

The vision teams in our story line completed their tasks. Next they needed to present and interpret their recommendations to their church constituencies, and help them manage the stress of transitioning to a new phase of their journeys with Christ. They had prepared the churches to make decisions about boards and leadership teams. The primary responsibility of a board is to sustain *critical mass*, and the primary responsibility of a leadership team is to sustain *critical momentum*. The work of the vision teams has involved both of those things, and it will help the future boards and leadership teams develop strategic plans and manage assets as each pair of churches comes together.

The vision teams have helped future boards to answer the most fundamental annual question: *Were we successful this year?* Consider Jesus's parable of the talents. The boards will be able to tell whether the two new churches have buried their resources in the ground or invested them to multiply disciples five, ten, or a hundredfold.

Similarly, the vision teams have helped future leadership teams to answer their most fundamental annual question: *How can we be even more effective to accelerate church growth and positively impact the community?* The leadership team will be able to align all programs and resources to pursue the vision God has given each pairing of merged churches. They will be able to train volunteers, shape programs, and disperse resources in the best ways to achieve results.

Stress Management **13**
Living between Grief and Promise

As the vision teams shared their comparative insights about the surrounding neighborhoods and current church membership, stress levels within the churches they represented went up. People inevitably pondered the connections and disconnections between current programs and emerging needs. They also began comparing hidden membership needs, tastes, and comfort zones against diverse community challenges, opportunities, and expectations. Was a healthy and faithful balance possible? How far outside their comfort zones would church members need to go?

Clearly, in order for any future merged church to grow, each church would have to give something up. Indeed, in order to be relevant to the mission field, all the churches would have to make changes. This was a real "gut check" time in the merger conversation. Churches would need to grieve the loss of some programs and some members in order to fulfill the promise of new programs and new people. At this time there was renewed lobbying in each merger conversation for a congregation to drop out of the process.

There are a number of key questions that need to be answered in the process of a merger. These questions force churches to recover and identify the real heart of the church, their unique place in God's plan to bless the world, and their essential courage for change.

- What is it about our experience of God that is most relevant to this community?
- Can we give seekers a good reason not to despair about the future?
- With our first breath and our last penny will it be "God's mission" or "me first"?
- Can we let go of control and allow others to use our assets to achieve God's purpose?

Each pair of churches stepped up with real courage for change. The representatives on the vision team were able to confront their own churches. If a church were to pull out of this merger conversation, it could not simply return to the status quo. There had to be a genuine alternative for strategic partnerships and a strategic plan. Simply stated: If the intended merger wasn't a good fit, what other kind of merger would make sense?

Merger 1: Wesley and Asbury

The first two questions were most stressful for this merger conversation. These questions forced the participating churches to directly confront their separate racial, economic, and educational stereotypes. Each church tended to focus on how *different* it was: *Your experience of God is different than our experience of God! Your life situation is different than our life situation! Your issues and answers are different from our issues and answers!* However, a more profound understanding of diversity through lifestyle segmentation helped them get beyond their stereotypes.

Yes, there were differences between church memberships, but there were also differences within church memberships. Younger generations were already crossing racial, economic, and educational boundaries in their relationships. There were degrees of difference among once homogeneous publics, so that attitudes, world views, behavior patterns, and lifestyle preferences varied even among people who shared a racial identity, economic status, or educational attainment. And lifestyle segments were already drifting from historic kinships and exploring new kinships.

So the supposed differences became less significant. Instead, church members discovered that they all shared fundamental anxieties about emptiness and meaninglessness, fate and death, guilt and shame, loneliness and abandonment. They also discovered that God was bigger than any of their preconceptions, and that there was plenty of room for people to experience God in different ways and belong to the same church.

Merger 2: Faith Temple and Pine Street

The second two questions were most stressful for this merger conversation. Faith Temple was already quite open to different experiences of God, and Pine Street was already aware of the universality of fundamental anxieties about life. They struggled over issues of radical generosity and surrender to God's mission.

A merger demands radical sacrifice, but the members of both these historic churches would only go so far. The percentage of their giving, you might say, varied between 3% (Pine Street) and 10% (Faith Temple), but it was still just a percentage. Most of their wealth in time, talent, and money, they kept to themselves. They expected the church to support a balanced lifestyle, but a merger demands an unbalanced lifestyle. It is a lifestyle that is radically generous, and it causes you to reshape your personal priorities.

The members of these churches had long histories of honoring membership privileges. Neither church was quite ready to go too far out of the box of their comfortable routines. Sacred cows abounded: sacred properties and technologies, sacred personalities and offices, sacred programs and reserve funds. Many members were unwilling or unprepared to surrender personal control to God's mission.

A more profound commitment to 24/7 spiritual practices, and a better understanding of biblical stewardship, helped them get beyond these reservations. Role models for sacrifice and surrender emerged from each church. Some of these role models were ninety-year-old veterans who remembered and still practiced the spiritual disciplines of the past; and some were teenagers who set new benchmarks for extreme living and social service.

The vision team in each merger needed to take time and intentionally honor the grief many church members felt about the past. The pastors and lay leaders helped people understand that a merger was not a judgment on their incompetence or seeming faithlessness, but rather another strategy to emulate the continuous learning and absolute faithfulness of their ancestors. The trouble with grief is that implies guilt. The more leaders removed the guilt, the easier it was to grieve.

Furthermore, the vision teams needed time to embed the new hope. The pastors and lay leaders needed to repeat the mantra of hope and multiply the stories of positive change in the histories of each church. Their good work to define a theme song, inspiring image, and motivational mission statement for each church bore fruit. Unity shifted from membership privileges to mission-mindedness.

Merging churches can be exciting when you think about the possibilities of a newly merged church: more people, more resources, perhaps a building out of which to do ministry, and so forth. But the excitement is also filled with stress. Those who were part of the declining church may still be in grief over the closing of their church. Those who were part of the growing church may be filled with excitement because they might have a permanent location in which to worship. The "honeymoon" may end once the practicalities of the merger need attention. The pastor and leadership of the church must help lead the people through grief to promise—the grief of losing what used to be and the promise of what God has to give.

The key to leading a merger between grief and promise is building healthy new relationships. Most merger processes design opportunities for church members to mingle, interact, and forge new personal relationships before a final decision is made. Such a process usually lasts about nine months (or roughly between September and May, which is the primary program year). Congregations worship together in the same space (or rotating spaces). Post-worship refreshments are more elaborate and encourage people to linger. Midweek activities bring together parallel groups from each church (e.g., women's groups, youth groups, choirs, Sunday school teachers, etc.). Other activities are creative initiatives that are new to everyone and include people in different ways.

Page's recent real-life experience of guiding a merger in New Orleans provides a simple example. Early in the merger of the Mosaic Church of New Orleans and Canal Street Presbyterian Church, the vision team guided the journey between grief and promise. In this example, Mosaic Church had been meeting in the sanctuary of Canal Street Presbyterian Church for several months before the two churches felt led to merge.

While most people in both churches were excited about the merger, several individuals on the leadership teams of both churches were worried about the two congregations getting to know each other and ensuring that they could all get along. The Canal Street Presbyterian Church family was dealing with grief over the loss of several church members during their decline of several years. While they were excited about the possibility of the merger, they also were apprehensive about a new community moving into their building. Several people in Mosaic Church expressed concern over whether the Canal Street members would fit in well with Mosaic's overall vision and mission to be a multiethnic church.

To manage the stress of change, Page and the vision team established several opportunities to allow the two churches to get to know one another. They crafted such events as fellowship meals, game nights, community mission opportunities, and worship gatherings. After each event, they observed that the two church families were getting to know one another. The leadership teams of both churches continued to encourage people with the message that the process was going well and that people needed to continue to reach out to one another during those events. By the time the merger officially occurred, the two congregations had established trust and fellowship. Within a year or two after the merger, there was rarely any reference to people of the former churches. The church as a whole established a new identity as one church.

This story may be relatively simple compared to other situations that may arise during a merger. But it provides an overall example of how the leadership of merging churches may gently but firmly guide two churches through the process.

Experiencing the Change

Despite the best attempts, there will always be some who are ready, willing, and able to embrace merging, and some who are not. Having a pastor or church planter understand the grief process and other stressors, which we will introduce later, will help to bring about healthy change. However, it is important for leaders to know that not all will embrace the change that is brought about by mergers.

It may be helpful at this point to return to the 20-60-20 rule. Although the percentages might vary from place to place, it is remarkable how accurate the rule is when church leaders anticipate change.[1]

- 20% are eager, restless, and impatient—and will leave if nothing changes.
- 60% are happy, content, and anxious about harmony—and will follow wherever trusted leaders lead.
- 20% are reluctant, resistant, and controlling—and will leave if anything changes.

When applied to a merger situation, leaders can expect similar attitudes. Whether or not a church is motivated to be externally focused on God's mission or internally focused on membership privileges largely depends on which 20% captures the attention of the 60%.

The first 20% of the congregation will be ready to embrace the merger. They have been eager, restless, and impatient ever since the first time they heard of the merger possibility. Leaders must help these eager members to have patience with everyone else, especially those going through the grief of the change. Some going through grief may even want to rush into the merger in order to hide the pain of losing their old church. Even so, leaders may harness these eager members to help build energy and motivation in others.

The second 20% are reluctant and resistant to any form of change. They have been anxious, negative, and pessimistic ever since the first time they heard of the merger possibility. They are often the ones who feel that they have the most to lose, such as power, control, position, or influence.

They are often most sentimental about past institutional glory, and struggle with the most grief for deceased friends, vanishing programs, or forgotten memorials. Leaders can answer their questions, counsel their grief, and reassure them of the continuing value of their traditions and contributions. However, leaders should be mindful that this 20% does not need to win their argument, but simply stalemate the process. If they can slow the process down enough, they know that the impatient 20% who want change will eventually become frustrated and give up.

The 60% majority of members are happy and content, but will follow whoever captures their attention most urgently. When credible leaders build trust and cast a bold vision that obviously blesses both church and community, healthy church members will follow. They will understand that fellowship will not be lost, but enhanced; that mission will not stop, but accelerate; and that faithfulness will not be compromised, but deepened. When leaders provide guidance through the stressors, trust is built, and most people will follow. On the other hand, when influential personalities replace trust with membership privileges and cast a self-centered vision that preserves the status quo, cautious church members will follow. They will become convinced that it is nobler to be a "righteous remnant" that eventually dies, than a diverse church that thrives.

People in the 60% may have the most merger-related questions of the three groups, as they are considering the information and trying to make a decision. The 20% who are eager for change must invest significant time, energy, and empathy to motivate people who are content to change and merge. More than this, they must intercept the reluctant 20% as they cross the floor of the refreshment room to spread negativity among the 60%, and intervene whenever the agenda of any meeting is dominated by dissent.

Someone will leave the church in the next five years. That is inevitable. If the merger fails, some will leave. If the merger succeeds, some will leave. And it is the hard choice of leadership to decide who that will be. The final decision must be guided, not by who might leave, but by who might come. If the merger fails, the impact of the church on the community will decline and disappear, and very few newcomers will join. But if the merger succeeds, the impact of the church on the community will accelerate and expand, and many new people will join. Leaders should practice a great deal of patience, even providing guidance to those who are resistant by way of answering questions, providing counsel through the tough changes, and developing strategies to manage the stress. At the same time, leaders should also realize that there will always be people who will leave in a merger process, though such persons may stay till the very last moment fighting the merger. The resistant few should not derail or alter the process once the majority have committed to merging.

The Stages of Grief and Merging Churches

Knowledge and understanding of the stages of grief may be helpful for the leaders of merging churches. Grief does not just happen to a person experiencing the death of a loved one. Grief may also happen when a person moves from one city to another for a job, when a family loses a pet, or when a church family decides to close the doors of a church. Grief happens because there is a loss of something or someone valuable to a person. Grief is the process a person goes through to come to the new reality of his or her situation. Christians are helped through the stages of grief by the knowledge and understanding that God is in control. God provides a sense of hope and purpose in the midst of questions that arise from loss.

Pastors, church planters, and other church leaders would do well to understand the stages of grief. For example, a visionary pastor who assumes leadership in a declining church may have a great vision for merging with another church. For the pastor, it provides hope, excitement, and a vision for what could possibly be great opportunities. But the people may not be as excited about the possible merger as is the pastor. If the pastor does not understand the grief process, a self-defeating cycle may follow. The pastor continues to preach and encourage members to get behind the new merger vision. The people delay commitment or refuse to budge. Soon, the pastor gets defensive about the new vision, frustrated by delay, and angry at obstinacy. People are repeatedly hurt by the pastor's words. The congregation becomes increasingly angry, the pastor becomes increasingly frustrated, and eventually the pastoral relationship is lost. This cycle is particularly damaging, because a church usually has only three chances for radical change. After that, the 20% who are eager for change have probably left, and the remaining members are convinced that the vision of merger is impossible.

The pastor who leads a successful merger must be remarkably flexible, and able to shift from one leadership role to another without loss of identity. The pastor must be a visionary in order to foresee the potential for merger and mission. Yet in order to fulfill the vision, the pastor must revert to being an enabler and caregiver to gently guide church members through the process of loss, come to the reality of their situation, and introduce them to a new hope that God offers the church and community. And finally the pastor must reinvent himself or herself to become a CEO who manages all the tactical details and moves the church forward into merger.

The stages of loss and grief were observed by Elisabeth Kübler-Ross in her 1969 book entitled *On Death and Dying*. The stages were not ones that people were *forced* to go through, but rather ones that she observed as typical of human nature. Not every person experiences the stages in the exact order, but most generally do. Not everyone proceeds through the stages at the same pace. Consider the stages she describes as a guide through the process of grief rather than benchmarks that a person has to reach at certain points in time. It is good for a merger leader to understand the emotions involved in the stages of grief in order to guide the church through the change process.

The first stage is denial. On the level of an individual, a person may refuse to acknowledge the loss of a loved one. Many times you may hear a person say, with regard to a death or other traumatic event, "I just can't believe it" or "I can't believe they are gone." It is a normal reaction to try to rationalize overwhelming emotions. It may also lead a person into isolation as he or she attempts to embrace the reality of what has happened. Such behaviors are normal defense mechanisms against experiencing too much of the immediate shock. Most of the time it is a temporary response that carries a person through the first wave of the pain.

Many church members may go through a similar process concerning a church merger. Leaders may see such a reaction both in individuals and the whole group; and in both the declining church and the growing church. When the idea of a merger is presented, it sometimes means that the hopes and dreams of one church may not have occurred. In Page's recent experience in New Orleans, for example, a merger meant that the established, declining church might not have successfully reached its community or did not have enough money to pay the bills and keep the church doors open. Merger for the newly planted and growing church meant the realization that, after several years, it has not been able to build a building on its own. It had to move into an already established church building that might not measure up to its standards.

Leaders must help individuals, and the whole group, embrace the reality of what has happened. The *facts* of decline are grasped intellectually early in the process of merger as the vision team discerns the realities of decline. But the *shock* of decline is often experienced emotionally later in the process. The shock occurs in the declining church because the members not only *understand* that they have lost years of hard work and even the building itself. Now they *feel* the loss of their dreams and even the building where so many precious memories were housed. Church members may have known for many years that "the day was coming" when such an ending would happen. But they may have unrealistically clung to the hope that the denomination would intervene or God would work a miracle. The quicker that a group can embrace the *shock* (as well as the *facts*), the better the transition will be. However, leaders must carefully guide and shepherd the group through that initial shock and denial.

Perhaps the best way to overcome shock and denial is to do preparatory work on the front end. Leaders must carefully share the vision of a merger and clearly present the reasons why a merger may be the best option. Showing statistics and data concerning church decline and community change helps planning, but showing compassion for the loss of dreams overcomes shock. Information sessions help people understand. Listening sessions help people express their feelings. Together these help individuals embrace the idea of merger. Denial is a natural reaction, but with preparatory work, the initial denial phase may be shortened and the shock lessened.

Leaders must be shepherds. An individual in shock over traumatic news does not necessarily need more facts but rather a shepherd to provide guidance. The shepherd is both rescuer (carrying the sheep to safety), but also gatherer (reuniting the sheep with the flock). This may involve intense listening and conversation, but such pastoral support will pay off further along in the process rather than merely presenting more facts and information.

The second phase is anger. As the shock begins to fade away, pain often sets in. The intense emotion felt by members is often redirected and expressed as blame. Anyone or anything can become an object of anger: God, family, inanimate objects, or even complete strangers. Anger is about a change that an individual did not choose, but that has been forced upon him or her. Even if the individual did choose it, it might be an unexpected change. Someone is to blame. This anger becomes apparent in a person when he or she loses a loved one, and the blame can be irrationally directed toward other loved ones. The resolution comes from acceptance that the loved one is no longer around, and that no one is to blame. The individual accepts the new reality.

In the context of a merger, members may have been generally open to change, but not for radical or unexpected changes in particular. Be aware that the anger from individuals going through the grief process of losing their former church to a merged church may be directed in various ways. Most commonly the anger is directed at the leadership of the congregation (past or present), or the leadership of a denomination (past or present). An older generation might blame a younger generation or vice versa. A faction may blame another faction.

What commonly occurs is that individuals will be angry, and church leaders assume the anger is directed at the idea of the church merger itself. In actuality, the anger is simply the grieving process happening because the person is having trouble accepting the new reality. How can the leadership best handle the anger phase? The natural reaction for church leaders may be to get defensive concerning their own leadership or the vision of a merged church. Rather, one of the best approaches leadership can take is to simply listen to the person or persons expressing anger, but model respect and sympathy for leaders (past or present) who were also trying their best to be faithful. Listen for the hopes and dreams that once were, but now have perhaps failed. There's no need to get defensive or even try to force angry people to see the hope a merger may bring. Instead, lament with them concerning past memories and expectations that were not met, but respect past decisions that were all made with the best intentions in a rapidly changing context. Lamentation can pave the way for renewed understanding and respect, healthy conversations in the future that will help the church move forward to embrace the new reality.

The next stage of grief is depression. Once anger recedes, depression often emerges as members begin to accept the reality of their losses. Depression can be characterized by a feeling of hopelessness and helplessness. An individual may feel that help is nowhere to be found or that his or her world is coming to an end. Depression is a natural part of the grieving process and should not be avoided. It should be noted that in the individual grief process, this stage of depression is not necessarily considered clinical depression. It is a situational depression that can be short or long in length of time.

For churches going through a merger process, members become depressed because of the loss of their hopes and dreams. Though individuals and groups may be excited about the possibilities that a merger can bring, there still may be underlying reasons for depression of the individuals in the declining church. Merger may be a recognition of radical changes in neighborhoods or communities where members have lived long and satisfying lives. It may reflect downturns in the economy, loss of employment, the distances between parents and children, and other circumstances beyond one's control. Members may feel that fate seems to have turned against them.

Leaders must be prophets if they are to take a church through this stage of grief. A true prophet is able to see grace instead of fate. Leaders must be able to see good emerging from the most difficult circumstances, and opportunities for grace even in the most trying times. A true prophet empowers the people. Leaders can help members regain their confidence (through God's acceptance), and retake control of their lives (with God's help). They can make positive decisions to retool, rebuild, and renew the church.

The last stage of grief is acceptance. Acceptance is the acknowledgment of what has occurred. In the loss of a loved one, the person accepting the death acknowledges what has happened and realizes that he or she must move on with life in order to find happiness again. This does not mean that the loved one will not be missed; rather, it means that the survivor(s) must make adjustments and develop new routines.

The same is true in a merger process. Acceptance merger is the most positive decision for a faithful future. Merger is happening or will happen, and a future thriving church can emerge from past declining congregations. Community change is happening or will happen, and a new and healthy community can emerge for past changing neighborhoods. Yes, memories of the churches and neighborhoods from long ago can still be preserved and honored. But a brighter future and renewed feelings of hope lay before all individuals in the newly merged church. Now the leader can become a CEO and manage the tactics to accomplish the vision.

Managing Personal Stress

Stress will come into any leader's life—that is guaranteed! During a church merger, leaders will experience victories and hear criticisms, and feel their own joy, depression, and every emotion in between. Some days you will believe you are in the center of God's will. Other days you will wonder if a merger was the right thing to do.

Knowing that stress will come from the merger experience, you must learn how to manage it. Managing stress involves anticipating what may come and being prepared with action steps when the stress happens. In a merger situation, keeping a proper balance within a possibly wide range of emotions is the key to developing proper action steps.

First, leaders must maintain a healthy spiritual life. Leaders need to establish daily life habits that help them move from humility and dependence before God, to reflection and dialogue with self and others, and finally to compassion for the world. Such a process involves scripture reflection and prayerful meditation, journaling, personal spiritual retreats, and personal service projects outside of the normal ministry schedule. These spiritual disciplines provide a stable spiritual foundation that helps to keep a proper balance in life so that when stress does come, the leader is ready for it.

Leaders recommit to spiritual disciplines when the stress starts. Prayer and scripture reading often increase during times of stress, but decrease when everything is going well. But in a merger process, you never know what situations or emotions may emerge on any given day, so it is important for your spiritual disciplines to remain constant.

Second, leaders need to maintain healthy intimacy within marriage, family, friendships, and mission partnerships. Fidelity in these relationships provides a strong support group for the leader when stress attacks. If married, the leader's spouse represents first-line support. If single, or married, strong friendships with others also provide first- or second-line support. Mission partnerships refer to those who are in similar ministry contexts, such as fellow pastors or church planters. Mission partnerships may also include denominational relationships that provide support. Maintaining these vital relationships during times of calm will help when stressful times come.

Third, leaders need moral support. Leaders need to gather an inner circle of like-hearted stakeholders who share the common vision and passion for the merger. This is why the joint vision team in a merger conversation is chosen with such care. But it also helps if the leaders in each participating congregation can fill the official decision-making body with like-hearted officers. It may take time for boards or councils to be reshaped with the election or appointment of new classes, but leaders should still have a support network of trusted colleagues who can provide wise counsel and encouragement during the merger.

Fourth, leaders need to keep their heartburst passion for seekers and strangers, and lifestyle segments underrepresented in the church, alive. Too many pastors define themselves by the tasks they perform, rather than by the mission to which they are called. They spend too much time doing things for the members, rather than simply immersing themselves in the lifestyles of spiritually yearning people who are seeking God and/or unable to connect with the church. They spend too much time in their office rather than in places where the public gathers. They are too preoccupied with ecclesiastical routines rather than significant conversations.

Leading a church merger will involve many tasks. Some will be new and unfamiliar. Some tasks that were so important for self-esteem and personal fulfillment become sidetracks that pull leaders away from the larger vision. Church leaders who guide mergers often feel drained and overwhelmed and incompetent. You are doing things you never did before, interacting with people and agencies you never met before, and risking your personal stability in ways neither you nor your family ever anticipated. Immersing yourself among the publics for whom your heart bursts renews your energy, expands your imagination, and gives you strength to carry on. Mergers must be a labor of love.

Last, leaders must keep focused on personal mission. A personal mission is greater than any particular church. It is one's calling to contribute to the realm of God. A leader's ultimate purpose cannot simply be to merge churches. A church merger is merely a means to the greater end of blessing a community in the name of Christ. Having a clear purpose will help a leader retain focus in the busyness of a merger. Personal mission drives every decision, shapes every environment, determines every reaction, and defines fulfillment in the leader's life. Focus will help a leader get through the stresses that accompany a merger by focusing on the mission and, ultimately, the larger picture. It provides a deeper sense of humility. At the end of the day, it's not about you, your career, or your reputation. It's about God's mission.

The New Board   **14**
Credible Leadership for Critical Mass

The time had come to make a decision. Each pair of congregations had made a decision to support a merger *in principle*, and had appointed a vision team to explore the possibilities and prepare the way. Each vision team had guided the conversations from trust to truth, and from truth to hope. They had uncovered the compatibilities of one church to another and to the wider community. And they had defined the priorities or measurable outcomes that would define a merger's success and ensure that the whole was *greater* than the sum of the parts.

Now each pair of churches needed to make a decision to support a merger *in practice*. The decision-making would be done in several stages. In the first stage, each congregation would be asked to approve several things. (For some churches, this would also require the approval of the relevant denominational body.)

- Affirm the merger's desired outcomes as defined by its respective vision team;
- Elect and appoint a new board for a new church;
- Approve the time-limited continuance of paid program and support staff (including ordered ministers) until a staffing plan was developed by the new board and approved by the new congregation (and relevant judicatories);
- Approve the time-limited continuance of the trustees for each church, until an asset management plan was developed by the new board and approved by the congregation (and relevant judicatories). Former trustees might be included among the trustees of the new church, but would not be able to serve consecutive terms.

The details of the strategic plan, including the development of a staffing plan and the distribution of assets would then be developed by the new board, assisted by staff currently in place. Recommendations would then be brought before the congregations and relevant judicatories by the new board for final approval as the second stage.

At this point, the decision-making agenda varied between the two merger processes. The churches involved needed to affirm a new name and mission statement. The timing, however, could vary based on the decision-making habits of the churches involved.

Merger 1: Wesley and Asbury

Wesley and Asbury were both Methodist churches, with an episcopal style of decision-making. In other words, big decisions like merger tended to be made within the hierarchy of leadership, and the future board was recruited to align the church with the mission. Therefore, at this time the vision team proposed the new name and mission statement for the new church, and it was approved simultaneously along with the election of the board.

Merger 2: Faith Temple and Pine Street

Faith Temple and Pine Street embraced a more conciliar style of decision-making. True, the "congregational" and "Presbyterian" methods were somewhat different, but in big decisions like merger the congregations relied on their boards to recommend decisions to their constituencies for approval. Therefore, the decision to approve a new name and mission statement was not made right away, but deferred for consideration and recommendation by the new board once it was installed.

Deciding on a new name and mission statement will be explored in the next chapter.

The Transition

A transition from two or more boards, corresponding to two or more churches, to one board for a new church is somewhat complex and always stressful. Each vision team found it helpful to consult with experts outside the church to educate, train, and facilitate the process. Wesley and Asbury were guided by denominational leaders from their conference, but also relied on an outside consultant familiar with contemporary board models for nonprofit organizations. It was Faith Temple's and Pine Street's lack of similar denominational support that prompted their reliance on their out-side consultant and the advice of Harvest Community Church, which had a reputation for an innovative board model.

Most churches are actually quite blind to alternative models of organiza-tion. They have lived so long with the same methods of decision-making that they assume it is the only way to manage a church.

There is, after all, more than one way to organize a church. Choose the model that is most effective for delivering the mission; most familiar to the merging churches; and most easily adapted to any denominational require-ments.

1. Council or Board?

Wesley and Asbury (Merger 1) decided that a "board model" resembling the habits of nonprofit organizations would be best for the merged church. People would sit on the board because of overall management expertise, experience, and maturity. This was already the practice of both churches. The new board would provide overall unity of integrity and purpose, but allow considerable freedom to pastors, staff, and teams to develop unique ministries.

Pine Street and Faith Temple (Merger 2) decided that a "council model" would be best for the merged church. Leaders would participate in a council because they led or represented different program areas. This would reduce some of the power politics that dogged each church in the past, improve communication and coordination, and hopefully allow the strongest pro-grams from each church to maintain continuity into the merged church.

2. Task Management or Policy Governance?

Both mergers believed that "policy governance" was the best organizational strategy. Their members were all tired of too many meetings, and they felt that a more decentralized model that gave real power to ministry teams might honor the greater diversity that each merger entailed. They wanted the board or council to refrain from micromanagement, and focus instead on establishing policies that would set measurable goals, describe decision-making habits, and protect executive limitations. These boundaries would free teams to do whatever worked, but still protect church integrity and safeguard members, adherents, and the general public.

Moreover, both mergers believed that the mission effectiveness of the merged church depended on an ability to interface with other social ser-vices and nonprofit organizations in the urban core. Most of these already operated with policy governance models. The board or council would gen-erally take responsibility to oversee the *critical mass* of the newly merged church.

Finally, both mergers believed that the actual management of a church should be delegated to a core leadership team. The team would generally take responsibility to oversee the *critical momentum* of the newly merged church. The team would be led by the senior pastor. It would have authority and responsibility to manage a discipling process (volunteers, programs, and assets) in any way that best accomplished the mission of the church, provided it honored the boundaries and policies of the board or council.

3. Automatic Representation or Nomination?

The tendency in a merger is to design a board of former leaders from each church in equal representation. In theory, this would build confidence that each constituency would have an equal voice, and eventually shape a new united identity. In practice, however, this strategy prolongs separate identities, undermines unity, and makes even small decisions fractious, tedious, and time-consuming, as both mergers knew from listening to stories of failed mergers. Therefore, each pairing of churches decided to identify an entirely new board.

Wesley and Asbury (Merger 1) wanted to move to a board model based on general organizational expertise. The committee developed common criteria for board leadership, including such things as spiritual disciplines, expertise or experience in long-range planning and policy development, maturity to mentor emerging leaders, and ability to network with social service and nonprofit agencies. Nominees would submit a written profile describing their suitability that would be circulated among both churches. As one church they would elect the new board.

Pine Street and Faith Temple wanted to move to a council model based on leaders of each program area. Since the program areas of the two churches generally paralleled each other, the committee recommended that leaders and participants in each program, from each church, gather to get to know one another and the parallel programs of each church. Once they knew and understood each other, they would vote as one group to elect the ministry area leader, who would also represent the ministry area on the council.

In addition to these decisions, the committees explored additional limitations or requirements that denominational bodies might have to shape a board. This included representatives to judicatory meetings, the role of the pastor on the board, and the focus and limitations for personnel committees.

Whether or not board members functioned as a nonprofit board or council, the nominations criteria in both mergers were the same. Committees would use them to choose chairpersons who would sit on the council; congregations would use them to choose board members directly.

The nomination process for the new boards was much the same as for the vision team with some new expectations:

- Experience with policy governance
- Skills in strategic planning and asset management
- Skills in systems of evaluation and accountability
- Ability to network with leaders in other sectors of the community
- Commitment to spiritual disciplines
- Readiness to mentor emerging leaders

The nominations criteria were made very clear to the participating conversations, and candidates were identified well in advance of congregational meetings for prayer. There would be *no* nominations from the floor.

Once the new board was approved, the old boards and councils of each church were thanked and dismissed. Some of the former members were nominated and did join the new board or new council, but this was based on the new criteria for nominations. Neither board nor council members represented their original congregations. They represented the merged church.

The new temporary status of paid staff did not come as a surprise. Personnel committees within each church indicated that mergers would bring staffing changes in the annual reviews. This gave some staff plenty of time to seek other positions if they chose. The vision team wanted to be clear, however, that *all staff* were given the same status, and that the board or council of the merged church would develop a comprehensive staffing plan rather than deal with each position piecemeal. This would maximize the cooperation and communication necessary for the merger to succeed.

Once formal decisions were made by the churches and judicatories to approve the mergers and new boards or councils, each merger celebrated together in a single worship service. They recognized and prayed for the new board or council of each new church emerging from the process of Merger 1 or Merger 2, asking God's guidance as they entered the next phase of strategic planning.

The primary responsibility of a board is to help the church sustain *critical mass*. The primary responsibility of a leadership team is to sustain *critical momentum*.

These two tasks tend to blend together when the organizational model is a council, which can be both a strength and a weakness. Positively, the council model can help smaller churches, with minimal paid staff that rely heavily on volunteer committees, to coordinate and monitor programs and resources. Negatively, the council model can involve everyone in management of processes, so that no one is doing long-range planning to sustain critical mass.

These tasks are more clearly distinct when the organizational model is a board, which, again, can be both a strength and a weakness. Positively, the board model is more efficient and effective for a larger church, with additional paid staff, to pursue mission. Negatively, the board model can conflict with the leadership team if the board is not clear about setting policies rather than planning tactics.

Remember that *critical mass* is all about sustaining the church to be an independent decision-making body that empowers sufficient volunteers to create and adapt effective programs, that sustains at least one full-time pastor, and that maintains and upgrades its own space. (See chapter 22 for more details.) In order to sustain critical mass, the board or council members must focus on *long-range planning* rather than *annual management*. They can delegate management to a leadership team because they have defined clear outcomes for which they must strive and clear policies (or boundaries) within which they must operate.

The need for long-range planning also draws board or council members into other roles. They must personally model and articulate the core values, beliefs, vision, and mission of the church. They must network with other agencies and mission partners in the community. And they must mentor emerging leaders for the future. Again, the council model tends to blend these responsibilities with the leadership team. In the council model, the pastor and staff often find themselves doing most of the networking and mentoring because the council must spend more time on program management.

Mergers provide an opportunity to streamline administration so that decision-making can be faster and more effective. But one of the great challenges in a merger is that people are already so burned out from attending so many meetings that they find it hard to give energy to the process. The burnout is a result of administrative bad habits that must be corrected if the new church is to thrive.

The first bad habit is that church councils and boards always tend to regress toward consensus decision-making. This is because church people (especially from education, health care, or middle-management backgrounds) are shy of conflict and don't want to hurt anybody's feelings. They simply can't say no. Every decision has to be discussed, revisited, and discussed again until everyone is in agreement.

The second bad habit follows the first. Church boards and councils are inclined to delegate responsibility without authority. They recruit a committee to do work, but withhold permission to adapt tactics. This ties the hands of the committee and causes frustrating delays because the committee has to keep going back to a board or council for approval. Eventually volunteers become frustrated and leave, and it becomes even harder to find more volunteers.

This leads to the third bad habit: As volunteer recruitment becomes harder, the council or board must do more management. Even the most trivial items demand additional meetings and more energy. The board or council members end up not only making decisions, but also implementing decisions. They then have no time or energy left over to evaluate and align all programs and personnel to the overarching congregational mission. Oversight is reduced to following processes slavishly and reporting information, but there is no time to measure results and evaluate success.

And this leads to the fourth bad habit: As councils and boards focus all their attention on tasks they become obsessed with time management and forget spiritual depth. Management and spirituality part ways. Board and council members are elected or appointed only for skills and not for spiritual leadership. Board or council members fret about "time wasted" in prayer, and are impatient to get on with the "real agenda." They never fail to come to meetings but are irregular in worship. They strive so hard to be *competent* that they fail to be *credible*.

Policy governance is a way to break those bad habits and embed good habits. It restores decisiveness and delegates both responsibility and authority with genuine trust. As board or council members step away from management, they can evaluate the systems that give the church *critical momentum* (see chapter 21). They can measure success and not just read reports. Most of all, they can devote real energy on prayer, theological reflection, targeting mission, and mentoring emerging leaders. They can claim the credibility of spiritual leadership that is so necessary for a thriving church (see figure 14.1).

This figure represents an "organizational map" for the merged church. It can provide everyone a fresh look at how responsibilities are divided. The *congregation* regularly defines, occasionally refines, and always celebrates the foundation of trust and vision of the church in every gathering and worship service. The *board* sustains critical mass by developing policies, setting priorities, and ensuring that every tactic and resource is aligned to the mission. The *core team* sustains critical momentum by annual planning, and managing programs, volunteers, and physical resources. *Committees* (or

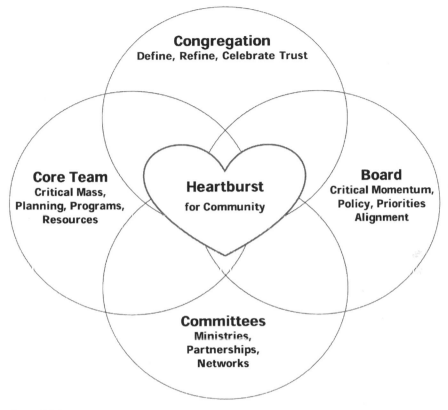

Figure 14.1.

teams) have responsibility and authority to discern, design, implement, and evaluate tactics that accelerate church growth and bless the community.

The real center of congregational life is not the perpetuation of an institution, but a *heartburst* for the diversity of lifestyles and cultures, and needs and yearnings that are constantly shifting and emerging in the community.

In a sense, policy governance is really about delegation and accountability. In a merger, the new board builds on the priorities and outcomes set by the vision team and takes them further to define measurable results: *This* will happen, rather than *that*. It then defines routines or protocols for making sound decisions that are incumbent on all leaders and committees: *Always think, pray, and proceed in certain repeatable ways.* Finally, it carefully selects limitations on action that, if consistently observed, will protect safety and guide learning and ensure coordination: *Never do this or that.* Boards don't tell people what to do. Boards point toward the destination, insist on integrity, identify specific pitfalls, and define boundaries within which leaders are turned loose to do whatever needs to be done.

The biblical example of such delegation and accountability is the story of the Israelites' exodus to the Promised Land. The vision, expressed metaphorically because its power and fullness cannot be contained in words, is to get to *a land flowing with milk and honey.* The measurable outcomes (or "ends policies"; see chapter 21) are that the Israelites will multiply as a nation and live in peace with their neighbors. The consistent protocol that will ensure wise decisions is that they should always remember the Passover and always love God with all their heart, soul, mind, and strength. They can be as innovative as they wish to get to the Promised Land, provided they do *not* do ten things (e.g., kill, steal, bear false witness, worship idols, etc.). If Moses, Aaron, and Miriam were the board, their job would be to stay on course, hold everyone accountable to love God totally and remember the Passover regularly, and avoid doing ten things. After that, the twelve committees of Israel could do pretty much as they pleased.

The declining churches that are brought together in most mergers have lived with bad administrative habits for so long that they often think there is no other way to run a church. (See figure 14.2.) As congregations become smaller, boards and councils become larger, and redundant levels of management absorb the energy of volunteers. They spend all their time debating and approving tactics and sustaining "essential services" like music

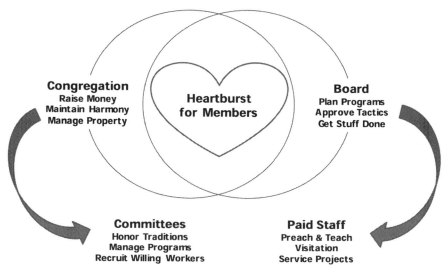

Figure 14.2.

programs and Sunday schools. Congregational participation involves more and more volunteers in efforts to raise money, maintain property, and protect harmony. Some committees function well, but many do not. They concentrate on honoring traditions and respecting membership privileges. Staff tend to dissociate themselves from the administrative struggles of the board or council, and they work in program silos for worship, education, outreach, and so forth, that are often in competition for limited resources. Churches become more and more inwardly focused.

Mergers usually shift the organization to a very different model. It may take a while for each piece of the organization to understand its appropriate role in governance. In the end, however, volunteer energy grows. The median age of the congregation goes down. The morale of the church goes up. The merged church becomes more externally focused. The community awareness and respect rises, and potential new partnerships emerge.

The New Identity   **15**
The Symbol of a New Beginning

The timing of the decision for a new name and mission statement can vary from merger to merger because of the different decision-making habits of the participating churches. For example, Wesley and Asbury came from a tradition of episcopal decision-making, and it made sense that the new name and mission statement would be approved at the same time that the new board was elected. However, Faith Temple and Pine Street came from a broad tradition of consensus building, and it made sense that their new name and mission statement would be developed by the new board after it was elected, and then recommended to the newly merged congregation. Beyond local timing and process differences, decisions such as these often require further denominational approval.

A new name does not simply come from the imagination of a hierarchy or the brainstorms of the new board. It emerges as leaders and members prayerfully reflect on the values, beliefs, vision, and mission of each participating church. Earlier in the merger process, each participating congregation in each merger defined itself using an inspiring image, a theme song, and a mission statement. Together this is what is often called the DNA—the unique identity—of this particular organism of the body of Christ.

The new board of each merger prayerfully discerned the revised DNA that became the corporate culture of its new organization. The values, beliefs, vision, and mission were articulated in words, modeled in deeds, and revealed in lifestyle, starting with the new boards and transferred to the emerging leadership teams and memberships. As each board clarified the new DNA of each new church, the new name and mission statement became clear.

It is the *external* or *missional* focus of an emerging organization that drives the change in name. This was true even in Christendom days. The names "Wesley" and "Asbury," for example, were originally chosen to reveal a method of spiritual life particularly relevant to working-class people, the poor, the addicted, and the marginalized. The name "Pine Street," for example, was taken by the Presbyterian Church in our story because its original mission field was thought to be the people living and working around that street. The name "Faith Temple," for example, was originally taken by the Baptist mission to proclaim safe sanctuary and provide new hope to the urban core neighborhoods facing challenging times.

Both board and council of the new churches immediately rejected keeping the original name of any of the original churches. They felt that a new church, representing a new beginning, was not well served by any lengthy, hyphenated name. For example, a name like "Faith Temple on Pine Street" would not be memorable, workable, or (most importantly) motivational for future generations of church members. Or for example, a "Wesley–Asbury Memorial Church" would be too confusing—and perhaps intimidating—to many of the lifestyle segments currently underrepresented or unrepresented in the churches. Most importantly, neither name would convey the real heartburst for mission for each new church.

They believed that the new names should unambiguously reveal the vision of the new churches rather than the history of the previous churches. The new names should be inspirational to the members and define exactly what they felt called to proclaim to the world. And they should be attractive and affirming to seekers, expressing exactly what seekers were longing to find or experience.

Similarly, the boards believed that their new mission statements should communicate clearly the blessing(s) the churches yearned to convey to the public. And they should be immediately relevant to the physical, relational, and spiritual needs of the lifestyle segments in their primary mission fields.

The new boards in each merger knew that not retaining any original names would disappoint the members who were most concerned about heritage. They also knew that they couldn't just invent or impose any names by themselves. Therefore, they went back to the theme song, inspiring image, and mission statements that were focused at each church, at the beginning of the merger conversations, as they built a foundation of trust. Those stimulated prayer and discussion about new names.

Merger 1: Church of the Good Shepherd (formerly Wesley and Asbury)

The denominational hierarchy suggested a number of options, and the new board finally chose the name "Church of the Good Shepherd." Board members knew that the metaphor of the Good Shepherd was prominent in the identity of each church. The Good Shepherd gathering the flock was a stained glass image high above the altar and dominating Wesley's sanctuary. The picture of Jesus as the Good Shepherd, who rescues the lost sheep and protects them from predators, was a key concept for the social conscience of Asbury.

They also chose a mission statement that was an abbreviated version of Asbury's mission statement, and implicit in the more intellectual version of Wesley's mission statement: "Christ SO BIG he can embrace all your neighbors!" Originally, the Asbury statement had referred to embracing "all your friends," but this was deemed too internally focused, so it was changed to "all your neighbors." The brevity and lettering of the statement suggested that such a mission statement could easily fit on the side of a bus, the back of a park bench, or the billboard along the interstate.

The name and mission statement were approved by acclamation in the congregations, and subsequently by the bishop, who led a worship celebration. The news was immediately released to the press.

Once the new name was announced, the congregations ceased using the old names and began worshipping jointly every Sunday. Since the former Wesley and Asbury churches were located about fifteen minutes away from each other in the expanding urbanization of the area, the worship site was rotated monthly between the two buildings until their asset management plan was approved.

Merger 2: Faith Community Church (formerly Faith Temple and Pine Street)

The new council named from among the credible leaders of Faith Temple and Pine Street recommended the name "Faith Community Church." This did not just preserve the name of one church, but communicated the clear commitment of both churches to faith formation and Christian maturity. The new board realized that both downtown churches had a clear heartburst for their surrounding neighborhoods, but the mission field today was much larger than just Pine Street.

Council members also recommended a mission statement that was less about programs and more about results, one that appealed to the gut more than to the mind. They felt that they needed to break a public misperception that their churches were old-fashioned and elitist. They recommended the mission statement, "Loving Our City with All Our Heart, Mind, and Strength." They felt the verb implied activity rather than passivity, and that the statement echoed the Great Commandment.

True to its conciliar tradition, the new congregation accepted the name wholeheartedly, but it debated the mission statement, which was eventually shortened to "Loving the City with Heart, Mind, and Strength." Some felt that the reference to "our" city was too condescending and exclusive of other faith traditions, and that the phrase itself had too many words.

Once the new name and mission statement were approved by the churches (and by the presbytery to which Pine Street belonged), the outdoor signs and weekly worship bulletins were immediately changed to proclaim the emerging organization and celebrate its potential for community impact.

Once the new name was announced, the congregations ceased using the old names, and began worshipping jointly every Sunday. Since the former Faith Temple and Pine Street churches were located so close to each other in the urban core, the worship site was rotated weekly between the two buildings until their asset management plan was approved.

What's in a name? Naming seems like a simple task, yet it is burdened by many shades of significance. Since the church is an organism, and not just an institution, it is helpful in a merger to reflect on how parents choose a name for a baby. They usually labor over it. They research names, experiment with names, pray about names, and test names with their friends and families. A baby's name should reflect the personalities of the parents, the history of each family tree, and the hopes and dreams of mother and father.

A name needs to "fit" the culture of the household. Specific concerns guide the decision. The baby's name should "seem natural" and be immediately recognizable and comfortable for family and friends to use. Moreover, the name should be safe from criticism, so that it will not be easily abused or mocked as a child matures to adulthood. Hopefully the name will reflect the personality and behavior patterns of the baby—eye contact, physical appearance, smile, and so forth.

If the parents feel lost in the crowd, left behind by culture, or excluded from upward mobility, then the name of the baby will likely be very unique. It will stand out, demand attention, and hopefully give the child a sense of pride and self-esteem. If the parents feel a kinship with a tradition, then the name of the baby will likely be very familiar. It will be shared by ancestry, claim authority, and hopefully give a child a sense of belonging and meaning.

Every lifestyle segment is shaped by particular anxieties and aspirations. Parents tend to name their children in a way that is sensitive to their unique fears and hopes. Some parents belong to lifestyle segments that are particularly anxious about emptiness or meaninglessness and particularly concerned to find purpose and friendship. Others belong to lifestyle segments that are anxious about fate and death. They may often feel trapped or vulnerable and yearn for hope and empowerment. Still others may be anxious about guilt or shame and long for wholeness and self-worth. And still others often feel displaced or abandoned, and long for responsibility and recognition.

Parents probably never think about this. Yet such considerations lie deeply embedded in their daily behaviors, world views, and religious sensibilities. When they are pushed by adversity or experience significant changes in their life cycle, they articulate their core values and express their bedrock beliefs in unique ways. Think of the most stressful moments in life: birth, adolescence, marriage, career change, relocation, retirement, and death. At each transition a person's identity is revisited, rearticulated, and in subtle ways reinvented.

Everything that is involved in the choice of a baby's name is also involved in the choice of a church's name. Church members often don't think about it, but there is a *reason* why the church is named the way it is. There is a *reason* why *this* stained glass window image, and not another one, dominates the sanctuary. There is a *reason* why a church chose to be associated with Pine Street rather than Peach Street, and it probably has less to do with a postal address and more to do with which side of the river or railroad tracks the constituency is from.

This is why the name of a church only emerges from the covenant of the church. In other words, it emerges from a shared understanding of core values (positive behavior patterns) and bedrock beliefs (convictions that give strength in times of stress). These shared assumptions provide the structure of accountability that is associated with a covenant. Church members hold themselves and each other to a certain standard. They rely on each other to remind, encourage, and strengthen one another when the going gets tough.

A name has *significance*. People always read a script or see a story that lies behind a name. It may not be the intended script or the right story, but churches choose a name to communicate something special. Even if they have to correct misperceptions caused by a name, they do not want to have to do that frequently. They want the first impression to be an accurate and lasting perception.

A name is always multidimensional. Think of a name as both a symbol and a portal. As a symbol, the name positions a church on the horizontal plane of daily life. It reminds and educates. It reminds the church members of where they come from, what they are about, and where they are going as a community. It suggests *these* measurable outcomes, rather than *those* measurable outcomes. At the same time, the name educates the community about the institution. Community members anticipate what kind of faith community they are entering, what kinds of preaching and programming they can expect, and how the church might (or might not) be relevant to their context.

All this is what we mean by a church "living up to its name." Seekers tend to join a church because a church lives up to its name. Members tend to leave a church because it fails to live up to its name.

As a portal, the name of a church positions a church on the vertical plane of incarnation. It reveals and proclaims. It reveals the soul of a church and the normative ways church members experienced, and are experiencing, the immanence of God in their lives. They are constantly experiencing grace in *this* way or *that* way. The stories cherished and told in the life of the church tend to be, for example, about healing, hope, belonging, growth, guidance, personal transformation, and/or social justice. The name proclaims what blessings seekers might experience when they connect with a church in the same ways. They are more likely to experience both the touch of the Holy and positive change in their lives, because they are healed, encouraged, embraced, matured, coached, freed from addictions, and/or vindicated.

This is also what we mean by a church "living up to its name." Seekers tend to visit a church because it has a reputation of relevance to their situation. Members tend to leave a church because it has become irrelevant to their situation.

In the days of Christendom, successful mergers usually chose a name that reflected their heritage (just as parents used to choose a name for their baby that came from previous generations). In those days, almost all Christians had some allegiance to a church tradition. Church growth was primarily driven by transfers of membership from church to church in the same "franchise," or by the baptisms of succeeding generations of church members.

In the days of post-Christendom, successful mergers usually choose a name that reflects their hope (just as parents today choose a name for their baby that comes from contemporary heroes, celebrities, and other role models). These days, many people either don't have a happy memory of church or any memory of church at all. People are more likely to join by affirmation of faith or conversion, or because they sense that a significant moment in their life (marriage or funeral) needs to be celebrated spiritually.

Here are other ways the significance of a church name has shifted from the Christendom to post-Christendom church:

- The name of the church used to be closely associated with the name of the denomination. Now the name of the denomination is barely mentioned, and the name of the church must have instant, positive recognition.
- The name of the church used to be connected with the name of the senior pastor. Both names were clearly visible on all signage. Now the name of the pastor is often missing from the outdoor signage, replaced by the name of some program or activity that is well known in the community.
- The name of a church used to be advertised in newspapers, along with the times of worship and Sunday school. Now the name of a church must appear regularly in social media, along with evocative images and powerful stories.

Perhaps the most important shift in the significance of a church name is revealed by the subtitle or mission statement associated with the name. In the past, the name of a church usually conveyed a sense of belonging. The name identified a meeting place or a fellowship, and often suggested a club or a friendship circle. The name was a rallying point, where the flag waved and everyone united around a principle or a cause. Members were never stricken from the rolls, and membership guaranteed certain benefits.

Yet the truth is that most lifestyle segments today are not looking for "belonging." The ones that are looking for "belonging" are often older, left behind by the mobility of the world, far from home, or painfully introverted. Everyone else has found ways to sustain significant relationships through clubs, gyms, sports venues, social media, and coffeehouses.

Today the name of a church usually conveys a sense of hope. It identifies a promise for the future. That is the one thing postmodern people miss the most in a global village threatened by violence, pandemics, global warming, economic downturns, meaningless employment, abusive relationships, chronic addictions, incurable diseases, and so many other problems.

This is not an age characterized by optimism. It is an age characterized by disappointment and the conviction that traditional institutions have let us down and scientific advance has fallen short. Therefore, the names of corporations, agencies, schools, retail stores, and so many other organizations (including churches) in all sectors (including religion) have changed. Gone are the old, reliable, brand names. Welcome the new, innovative, catchy names that are bright with promise.

Asset Management

16

Resourcing Teams and Ministries

The mergers had been approved *in principle*, then approved *in practice*, and now needed to merge *in fact*. A sense of pride and confidence was also emerging. The churches in each merger (Wesley and Asbury to create Church of the Good Shepherd, and Faith Temple and Pine Street to create Faith Community Church) had discovered that they were indeed willing to pay the cost of discipleship and could be faithful to follow God's mission in new ways. They were willing to change attitudes and traditions, organizations and leadership teams. And now they felt a deeper trust that would help them change properties, technologies, and financial strategies.

All four churches had been warned at the very beginning that discussion of what would happen to property, facility, and money in a merger would be very difficult. However, the mutual respect and sensitivity that was generated in the ensuing months made this conversation easier than feared. They had built trust and focused mission. They had set priorities for leadership and program. Most importantly, they had already reduced the power of controllers and factions in each church. This meant that discussion of assets could be calm, respectful, and, most of all, missional.

Merger 1: Church of the Good Shepherd (formerly Wesley and Asbury)

The biggest challenge for Church of the Good Shepherd was that neither the former Wesley property nor the former Asbury property was particularly suitable. Aside from limited parking, both were constructed in such a way as to make renovations very difficult. Neither sanctuary had particularly good acoustics. The space was not versatile enough to offer the worship options the new board envisioned. The offices were cramped. The nurseries were located in the basement or near exit doors that could not be secured.

The Wesley property did have a good traditional pipe organ, but it would probably not be versatile enough as an instrument for future worship. Good Shepherd could sell the organ to another church and use the income to purchase keyboards and other instruments. The Asbury property did have a gymnasium, but such space was hard to maintain and unsuitable to hospitality and fellowship ministries that would need to be higher quality.

The denomination could transfer ownership of the Asbury property to another ethnic church in need of space and sell the Wesley property at a good price to a developer to build condominiums. The real challenge was to locate a suitable, affordable place for Church of the Good Shepherd that would be centered in the primary mission field. Church leaders ultimately found an opportunity to purchase: a renovated former home-improvement box store. It would provide excellent parking. An architect connected with the conference could design it to suit their needs. Best of all, a member of the former Wesley Church was a director on the board of the holding company that owned the former home improvement store and could arrange acquisition at a good price!

Reserve funds and financial accounts could be merged fairly easily, and the trustees from each former church organized the process. However, Asbury carried a significant debt left over from the building of the gymnasium ten years ago. The conference was able to help the church discharge much of that debt and reassign the rest from the bank to the denomination.

The asset management proposal for Church of the Good Shepherd was now shared with the church and their denominational parent for approval. The board and trustees could now follow through with changes related to state government requirements and nonprofit status.

Merger 2: Faith Community Church (formerly Faith Temple and Pine Street)

The biggest challenges for the new Faith Community Church involved location and facility. Each former church was located on highly visible corners in the downtown area, and each church struggled to provide adequate parking. And of course, the members of each church loved their own buildings. The newly formed council paid for professional engineers to thoroughly evaluate each building. The engineers concluded that the Faith Temple property was in much worse condition and would cost more in renovations than the Pine Street property. The council would recommend the sale of that building, with the congregation centering on the Pine Street location.

In the end, this was good news for the charter school of the former Faith Temple. Not only were there better facilities at Pine Street, but the income eventually generated from the sale of the Faith Temple property would provide significant capital infusion for the ministry. On the other hand, this was stressful for Pine Street, because it had to terminate the lease of a number of fledgling ethnic churches housed in that building. The council would do whatever it could to relocate them.

Faith Community Church also needed to update a number of technologies, including audio systems in the sanctuary and plumbing in the washrooms. And plans were developed to remove, relocate, and preserve a number of "sacred" objects—stained glass, sanctuary furniture, and archives—from Faith Temple.

There were reserve funds held in trust by both former churches that needed to be brought under the supervision of the new church. Lawyers who were already members of Pine Street volunteered to undertake the necessary legal procedures. The most complex task was to protect the financial "firewall" between the church and the charter school (which was separately incorporated and received state grants and public donations).

The sale of the old Faith Temple property might take some time, given the economic realities downtown. For the time being, it could be rented to various religious and social service groups, and the sanctuary could still be rented for concerts. The good news was that Faith Community Church could sell the air rights to a developer who wanted to protect several corporate buildings near the church.

The asset management proposal for Faith Community Church was now shared with the church and the denominational parent of the former Pine Street Church for approval. Council and trustees could now follow through with changes related to state government requirements and nonprofit status.

For many church members, a merger only becomes *real* when the control of assets is transferred to a new church (with a new name, a new board, and new trustees). Once again, stress levels rise. The new reality challenges their fundamental attitudes about mission. This situation comes to the surface when trustees and financial managers of each former church actually list the assets that are to be merged.

Our case studies have assumed that the books of each church have been professionally audited and the assets of each church have been accurately and comprehensively listed. While it may seem obvious, this in itself is often a problem. Older, smaller, declining churches often neglect professional audits, cut costs by relying on internal audits, or forget audits altogether. Professional audits may bring unpleasant surprises. They may reveal that financial assets were not as large as supposed, that reserve funds have conditions that were forgotten or ignored, or that debts have been forgotten and payments outstanding. Occasionally audits may offer pleasant surprises and reveal bank accounts and hidden funds that have been forgotten and can be recovered.

Similarly, our case studies have assumed that each of the churches has a clear list of physical assets and liabilities. This also seems obvious but is often a problem. Many churches own multiple properties (manses or parsonages, parking lots, education centers) that have long been unused or were loaned to other users long ago. There may also be more portable assets like pipe organs that were in use for a long time but not owned by the church. The title to some assets may also be unclear. There can be liens against properties that are outstanding. Some church buildings house artifacts that in fact belong to a parent denomination or historical society. Other church buildings have been designated as historical sites with limitations imposed by state and local governments on how the property can be changed or how ownership can be transferred. Even if legal title is clear, outside organizations that have used a facility for decades may assume they own it and are shocked when it is taken away. Even if they are clear about ownership, they may expect to have the right to purchase the property prior to any merger.

The more complicated the situation, the more important it is to seek professional financial and legal advice *from outside the memberships of all churches participating in the merger.* This requires absolute objectivity, so that audits and reports have absolute reliability. Even if there are legal and financial experts within the memberships of the churches, there must not be any possibility of intentional or unintentional bias. Moreover, if any of the participating churches belong to larger denominations, their lawyers and financial officers must be consulted as audits and asset lists are created. There may be petitions to governments that need to be filed or requests to denominations that must be approved.

As audits are finished and assets are listed, stress within the churches can rise again. This time, it is usually from older or inactive members with significant family history in the church. Despite the best communication efforts, they may simply have missed news of the merger. Now, however, they may lay personal or family claims to specific assets (property, musical instruments, stained glass windows, communion wares, etc.) that they may have given to a church as a memorial. In most cases, a memorial is a gift with no strings attached—but not always. Even if a member family has no legal claim to a memorial, it may be kind and generous for a church to return a portable object to the family. Or it can at least return memorial plaques placed on fixed assets. However, a church cannot be expected to pay for the added costs of removal, demolition, and/or transportation of memorial objects.

The emotional attachment to physical assets of older members and families with historical connections to a church should not be treated lightly. This is why many mergers intentionally include a strategy to dedicate a museum, archive, memory garden, or some other special location or method to preserve memorials. A special worship service will be held to celebrate the past *before* any change, renovation, or demolition occurs. In some traditions, the denomination will have special requirements to deconsecrate sacred space or sacred objects. Merger participants can cement their trust in each other by attending all such services among the partners.

As emotional as this process can be, it is also an opportunity for church leaders to emphasize once again the missional purpose of a merger. After all, even the oldest churches were originally founded out of a sense of *mission*. However *internally* focused churches might have become over the decades or centuries, they were all originally founded to be *externally* focused to bless the community.

Biblical Principles of Asset Management

During the transition from merger *in practice* to merger *in fact*, merging churches often share a preaching series and/or Bible study program. The preaching series is based on the same texts, at the same time, in each church. The sermons might even be jointly written by the pastors as a team. The Bible study program intentionally mixes members from each participating church so that they might not only study together, but create new friendships. The text from 2 Corinthians 8–10 can reinforce basic biblical principles about faithful stewardship.

- Our possessions and assets should be used for the sake of the Gospel (2 Corinthians 8:1–3). Paul offers the example of the Macedonian church, noting that the purpose of giving was to help the work he and the other apostles were doing in their missionary journeys. Paul stresses that the Macedonians gave even out of their own poverty. A missional mindset means that the assets we have, and the sacrifices we make in the future, are part of God's larger plan to bless the world. Our security depends on sharing the mission, not holding property.

- Our assets should be used to bless others first, and ourselves second (2 Corinthians 8:4). Sometimes it is hard to differentiate between money used for mission impact and money used for church growth. Yet the real priority for building or renovation is primarily to multiply options for ministries to the community. Only as the church succeeds in mission does it grow itself.

- Christ is our example for wealth management. Paul writes: "For you know the generous act of our Lord Jesus Christ, that though he was rich, yet for your sakes he became poor, so that by his poverty you might become rich" (2 Corinthians 8:9). Jesus chose this passage from Isaiah for his first sermon: "The Spirit of the Lord is upon me, because he has anointed me to bring good news to the poor. He has sent me to proclaim release to the captives and recovery of sight to the blind, to let the oppressed go free, to proclaim the year of the Lord's favor" (Luke 4:18–19). When churches use their material possessions in order to minister to others, then truly they become the "body of Christ."

- God's purpose is parity between the rich and the poor (2 Corinthians 8:14–15). Paul states that some believers will have much, and some have little. Yet, God has supplied those with much to help those with little. In some merger situations, the church with a greater amount of money may feel a sense of privilege or authority over the church that has little. The church with much may feel as though it should have greater influence over decisions. The wealthy church not only shares resources equally with another church but also shares authority equally with the other church. God has blessed one church in order to be a blessing to the other church.

- The best way to maximize the harvest is to sow liberally (2 Corinthians 9:6–9). Paul touches upon a parallel Old Testament concept: God, through Malachi, challenges the nation of Israel to bring the full tithe into the storehouse and only then receive God's blessing (Malachi 3:10). The New Testament principle is much the same: Give to God the resources God has first given to us and see how the blessings flow. The more generous the church is toward the community, the greater the harvest that deepens faith and positively changes society.

Missional principles allow churches to keep their focus on goals and values higher than themselves. Asset management all too easily becomes territorial. Mergers are always easier when people are willing to let go and allow their assets to be used by God.

Property Development

Throughout the process of merger, leaders constantly remind members of the proper order of planning: foundation and function, and then form and finance. The order of planning parallels the priority list of seven cost centers: tradition, attitude, leadership, organization, property, technology, and money. The merger first laid a solid foundation of trust, discerned God's vision for the future, and then defined the mission and name for the new church.

The physical form of a church (i.e., properties, facilities, and technologies) emerges out of its vision and mission and is shaped by the values and beliefs of the church. The assets of a church are not precious in themselves; they are precious only as they effectively follow the vision and deliver the mission. Therefore, there is no single and correct way for a church building to be designed. There are many choices: The best way to reveal church identity and deliver mission results should be determined pragmatically.

It is rare for a merged church to have complete freedom to design its facility. Often, one property becomes the location of the new church and any renovations are limited by engineering and financial realities. If the new church relocates to an entirely new site or structure, there are additional limitations due to zoning or leasing requirements. Nevertheless, it is helpful for the board or council of the newly merged church to understand that there are six basic pieces in the pattern for an effective church building.

1. Hospitality and Communication

An effective church property needs a central, accessible, hub of communication and fellowship. This space is often an intersection of hallways in the building, at the center of the natural corridors of movement as people go from here to there. It is also clearly visible as people enter the main doors of the building. This is where a welcome center is placed, along with any displays of books or other literature. This is where food and refreshments are located and people linger to talk before, during, or after events. This is where the pastor and staff can be found for introductions or brief conversations. There may be a small kitchenette or preparation counter with running water. Note that this space is almost always on the main floor when you enter the building and is accessible for those with physical handicaps or young families with strollers.

2. Nursery

In the past, churches generally thought of the nursery as part of Christian education. Therefore, the nursery was located in the midst of Sunday school space downstairs, upstairs, or down a corridor. Today, the nursery is considered part of hospitality space. Ideally, it is located on the same floor and adjacent to the hub of hospitality. This space is usually more central and more secure. Parents are more likely to linger before or after worship if they are closer to their infants and toddlers. Since running water and washrooms are also part of hospitality, these utilities are convenient for the nursery. The kitchenette makes it easier for nursery caregivers to warm bottles or prepare snacks.

3. Worship

An effective church property needs to provide flexible gathering space for worship. The general rule is that once regular worship attendance reaches 80% capacity, it is time to start a second service. Leaders in the newly merged church need to estimate regular worship attendance based on the records of each of the previous churches. Whatever that number is, add 15% in order to anticipate an increase in visitors that usually follows a new church opening. Worship space can certainly be sacred space, but it does need to be changeable space. Today's church that adapts to diversity cannot assume that the style of worship preferred by the past members of the participating churches will remain the same in the future.

4. Education and Group Space

One reason Sunday Schools have declined is that churches have not recognized the different learning methodologies and technologies that have evolved in postmodern society. Today classrooms are designed more for conversation or interaction than presentation or reading. And effective church property usually provides more and smaller rooms in the same square footage where once there were fewer and larger rooms. Classrooms tend to be less formal, with less furniture, so that learning can be more experiential. Desks have been replaced by craft benches. Blackboards have been replaced by computer and video technologies. Parents today have much higher expectations for the cleanliness, safety, and technologies of educational space for their children.

5. Outreach

Now that churches are focusing on major signature outreach ministries, they often need to create or customize space especially designed for continuous use by outreach leaders seven days a week. The space is renovated for whatever the outreach ministry needs, but there are certain necessities. There should be a separate entrance to the space, and access to the rest of the building should be limited for security reasons. Exterior and interior should be well lit. Washrooms should be located conveniently close to the outreach center, accessible for wheelchairs and baby strollers, and uniformly equipped with infant change tables. The only reason to have a large kitchen is for outreach purposes. And many outreach ministries don't really need one. Running water, refrigeration, and microwave ovens may be all you need.

6. Administration

Offices can often be located in different parts of the building and configured in any number of ways. However, there are three important priorities. First, the receptionist (or church secretary) space needs to be the highest quality. This space is not only convenient to visitors, but it provides an important "first impression" of the values and beliefs of the church. Furnishings, decorations, and even storage space need to be arranged by the church, and not simply by whoever happens to occupy the room. And of course, a counter, window, or larger doorway should allow the receptionist to both see and be seen.

Second, the pastor's office also needs to be centrally located (preferably near the receptionist or church secretary space). This is partly for communication, but mostly for the security of visitors and the protection of the pastor. Do not provide a private entrance to the pastor's office. Although the offices for other staff may be located anywhere, it is best to cluster them so that no staff person is isolated in the building.

Of course, the above recommendations for space are ideal. The reality is that compromises must be made. In a church merger, either the *most* useful property will be chosen from the existing properties or the new church will move into a *different, used* space. It is rare that the newly merged church can build its own facility. This is a time of fluidity and flexibility, however, and church leaders should take advantage of it. Make as many renovations and changes as soon as possible. It will become much harder to make changes even just a few months later. The new church quickly "solidifies" with new habits and structures.

Now is the time to jettison unusable items. Don't "take it with you." Eliminate the old curricula, ragged and broken toys, old technologies, old-fashioned furniture, and rummage sale leftovers. Have a shared, giant yard sale, or, in some contexts, just give everything away to people who really need it.

There is one final caution: Don't start renovating without consulting a professional engineer or architect. Old buildings cover up many unpleasant surprises. Electrical wires and plumbing hide in unlikely places, and often need to be updated. It is often difficult for an amateur to know which walls are bearing loads and which are not. Some church buildings, in whole or in part, are heritage sites and protected from radical change. Building codes are complicated, and many old churches that have been "grandfathered" into the system may cease to be exempt and have to do significant upgrades under new ownership.

Financial Management

Once the assets and liabilities have been comprehensively listed and audited and a property plan has been developed, church leaders can develop a financial management strategy. Every context is different. Denominational policies vary. A new church will want the best people available to develop the plan—people who are knowledgeable about *current* accounting procedures, investment guidelines, and fundraising strategies. It may be very helpful to have a short-term contract with an outside professional who can lead the development of a plan and coach church members for future responsibility. There are four important things to consider.

1. Reserves

The comfort zone of church leaders varies. Some leaders (including church planters) are comfortable with smaller reserves to cover acute emergencies. This might mean sufficient funds to cover salaries, utilities, and other essentials for three months. They assume that their faithfulness and creativity will help them solve an emergency in that time. They do not want large reserves to reduce motivation for weekly giving, and they want to minimize overhead and maximize mission. Other leaders (including older, veteran leaders familiar with older, used buildings) are only comfortable with large reserves to cover chronic deficits and expensive maintenance. This might mean sufficient funds to cover salaries, utilities, and other essentials for at least a year. They assume that their faithfulness and determination will solve, or at least manage, the problem in that time; they do not want large deficits to reduce motivation for weekly giving, and they want to be prepared when something expensive in the old building breaks down or falls apart. Obviously, leaders of the newly merged church need to make the best compromise possible. Three things are clear, however.

- The new church *must* break the habit of many declining churches that accept year-end deficits as a fact of life. You cannot use either the interest or the principal of reserve funds simply to bail out the church at the end of the year, and you cannot rely on extra rummage sales or fowl suppers that drain the energy out of volunteers for little financial return.
- The new church *cannot* maintain reserve funds that are so large that they damage the credibility of the church. Unnecessarily large reserves are a sign of institutional privilege and hypocrisy to postmodern people. They may use church programs, but they will not consider church membership, nor will they support the church's budget
- Reserve funds that are restricted or limited in any way *cannot* be continued. Many churches will bring to a merger reserve funds that are restricted by conditions imposed at the time the money was raised (e.g., "organ funds") or by conditions imposed as part of a bequest (e.g., "memorial fund"). The policies must be changed to allow the church freedom to use the money as needed. In extreme cases, it is better to return large sums to the original donors of a bequest rather than allow outside parties control over the budget.

Of course, it is also possible that one or all of the churches involved in a merger have no reserves to bring to the merger. In that case, the financial plan must include a strategy to build reserves over time. If this is partly done through bequests, grants, or designated giving, the policy of the church must give the church freedom to reallocate money as needed.

2. Debt

Once again, the comfort zones of church leaders vary. Some leaders (including church planters and leaders from some evangelical traditions) are comfortable with larger debts because they are highly committed to adult faith formation and radical discipleship, maintain high expectations for tithing, and are confident about church growth. Other leaders (including veteran pastors and leaders from mainstream traditions) are only comfortable with low debt because they are highly committed to lifecycle ministries and pastoral care, maintain low expectations for percentage giving, and are less confident in church growth. There needs to be a compromise, but three things are clear.

- Annual debt payments for a merged church *should not exceed* about 15% of the budget. Church plants and healthier established churches might sustain higher debt, but a church merger has more risk.
- A healthy church always has mission-driven debt. In other words, the church's "mission reach" should always exceed its "financial grasp." However, *this must be clearly mission-driven and not maintenance-driven* debt. Church members and community members are always more motivated when churches take risks for the sake of mission.
- Church debt is *not* household debt. It is not even the debt of multiple households. The confusion stems from the misinterpretation of what it means to be a "church family." The total debt (principal and interest) may seem overwhelming, but it is funded not only by member households but from outside sources.

In many contexts, the choice of the loan is more important than the amount of the debt. The church can choose to be indebted to the bank, to a denomination, to individual members, and/or to mission partners. Banks may be inevitable lenders, but they are usually the least flexible. A denomination usually offers low-interest loans (and may even forgive repayment in time) but often in not very large amounts. Church members can also lend money in the form of personal debentures or bonds or as part of a strategy to match denominational giving, but bonds can usually be redeemed at the request of a member donor in case of family emergencies. Some mission partners working with the signature outreach ministry of the church may offer short-term loans to sustain a program. In other words, a church may not have *a* debt, but *many* debts, because it is financially beneficial to negotiate with multiple sources.

3. Budget

In the past, most churches developed line item budgets that were extraordinarily detailed. In a sense, the budget for the coming year mirrored the financial statement from the previous year. Annual congregational meetings compared the two, and scrutinized each line item before approving the budget. This custom is due, in part, to the desire of some members to treat the church like a business, applying the same accounting practices of the corporate sector to the religious sector. It is also due, in part, because some members persist in thinking that a church budget is the same as a household budget, applying the same accounting practices from personal lifestyle to organized mission. Note especially that this practice is most common in *low trust* churches. The members are compelled to review every line of a financial statement and budget because they are actually not that confident in their leaders.

The difficulty in a merger is that the items in the financial statement and budget of one church do not easily match the items listed for another church. This makes it almost impossible to simply take multiple budgets and combine funds accurately and fairly. Moreover, a church merger is, and must be, a *high trust* church. There are too many complications in a merger, and things are happening too fast, for the members of several different churches to understand and approve a line item budget.

An emerging practice for churches is much more suitable for church mergers. The budget for the coming year does not have to mirror the financial statement of the previous year. Yes, the annual financial statement needs to be very detailed; and yes, church members should be able to see it. The budget, however, is really not an item-by-item list of anticipated expenses. Instead, it is a series of capital pools. Each capital pool generally matches the steps in a discipling process that sustains critical momentum. For example, there is a capital pool for hospitality, worship, education, small groups, and outreach; and a capital pool for property maintenance and technology upgrades, administration, and communication. The sum in each capital pool is calculated with reference to various line items related to each area of ministry, and with reference to the strategic plan for growth in each area of ministry. However, the leadership teams for each area of ministry have the flexibility to spend that money as needed to get mission results. Policies of the board both block and guide spending from each capital pool with executive limitation and administration processes.

This kind of budget is more suitable for a *high trust* church. The members can see financial statements and approve them. The members can ask what the strategic plan or capital pool entails in each ministry. And the members can learn and modify the policies of the board. However, they do not have to review and approve every line item because, fundamentally, they trust the leaders. This means that the budget of the merged church can be created as a fresh and original budget for the new church and not be encumbered with the line item budgets of the former churches. They can then create annual financial statements that explain how capital pool funds were spent, without tying the hands of ministry area leaders to repeat the same strategy all over again.

4. Fundraising

As the years, decades, and perhaps centuries have gone by, established churches have become increasingly lazy about stewardship. At best, many churches simply mail out financial statements and pledge cards to the members in November. The members listen to one sermon about the faithful use of money, send their completed pledge cards to the church office, celebrate how much of the budget has been underwritten while anticipating periodic reminders to fulfill their pledge, and brace themselves to volunteer in an urgent fundraising program to make up inevitable deficits. Again, this habit reveals the hidden assumption that the church is a "family" and the budget is a household budget. But this practice will almost certainly guarantee the failure of a church merger.

The newly merged church must develop a year-round, comprehensive, fundraising strategy. It needs to appoint a stewardship team that is separate from the trustees or finance committee, and specifically focused on fundraising throughout the year. A year-round strategy usually includes the following elements:

- An annual leadership strategic planning retreat that defines measurable outcomes for the year, and stresses that leaders must lead the sacrifice to support the church
- Keynote speakers or programs on Christian financial management, credit card debt relief, and tithing tax refunds
- Volunteer Opportunity fairs to help members follow mission money with hands-on involvement
- Appreciation dinners for the top givers and most energetic volunteers
- Advanced pledging by leaders to publicly underwrite the life and mission of the church
- A month of preaching and small-group discussion on the seven cost centers of discipleship (i.e., tradition, attitude, leadership, organization, property, technology, and money)
- A celebration *weekend* of fellowship and prayer

The stewardship strategy needs to offer multiple choices for giving and financial management because the merged church is now much more diverse than any of the previous churches. Some members will prefer to simply give a lump sum to a unified budget, while others will prefer to designate giving to particular ministries. Some members only want information, not conversation, so that they can make informed philanthropic decisions. Other members want a conversation, not just information, so they can be coached in an overall Christian lifestyle.

One reason that churches today focus on a single, major, signature outreach ministry (rather than sending small amounts of money and energy to multiple missions) is that people are always more generous toward missions in which they actually participate. Moreover, a signature outreach ministry can often be transformed into a separately incorporated faith-based nonprofit. Church leaders and members are still involved on the board and nonprofit activities, but the nonprofit can function with an independent budget and receive donations from the community or grants from government and denominational agencies. The nonprofit then contributes financially to the maintenance of property and perhaps contributes to a staff salary.

Perhaps the biggest shift in stewardship is the changing attitude of church members. In the past, churches tended to adjust the mission to fit the finances. Going forward, churches will find creative ways to raise the finances in order to fit the mission. The shift reflects the new culture of a merged church that is revealed every week in worship. The church is no longer bashful about talking about money, because the money is always tied to mission. The church is always sharing stories of successful ministry funded by the church. A person may share a testimony about how a certain ministry of the church impacted his or her life. The pastor may then tie the ministry to the financial plan to show how it is funded by the church budget. A testimony about spiritual life and lifestyle from an individual motivates the faithfulness of others. Authentic witness and financial transparency are especially motivating for younger generations, and they build credibility in the community.

Above all, consistently communicate the teaching of the early church that every gift is valuable in God's realm. It is not the size of the gift that matters but the willingness to share the sacrifice. The smallest or the largest gift is acceptable when everyone gives together as a community.

Building a Core Team
17
Competent Leadership for
Critical Momentum

The two mergers had now been approved *in principle*, then *in practice*, and finally *in fact*. The surrounding community, church members, state, and denomination now considered the merger accomplished—except *in ministry*. Up to this point, the program and support staff from the former churches had been carrying on with the understanding that all offices were time-limited. Now the time had come to unite in ministry and finalize a staffing strategy.

The essential identity, purpose, and basic organizational structure of the two new churches became clearer. Church of the Good Shepherd had chosen a board model, and Faith Community Church had chosen a council model. Both models would focus on sustaining the critical mass of the church. In other words, in their respective churches they would make critical decisions to grow membership and participation, manage financial resources, update facilities and technologies, build and network with mission partners, mentor emerging leaders, encourage creativity, communicate within and beyond the church, protect the core values and bedrock beliefs of the church, and align everything and everyone to the vision God gave the church—and nothing else.

However, there was much those entities could not do and would not attempt to do. The task of sustaining critical momentum for each church would be entrusted to its *core leadership team*. This team would run the day-to-day, week-to-week, year-to-year ministries of the church. The board (used generically) together with the leadership team would define measurable outcomes in a changing world, but it would refrain from micromanagement. It would delegate both responsibility *and* authority to the leadership team to achieve the measurable outcomes in any way that worked (within the policies and executive limitations it defined).

Critical momentum is basically about sustaining a discipling process. Earlier the vision teams for each merger had used a similar concept to define measurable outcomes for the new church. Now a core team will oversee each critical step required to grow a seeker into a servant and a member into a volunteer.

The core team consists of leaders who each take responsibility and authority to manage one step in the journey of spiritual and missional growth. An individual leader would innovate and evaluate tactics, build and train his or her own team, coordinate with other leaders, network with related agencies and partners, and generally ensure that the outcomes expected by the board and senior pastor were achieved.

Earlier the two pairs of churches had approved the first stage of the mergers, which included the continuance of the existing program and support staff from each church until a new staff strategy was devised. However, the design of a core team is not just a staffing strategy, but a leadership team strategy. Some leaders are paid full- or part-time, while others may be unpaid even though they share the same responsibility, authority, and accountability of paid staff.

Merger 1: Church of the Good Shepherd (formerly Wesley and Asbury)

The Church of the Good Shepherd required a staffing strategy that could both model and develop the bi-racial character of the new church, and also relate to the growing multicultural population of striving singles in the emerging mission field. The new board proposed the following staff configuration:

- The senior pastor of the former Wesley Church, who was retiring anyway, recommended that Church of the Good Shepherd ask the bishop to appoint a veteran African American minister with strong administrative and preaching skills.
- The part-time youth pastor from the former Asbury Church would be hired as the full-time youth pastor for Good Shepherd. However, in order to connect with the diverse mission field, this youth pastor would be retrained to specialize in small-group multiplication. The goal was not to create a youth ministry, but to multiply cross-generational affinity groups.
- The new church needed musical leadership that could competently include multiple musical genres and instrumentations. The former paid music director from Wesley was too narrowly focused on classical hymnology, and the former unpaid choir director from Asbury was not

available for extra training or additional time. The board proposed that both be replaced by a younger music professional found outside the conference through a national search.

- A combination of early retirements and extra training would allow the church to reduce secretarial support staff to a full-time position supplemented by a team of volunteer receptionists. Since they anticipated moving into a completely different space (more on that later) the board of Good Shepherd decided to contract with an independent custodial service.

The former churches both had strong lay visitation teams, and they expanded the *Stephen Ministries* program from the Wesley Church to delegate most of the caregiving to laity. Stephen Ministries (www.stephenministries .org) is a nonprofit organization that trains and resources one-on-one lay caring in local congregations. The ministries provide personal support for people experiencing a difficult time in life, such as the death of a loved one, divorce, job loss, chronic or terminal illness, relocation, or separation due to military deployment. Stephen Ministries has a high reputation for confidentiality and accountability.

Merger 2: Faith Community Church (formerly Faith Temple and Pine Street)

Faith Community Church (formerly Faith Temple and Pine Street) required a staffing strategy that supported its strong emphasis on faith formation and interfaced well with the social service agencies downtown. The new board proposed the following staff configuration:

- The senior pastor of the former Faith Temple was near retirement and had announced his intention to move to a smaller church in another state where he could be closer to grandchildren; the minister at Pine Street was an interim, anyway. Council proposed calling a new pastor who was an excellent expository preacher and an adjunct faculty member at the nearby college. He also had experience developing nonprofit organizations and understood policy governance.
- The part-time Christian education director from Faith Temple would be made full-time in the new church. Her salary would be supplemented by the charter school through grants to that separately incorporated nonprofit. This would allow the new Faith Community Church to afford a half-time youth minister, with the hope of expanding the position to full-time in five years.

- The underpaid music director from the former Pine Street church was so talented, and had such a reputation in the arts community downtown, that the council encouraged him to stay with the new church and proposed a higher salary to ensure his tenure. He would also be integrated into the curriculum of the charter school as a music teacher.
- Secretarial and custodial staff were sorted out easily. The big challenge, however, was that the church needed to boost hospitality in order to get traction for growth in the urban core. Council proposed stretching its budget to hire a Christian with experience as a restaurateur on a part-time basis, who really understood how to welcome and honor guests. She brought her experience training hospitality teams to the new church.

Caregiving demands would continue to be high in the urban core, but the church couldn't afford paid chaplaincy. Fortunately, there were two retired, active ministers in the neighborhood who volunteered to oversee wedding and funeral ministries.

In order to meet the challenge to develop a staffing strategy, Faith Community Church was forced to build a more experienced and better trained human resources team than either church had formerly known. None of the people from the former personnel committees were asked to continue. Instead, new team members were recruited with a much higher accountability to excellence. Some emerged from within the membership; some were borrowed from the board of the charter school; and the chairperson, who was Roman Catholic, was recruited from the nearby city hospital administration.

The staffing strategies were approved by the two new churches and implemented with the assistance of relevant judicatories.

Building a core team in a church merger is the key to long-term success. The transition to forming a core team is one of the most important steps on the merger journey, because the DNA of core values, vision, and mission must be embedded in the core team. The DNA embedded in a core team will make or break the church for the long haul.

The composition of a core team in a church merger depends on the context of each community and the situation of each church. If the community context is transitioning quickly, then past leadership teams may not reflect the ethnicities and lifestyles that are emerging in the mission field. This was the case in both of our case studies. It is important that the core team reflect the diversity of the community, so that leaders are not only skilled, but also empathic, with the emerging lifestyle segments. Credibility is crucial.

If the community context is very stable, with slow to little change anticipated, the leaders from past churches are more easily incorporated into the new core team. This is often the case in small-city urban centers and small towns that are beyond the urbanization of major regions of the country. Credibility is already established, but leaders may have to be trained with new skills.

In any event, note that community needs are considered first. Strategic planning always begins with mission field needs and expectations, rather than membership needs and privileges.

The situation of each church in a merger is different. This is revealed in the assessments of "cost of discipleship" and "prioritization of measurable outcomes" that were part of the earlier visioning process. They identify strengths and weaknesses in leadership and programs that will need to be appreciated or addressed in a new leadership team. If the situation of a church is very weak (e.g., with staff and volunteer burnout, controversy and conflict, or low credibility), then it is better to build a new core team based on the leadership of the stronger churches in the merger or with new leaders altogether. If the situation of a church is relatively strong (e.g., with staff and volunteer energy, peaceful and healthy relationships, and high credibility), then it is possible to build a new core team with a retraining or redeployment plan for the existing leaders.

Note that choices for leadership are more about "mission" than "mercy." Do not include past leaders on the new core team simply because you feel sorry for them, are afraid to hurt their feelings, or doubt that they have any other career or work options. You can provide counseling and career coaching, but decisions must be made for the greater good of God's mission to the community rather than misplaced compassion for an individual. When leaders are retained in a new mission team merely out of pity, not only is the future mission jeopardized, but the individuals eventually suffer more through conflict and failure.

In Page's experience in New Orleans, the merger of Canal Street Presbyterian Church and Mosaic Church, the leadership teams from both churches were carefully blended together. The people from Mosaic Church were needed to infuse a new church-planting attitude into the merged church. At the same time, the institutional knowledge shared by the members of the established Canal Street Church was needed to understand the liabilities and opportunities of the property, financial investments, and stewardship practice in financial management. Both parties in the core team agreed to the new vision, mission, and values statements and worked tirelessly to pursue them.

Regardless of the makeup of the core team, every leader needs to embrace, model, and communicate the core values, beliefs, vision, and mission of the new church.

Pastoral Leadership for the New Church

One of the most challenging decisions in forming the core team is about pastoral leadership. In our case studies, the decision was fairly simple. The senior pastor of the former Faith Temple was retiring, and the pastor at the former Pine Street Presbyterian church was an intentional interim, so the way was clear to call a new senior minister following traditional Presbyterian methods.

The senior pastor of the former Wesley Methodist Church was retiring, and the pastor of the former Asbury Methodist Church was a young African American minister who had come to leadership following several controversial years. Here, too, the pastor was for all intents and purposes an interim. The new church needed a more veteran CEO kind of leader, and while the bishop and district superintendent considered training for the young Asbury minister, they decided to appoint a more experienced African American pastor.

There are many other variations in the choice of the new pastor. The choice is crucial, because the senior pastor will collaborate with the board and have enormous influence on the development of the core team. Several considerations should be taken into account when choosing a senior pastor.

One consideration for senior pastor is *giftedness*. Pastors have various gifts that often flow together, among them, shepherding, administration, teaching, preaching, and mercy. The gifts can be considered spiritual or natural. For example, a pastor may have the spiritual gift of mercy but also be more of a people-person. Or a pastor may have the gift of leadership but also be more introverted.

Another consideration is *experience*. Some pastors come with more or less experience due to age. But another side of this factor to consider is if a person has experience leading a merged congregation, or if previous experience will help the person to lead an upcoming merger. As in the example of the Methodist churches above, the right type of experience is necessary to lead a merged congregation forward.

A third consideration is the *standing* of the pastor with the members. The merged church will go through many challenges ahead, and the pastor of the merged church needs to have good standing with the members, adherents, and active participants of the church. The pastor will need to confront challenges and encourage the members of the core team. The pastor's background will play into this consideration a great deal. One of the pastors from the merging churches might be able to lead the core team better due to a deeper empathy and broader respect with the church people.

A fourth consideration is the *credibility* of the pastor with the public. The merged church must have a positive reputation for empathy with the surrounding lifestyle segments and be able to work well with other community organizations. The pastor's background will play into this consideration as well. One of the pastors from the merging churches might be able to coach the core team to be relevant and sensitive to the diversity of the mission field.

Given the considerations above, merging churches need to have a holistic view concerning the future pastor of the newly merged church. A pastor that is younger but with a little experience might carry the merged church further in its mission than an older, soon-to-retire pastor. However, if the young pastor is too young, a more seasoned pastor might be better, even if the seasoned pastor does not have merged church experience.

To cite one example of merger known through Page's personal experience, the former pastor from one of the merging churches became the lead pastor of the merged church. However, the pastor was more gifted in pastoral care and counseling than in leading a larger and more diverse organization. After a few years, the church went into decline, even though the merged church had several hundred people. The pastor had experience and good standing with the people, but the gift set was wrong for the context.

In another example from Tom's experience, the former pastor of one of the merging churches became the lead pastor of the merged church because he had strong administrative skills and a successful record sustaining traditional churches. However, the present community was much more multicultural, with a higher proportion of young singles and nontraditional families, than in the past. The former pastor did not have the credibility necessary to lead the church into the future, and the merged church only continued to decline.

Many merging churches will try to have the pastors of the churches serve as co-pastors. Let us give a word of warning in this type of scenario: We have seen several cases in which conflicts of control and influence happened because there were no clear lines of leadership. While co-leadership or shared leadership can sound good during the dreaming stages of a church merger, it often fails on the pragmatic end once the merger occurs.

Allow us to offer some alternatives, in which one pastor or staff member will always emerge as a leader, however small or great the church may be. One option is to have pastoral titles that reflect the shared leadership. For example, one pastor might be "Pastor of Administration" while another one may be "Pastor of Teaching." Such titles avoid the ominous "Senior Pastor."

Another alternative is based not on titles but on shared votes on and accountability to a leadership entity. While a pastor may have the title of "Senior Pastor," he or she has one vote just like any other leader. Shared authority is there along with shared vision. But one pastor is allowed to take the lead in setting the pace of and maintaining the merged church.

In one successful church merger in Kentucky, two pastors (one black and one white) merged two churches to create a multiracial congregation. Both pastors had been successful in their respective churches, but they took an honest assessment of their gifts, abilities, and contexts. They determined that the black pastor had the gifts to become the lead pastor. He was visionary, could preach and teach well, and had a good standing with the people. The white pastor could also teach well, but had gifts more in the area of administration and counseling. They also felt strongly that since the congregation would have a slight majority of white members, a black pastor would help maintain the diversity.

While there is no magic formula for pastoral leadership in a merged church, the situation does need to be addressed carefully. A merger is a situation that needs clear lines of communication, responsibility, and accountability. Pastors need to have a clear vision and strong coaching abilities. Selection of pastors can make or break the merger.

The Focus of the Core Team: Discipling

The process for forming a core team begins long before people are asked to serve. The merging churches must agree upon a vision, mission, and values that will shape the new church. We want to focus on how to create a core team around the need to sustain critical momentum—making disciples.

Churches in general, but North American churches in particular, have become too focused on programs, numbers, budgets, and buildings. Preoccupation with material things does not necessarily produce disciples. Vital congregations actually focus *less* on program development and *more* on personal growth. The real goal is not maintaining an institution, but making disciples in fulfillment of the Great Commission, in order to bless the world in fulfillment of the Great Commandment. A church's vision and mission statement can vary according to the given context. But every vision statement should reflect how the church intends to make disciples, given their context and location.

Why should making disciples be the ultimate goal? First, of course, it is biblical. The example given to us in the Gospels is of Jesus making disciples of the first apostles. The example given to us by Paul in his letters is of teaching the precepts of the Gospel to other people by making disciples. The older are to teach the younger: the older men to younger men, and older women to younger women. Paul commanded Timothy to pass on the doctrine to faithful preachers whom he led. These are just a few examples of how the idea of discipleship runs throughout the New Testament.

Just as critical mass depends on people rather than property, so also critical momentum depends on volunteer empowerment rather than membership recruitment. The impact of the church on the community relies on *servants* rather than *programs*.

When churches focus on buildings and programs, they focus on tools rather than servants. Buildings and programs are merely tools that are useful to a certain context when doing ministry. Buildings are only meant to house worship and offer a location for programs and ministries. Programs and ministries are constantly adapted to a specific context and a particular time and place. Both buildings and programs, while important, are only meant to be the vehicles by which discipleship can be administered.

When churches emphasize buildings and programs to grow their ministries, people are attracted to churches for the wrong reasons. Too often individuals and families will attend a church because it has the right facilities, such as play areas for the kids, or the right programs, such as youth activities. While such facilities are important to individuals or families *at the time*, they don't necessarily mature Christians, grow disciples, and deploy servants *over time*. People use the facilities and enjoy the programs as long as they are relevant to a particular stage in their lives, but often drop out of the church (and out of God's mission) when their temporary needs have been met.

Churches need to grow people, not programs. Churches grow and mature believers by discipleship, not just by membership. Paul writes in such passages as 1 Corinthians 12 and Ephesians 4 that the focus of the church should be on growing people to be more like Christ and live their lives using the spiritual gifts that have been given to them. The growth of a church depends on maturing believers, equipping them to use their spiritual gifts, and then setting them free with their passion for the ministry. Obsession over properties, facilities, and technologies—or over specific programs and pet projects—encourages "sacred cows" and "controlling personalities," both of which lead a church back into decline and irrelevance. Discipling accelerates church growth and maximizes impact for community change.

Churches in North America would do well to invoke a multicultural test when it comes to ministry. In many parts of the world, a local church might meet in a home, a tent, or even under a tree. When our ministry becomes too attached to a building or a certain program, we should examine the discipleship process to see if it is truly focusing on building up believers, instead of relying upon other things. If a discipleship program cannot be done in a variety of cultural settings, it probably needs to be reevaluated as to its biblical faithfulness.

The newly merged church should build a new core team that connects the overall vision and mission with a strategy to change lives, mature faith, call ministers, equip volunteers, and send servants. That's disciple-making. Immediate growth may be slower in the short term, but disciples will be grown and matured in the long term. Disciples connect with seekers; mature members connect with newcomers; servants are released into the community who model, mentor, and work in the image of Christ.

Selecting the Core Team

The right composition and structure of the core team is essential. The core team is the group of individuals, including staff, pastors, and laypersons, who will discern mission opportunities, design and manage relevant ministries, and evaluate the various programs, within the boundaries of policy and executive limitations defined by the board, in order to achieve the measurable outcomes for ministries expected by the board. They will also be role models and mentors for volunteers as they lead ministry teams. Think of the core team as the first generation of what it is hoped all members of the church will become. The second and third generations of people joining the merged church for ministry will flow from the model of the core group.

The core team may be formed in several ways. However, the core team must be carefully selected so that the mission attitude for the community and the integrity of the church are embedded in the team, relevant skills interface within the team, and everyone works harmoniously as a team. While the church board or council and pastors of the legacy churches have a part in choosing the core team, it should not be chosen based upon church politics or popularity.

There are several ways to select the leaders of the core team. The methods often depend on the style of governance chosen by the merged church, and these are illustrated in our case studies.

Individual Program Functions

Faith Community Church chose a council model of governance, in which key people were selected to serve on the council due to their leadership of key committees. In order to do this effectively, the following question must be answered: "What key ministries do we need to grow and multiply disciples in the context of our vision and mission?" Leaders are then selected based upon key committees that are needed in order to design and manage the program and resources of the church.

This approach develops a core team primarily based on program function. The leader of the team (or chairperson of the committee) sits on the church council in order to ensure smooth cooperation, proportionate distribution of resources, and calendar-planning with the other representative team leaders on the council. A core team structure might look like this:

- Hospitality and Communications
- Worship
- Christian Education
- Midweek Groups
- Caregiving
- Outreach
- Facilities and Technologies
- Financial Management

Depending on the community context and strategic plan of the church, there might also be leaders for capital campaigns, Sunday schools, nonprofits associated with the church, and so forth. True to policy governance principles, each team leader has responsibility and authority to design and manage his or her respective function. However, evaluation of programs is often referred back to the council as a whole.

Total Program Management

Church of the Good Shepherd chose a nonprofit board model of governance, in which board members were chosen solely for their abilities to focus vision, align mission, protect and model values and beliefs, and network in the community. Authority and responsibility for program management is entrusted to the core team. In this case, the core team is chosen for its ability to lead a particular step in the disciple-making process, and not just manage a set of functions. Team leaders have a larger role. Team leaders will be able to handpick their own teams, mentor each of their team members, oversee the work relevant to their particular step in discipling, and ensure that people involved in that step can move on to the next steps of spiritual growth and volunteer empowerment. A core team structure might look like this:

- Encounter Christ—Evangelism, hospitality, communication, and any activity that helps people connect with the church and feel the immanence of God
- Experience God—Worship, prayer, spiritual direction, and any activity that helps seekers experience the healing, guiding, vindicating, liberating, teaching, transforming, promising power of God
- Grow in Faith—Christian education, Sunday school, Bible study, structured learning, and any activity that helps to mature Christians
- Discern Call—Small groups, mentoring relationships, spiritual discernment, and any activity that helps Christians discern their place in God's mission
- Equip Disciples—Financial management, property and technology upgrades, leadership training, and any activity that applies the physical resources of the church to prepare ministers for mission
- Send Servants—Any form of outreach, local, regional, national, or global that involves personal participation in addition to charitable giving.

Note that in this structure, each leader of the core team is deployed systemically rather than just functionally. All have authority and responsibility to discern, design, implement, and evaluate mission without returning to the board, and are free to terminate old ideas and innovate new ideas that move people along in discipleship.

In either choice, the core team may be selected in several ways. A senior pastor may handpick the members, all the leaders from the original churches might become a single large core group, or leadership may be open to any volunteer. Even in such scenarios, care should be taken to embed the values, beliefs, vision, and mission in every team member; and focus the entire core team on the discipling process.

Team members are always acquired, trained, evaluated, and, if necessary, fired or dismissed with reference to the shared values, beliefs, vision, and mission of the church. Newly merged churches are apt to make leadership decisions too quickly, and their haste creates problems down the road. Inappropriate behaviors, contradictions about beliefs, inability to align lifestyle and work to vision, and actions that favor personal agendas over mission emerge, and they both fracture the teamwork of the leadership core and undermine their credibility in church and community. Look at it this way: You can't fire or dismiss a leader who has not been properly evaluated, you can't evaluate what you have not adequately trained, and you can't train on what you have not explained clearly in the original job description. A great deal of stress can be avoided if churches choose the core team with due diligence in the first place.

Whatever the method used for choosing the core team, three principles should be kept in mind. First, the core team should embody the DNA of the merged church. Second, the structure of the core team should flow so as to facilitate ministries. Third, the selection process should not be based upon politics or favorites, but rather mission and vision for the context of the merged church.

Who should be on the core team of a newly merged church? Three categories of people may serve, depending on needs, vision, and local context. If a merged church has a honed vision and mission statement, the structure and ministries should naturally flow from them. The following questions may help: What type of pastoral leadership is needed to lead the church? What ministries are of highest importance to accelerate church growth and/or profoundly impact the community? Who can lead the important ministries? What significant laypeople are equipped to be part of a newly merged church and provide nonpaid or volunteer leadership?

First, staff and pastors need to serve on the core team. Borrowing from a common practice in church planting, it is recommended that core team members include a lead pastor and worship designer/music director. Depending on context, the third staff position is either a children's pastor, Christian education director, or small-group developer. These combinations of paid staff are key for initial success in building the merged church. The lead pastor is the person who sets the vision and mission, sets the pace in mission to the community, and monitors the spiritual growth of church members.

Many mergers achieve critical mass but can only afford to pay one full-time pastor. The worship, children/youth director, and/or small-group positions may be filled with either paid or volunteer people. Worship is the key ministry that motivates spiritual growth and embeds DNA for the unity of the church and therefore is a central component in the life of the church. Children and youth ministries are important for both church plants and mergers, especially for those seeking to bless lifestyle segments with children living at home. The discipling system for these churches tends to develop generationally. Small-group ministries are important for churches that prioritize singles, empty nesters, and "unchurched" publics.

Laity who are not paid but are in a volunteer capacity for leading ministries may also serve on the core team. The expectations for unpaid leadership on a core team are much the same as for paid leadership. They, too, are acquired, trained, evaluated, and dismissed with reference to the congregational DNA; they will also be expected to align to vision, model integrity, improve skills, and collaborate with the team in the same way as paid staff.

Unpaid leaders should be church members who are experienced leaders and highly committed to the merged church. They should be as committed as paid staff, but may receive more coaching than paid staff. Since they are volunteers, unpaid staff may be evaluated more frequently to enhance their continuing education, and may be rotated more frequently to avoid burnout. For example, it might be a good idea to ask a person to commit to leading a ministry for a certain amount of time, such as eighteen months, and then ask another leader to rotate into the position.

Other volunteers may join the core team who are not necessarily ministry-team leaders. These core team members may be highly committed to the vision but fulfill a very specific, although equally important, task. For example, volunteers may join a core team because of their skills in administration, financial management and fundraising, technology, and so on. These "helpers" can make a huge difference to the new church.

A careful balance of ordered minister leaders (e.g., clergy), program ministry professionals, and volunteer leaders should form every core team. The balance depends on context. The size depends on missional strategy. However the core team is designed and whatever its size, these leaders function as role models and senior managers. They are the leading edge of ministry and mission. The core team needs people who are committed, energetic, and willing to sacrifice in order to carry out the vision and mission for Jesus Christ.

Group Growth and Cohesion

The core team will follow a process to build trust and habits of collaboration just like any other group in the merged church. Individual leaders bring history and habits from their former church context; a merged church core group may present unique challenges, because the groups from the former churches already have established cultures. While individuals may bring their own unique cultures, two churches bringing together very strong, independent cultures must find common ground in the unified vision and mission of the merged church.

A common way of thinking about core team formation is found in the phases of *forming, storming, norming,* and *performing.* The senior pastor usually guides the newly formed core team through these stages. This energizes the core team for future leadership, and helps the core team correct previous weaknesses in the former churches.

In the *forming* stage, the core team comes together around a unified vision and mission for the newly merged church. During this phase, the pastor needs to exercise a great deal of guidance. Team members may need to confront and overcome past expectations from their former churches, and embrace the new priorities for the new church. Roles may be unclear in this phase of team development, and the senior pastor clarifies the new roles.

In the *storming* stage, the vision and mission of the church will become clearer, but the relationships between team members may be fuzzy. Sometimes teams form around naturally existing relationships. In a merged church, however, the core team must come together around shared vision and commitment to discipling process. The pastor needs to keep pointing people to the vision of the merged church, but also provide opportunities for the group members to build relationships. As the relationships continue to form, trust will be built.

In the *norming* stage, relationships have been built and the team as a whole has a sacrificial commitment to the vision. At this point the senior pastor concentrates on leadership empowerment. Functions or systemic stages of discipling are defined for each team member. Leaders realize that they have both responsibility *and authority* to discern, design, and implement mission, and understand the boundaries for action that are set by governance. This stage is about developing consistent attitudes and habits:

- Personal growth is more important than institutional survival.
- Volunteer development is more important than program efficiency.

- Teamwork is more important than personality.
- Credibility is more important than popularity.

The flow of seekers who become disciples, connecting with the church, experiencing God's love, growing in faith, discerning their place in God's mission, getting equipped to do whatever they are called to do well, and moving out as servants to bless the world in Christ's name—all that activity is what is normative for the church.

The last stage is *performing*. At this point, the team has formed strong relationships that are aligned sacrificially to a shared vision, and team members understand the extent and limits of their authority. Now they focus on strategy and the execution of the vision. Each team member shares with the team a basic plan for future work. Usually this includes measurable outcomes, a keen awareness of opportunities and obstacles, an updated understanding of demographic trends and lifestyle expectations, particular needs for extra training or education, and some anticipation of resource needs regarding technology, facility, and budget.

Core team formation is a huge opportunity for a newly merged church. The team can overcome the weaknesses of the past churches. It can out line a process for engaging their community in ministry. In the merger between Canal Street Presbyterian Church and Mosaic Church, Page realized that both groups brought values that were helpful to the newly merged church. Canal Street had values that were internally focused on taking care of people. Mosaic had values that were focused on reaching the community. Page created a core team that brought both sets of values together and created a new culture for the merged church that was both internally and externally focused. In other words, the culture was about reaching people and caring for people at the same time.

Core Team Virtues

There are common virtues that every member of a core team must support. These can be summarized and advertised to sustain and recruit core team members.

Unity

The core team reveals the unity of the church as a whole. This does not mean that the team members never disagree, but it does mean that at the end of the day, they support the senior pastor, follow the policies of the board, back shared decisions, rally around the vision, and trust one another. Temptations for disunity are always present, but the core team works for unity. It does not tolerate divisive conversations, gossip, or power struggles. It also works for reconciliation of relationships as quickly as possible when divisiveness does occur.

Giftedness

Core team members bring various gifts to the new ministries of the merged church. While all core team members should strive for unity, they should also acknowledge differences in gifts and abilities. Such differences should be celebrated, as various sets of gifts balance out other sets of gifts. The individual gifts of core team members should match the diverse expectations of the mission context. In addition, the gifts of each individual core team member should balance the gifts of the others. For example, if the pastor is a strong visionary, then he or she needs to be surrounded by administrative and detail-oriented people. Or if the worship designer is all about performance, then other team members need to be all about compassion.

Coachability

Core team members must all be coachable or teachable, that is, they should embrace a culture of continuous learning. The value of coachability or teachability starts with regard to the senior pastor and trickles down to every other core team member. Only through constant learning can the core team engage in new challenges. Team members coach and are coached by, learn from and teach, one another to align mission, model integrity, improve skills, and work more effectively as a team.

Selflessness

The core team values selflessness and humility. A value and attitude of selflessness means that the team members recognize that they should place themselves last and others first with regard to personal relationships. They are seeking the betterment of others first and foremost before themselves. It also means that team members place the vision and unity of the merged church before their own vision and desires. Many problems in core group formation can be headed off by establishing an attitude of selflessness from the beginning.

Think of the formation of a core team as laying the foundation for the newly merged church. Establishing the right culture of vision and values, attitude and integrity, overlapping skills and teamwork, is crucial. The core team unites the members of the former churches and models the identity of the new church for the next wave of people who join the church. While not all problems can be avoided by instilling the right virtues, the core team can define the culture of an entire church as its members travel together into the future.

Strategic Planning   18
Traction and Steering

The core teams in each new church needed to develop a strategic plan for future ministries. This was accomplished with the active collaboration of the former vision team members. After all, it was the vision teams from each merger conversation that defined the basic measurable outcomes that would make the mergers successful.

The strategic plan was intentionally built on the foundation of trust, clarity of vision, and contextual analysis that prepared the churches for merger. The plan was also created with the policy governance model in mind. This meant that the strategic plan did not have to identify every single tactic to be used by the new churches. Tactics could be delegated to teams. It did mean that key strategies needed to be identified that would give the new churches traction and direction for the immediate future.

The core teams for each merged church evaluated the programs from their respective former churches. They wanted to merge and accelerate programs that were working well, improve on programs that were important but less effective, initiate new ideas to achieve the outcomes defined by the vision team, and terminate tactics that were no longer relevant or effective.

In order to do this, they used a simple model for traction and steering, which were the "mechanics" that would move the vehicle of the church forward. Certain programs would give the church "traction." These would engage the targeted lifestyle segments, inject the power of the Holy Spirit, grip the road, and move the organization to positively impact the world. Other programs would give the church "steering." These would mature Christians and concentrate outreach, and equip servants for faith witness and social service. The idea, simply put, was: better traction, greater impact; clearer direction, increased growth.

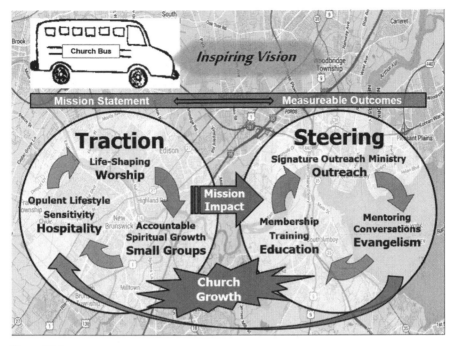

Figure 18.1.

Traction

The core teams in each new church explored how effectively each former church was getting "traction" in the community. They looked specifically at programming for hospitality, worship, and small groups (or other forms of significant spiritual conversation that integrated lifestyle and faith). Then they explored the quality of caregiving throughout the church.

Merger 1: Church of the Good Shepherd (formerly Wesley and Asbury)

The core team for Church of the Good Shepherd discovered that each former church had struggled to get traction for different reasons. Wesley had struggled with radical hospitality, but midweek fellowship groups and study groups were quite strong. Asbury had strong hospitality, but there were few midweek small groups. The result was that visitors came to the former Wesley church via midweek group relationships, but then felt ignored by the congregation as a whole; and visitors came to the former Asbury church because of their outreach but failed to go deeper into faith formation.

There were quite different styles of worship in the previous churches, but the real issue was not so much about style as purpose. Worship at Wesley had been informative but tended to satisfy curiosity rather than generate urgency. Worship at Asbury had been motivational, but tended to draw people into advocacy without disciplined spiritual growth. The core team's "Aha!" moment came when it realized that the Sunday morning habits of each church only led to friendly chatting about family, weather, and sports during post-worship refreshments. There were few truly significant conversations about God, life, mission, and so on. The new strategic plan needed to reshape congregational habits.

The new church required several layers of trained greeters before and after worship; a worship service that was more inspirational, with strong musical rhythms and down-to-earth coaching about faith and daily life; and multiple choices for high quality refreshments that would encourage people to linger longer, so that the church could make connections for midweek small groups. Follow-up on visitors would need to combine face-to-face conversations and social media.

Midweek small groups instead of classic Sunday school had to become the cornerstone of Christian education and faith formation. Neither church was very experienced in this method. So the merged church would need to adopt a model of designated and well-trained small-group leaders. It would need to develop a variety of study and affinity groups, with the common goal of serious spiritual growth.

Finally, the core team recognized that the lifestyle segments comprising the original two churches were actually diminishing in the mission field. In order to be relevant to the emerging segment of multicultural singles, it would need to develop a second worship service that was completely different in message and format than the more traditional service. Message, music, place, time, and leadership would be different in each worship option. One option needed to be very inspirational and presentational; the other option would need to focus on coaching tips for daily living and be more dialogical.

Merger 2: Faith Community Church (formerly Faith Temple and Pine Street)

Meanwhile, the core team of Faith Community Church discovered that the systemic strengths and weaknesses of the previous two churches were actually quite similar. They could now gather more resources to overcome weaknesses and build on strengths.

The original two churches were really not as friendly as they thought they were. The people all tended to gather in cliques, making it difficult for newcomers to fit in. They needed to learn how to be sensitive to generational differences; be intentionally respectful to men, women, and alternate lifestyles; and learn to at least welcome and give basic directions in Spanish. These realities explained why the core team included a paid leader with a background in hospitality planning from the restaurant business.

The original two churches also assumed their worship was more inspirational and engaging than it really was. In fact, at both churches, worship was a blend of education and caregiving—and the didactic order of service and long announcements were, frankly, boring. They needed to combine education with more inspiration in order to be more relevant to the lifestyle segments of the mission field. This meant more music in multiple genres and instrumentations, more still and moving images, and updated technologies to provide those enhancements.

Issues involving brokenness were huge in the urban mission field, and the core team decided that the church would need to add an additional healing service during the week. This worship option would not be a "preaching" service so much as a "praying" service aimed toward people who were physically, mentally, emotionally, and relationally broken, and looking for wholeness and hope.

Ironically, the greatest weakness in both churches was the inability of the laity to be confident and courageous in engaging newcomers in conversations about faith and other serious life issues. Sunday morning refreshment time was notable for the lack of significant conversations about matters of substance and, instead, chatter about sports and the weather. An additional team of "minglers" would need to be trained and deployed to introduce visitors and members, and to kick-start conversations that mattered.

Steering

The second strategic synergy was about how each new church could "steer" toward the outcomes of a clear mission. Each core team looked specifically at Christian education, outreach ministries, and evangelism. Then they explored how they could improve leadership accountability among staff and volunteer leaders.

Merger 1: Church of the Good Shepherd (formerly Wesley and Asbury)

The core team focused on membership training, signature outreach ministry, and mentoring for emerging leaders. Then several more priorities were identified.

Membership training had been Bible-based in both former churches, but tended to focus on denominational polity, doctrine, and public policy. The core team recognized that the priority in the postmodern world needed to be on spirituality, lifestyle, and conversation with culture, rather than theologies, ideologies, and confrontation with culture. And training would probably need to be offered in smaller, incremental programs, with options for time, place, and media.

Asbury had always wanted to develop a youth ministry as a signature outreach, but did not have the financial resources or managerial talent to create a comprehensive ministry that could offer options to the full diversity of young adults in the mission field. The fact that the merger now provided the resources to develop this major mission was why the staffing plan boosted the youth minister to full-time status and retrained him in small-group ministries.

Intentional mentoring for emerging lay leaders would need to be added by policy to the expectations of board membership and team leadership. Each board member would be expected to mentor at least three emerging leaders in spiritual life at any given time; and every team leader would be required to have an apprentice. Evangelism and spiritual disciplines needed to be emphasized, because former members of Wesley Church were timid about sharing faith; and former members of Asbury church were vague about deepening faith.

The committee began to compile a list of education and training goals that would be needed to help members of each church understand and implement these shifts in priorities.

Merger 2: Faith Community Church
(formerly Faith Temple and Pine Street)

Once again, the core team identified common weaknesses and strengths in the former churches and developed a strategy for future mission.

Both churches had strong Christian education programs for all ages that could be merged with relative ease. However, adult Sunday schools had uniformly plateaued and stagnated. Some of these would need to be terminated so that new ones could flourish. There were also serious concerns about the nursery and preschool ministries. Training was poor, equipment was old and broken, and security was lax. An all-new leadership team needed to be developed, and any future space would need a significant budget to make it secure and "state of the art."

Both churches had signature outreach ministries for which they were known in the community. Faith Temple housed the charter school, and, while it needed a cash infusion to upgrade technologies and materials, it was strongly supported by young families and single parents. Pine Street had a reputation for music and the arts that would need to be sustained by professional staff. These outreach ministries could work very well together. In fact, the merged church could add free music lessons and develop a community youth orchestra and choir, or expand into specialized tutoring for high school students.

Both churches had groups of matriarchs and patriarchs who were mature in their faith and informally mentored emerging generations. The challenge was to make this more intentional and then sustain the practice through future generations as the elders passed on. The pastor would need to be freed from many visitation and pastoral care responsibilities, and to minimize the number of administrative meetings, in order to invest energy in teaching and mentoring groups of adult members. The core team developed a list of education and training goals. Team members recognized that they would need to look outside both churches—and perhaps beyond their denominations—to learn "best practices" from growing churches in urban contexts across the country.

Perhaps the greatest challenge for both core teams concerned the "hubs" of the two wheels. Traction rotates around excellent caregiving, which had become too pastor-dependent in all four previous churches. Both Good Shepherd and Faith Community would need to develop a more sophisticated network of lay visitors and recommended counselors.

Steering rotates around leadership accountability. There was widespread misunderstanding and fear of strong accountability. Both Good Shepherd and Faith Community needed to create credible nominations processes, friendly and collaborative practices of oversight, and ongoing coaching for paid and unpaid leaders.

Strategic planning is all about *acceleration* and *impact*. Traction provides the acceleration. Steering provides the impact. The balance between the two resembles the art of driving a motor vehicle. Sometimes the driver needs to adjust speed in order to maintain steering. Sometimes the driver needs to adjust direction in order to get traction. The same is true for a church. Sometimes a church must accept slower growth in order to concentrate on changing the community. Sometimes a church must step back from a particular mission in order to grow the church.

Both *acceleration* and *impact* are important. The synergy between them is what sustains the organization for the long term. In the short term, one may become more important than the other, but in the long term, both are necessary. There is really no point to church growth if there is no positive change in the community. Eventually people will wonder why they should spend so much time, energy, and money perpetuating an organization that doesn't accomplish anything beyond itself. On the other hand, an organization cannot continue to bless the community without fresh resources of volunteers, consistently effective programs, constantly updated technologies, and year-round stewardship. Eventually the church will die and all that momentum for community change may die with it.

It is the primary responsibility of a core team to manage *acceleration* and *impact*. In a church merger, the vision team point outs the destination for the drive, but it is the core team that actually takes the church from point A to point B. The vision team delegates the details of strategic planning to a trusted, gifted few, who have three purposes:

- They reinforce effective programs; improve necessary but ineffective programs; initiate creative new ideas; and terminate ineffective tactics.
- They coach effective leaders and teams; train well-meaning but ineffective leaders and teams; recruit, train, and deploy new leaders and teams; and close and redistribute leaders and teams that are no longer needed.
- They preserve effective financial resources and technologies; raise funds and upgrade resources to help leaders and programs become more effective; invest money and resources to develop new ideas; and redistribute resources from teams and programs that are no longer needed.

The point of all that day-to-day, week-to-week, and even year-to-year management is to achieve the outcomes that fulfill the vision of the church.

The principle of *acceleration* requires a church to prioritize anything that promotes spiritual disciplines, deepens personal relationships, grows membership, expands the pool of volunteers, raises more money, and upgrades property and technology. It may also be called the "principle of zoom": The strategic plan should make the church *zoom* so that it flies higher, goes faster, dives daringly, swoops creatively, and glides on the wings of the Holy Spirit.

The principle of *impact* requires a church to prioritize anything that positively transforms lives, shapes marriages and families, encourages all generations, includes all cultures, changes the neighborhood, combats evil, pursues justice, and generally makes life in this world better in the name of Christ. It may be called the "principle of punch": The strategic plan should make the church hit harder, bite deeper, sculpt a healthy community, knock out the devil, and make the world resemble the realm of God.

The overarching twin purposes of any church, of course, are to multiply disciples and bless the world. In the two mergers that are part of our evolving story, the core team of each church develops a plan that will help each church zoom and punch in its own unique way, in its own special context, with the resources God has provided.

The Church of the Good Shepherd (Wesley and Asbury merger), for example, is going to grow the church (and every member in it) through adult faith formation and mentoring strategies, so that the community will be blessed, and members of specific lifestyle segments who feel especially lost, trapped, or hopeless can experience Christ, who can guide people through the ambiguities of life, liberate captives, and promise life eternal.

Faith Community Church (Faith Temple and Pine Street merger), for example, is going to grow the church (and every member in it) through powerful educational and artistic strategies, so that the community will be blessed, and specific lifestyle segments that feel especially lonely, broken, or abandoned can experience Christ, who accepts them as they are, guides them toward truth, and promises abundant life.

It all sounds glorious. The question is, how, exactly, will each church accomplish this? What will the churches do—and what will they *not* do? Where will leaders lead—and where will they *not* go? How will teams be deployed—and how will they *not* be deployed? And what will it cost—and what will it *really* cost?

There are several mistakes in strategic planning that must be avoided, especially when planning a merger. The following common mistakes often sabotage effective planning so that the merger is literally set up to fail.

The first mistake is to begin with brainstorming. A bunch of people in a room throw ideas on the table. There is no discernible method to separate the simplistic from the overly complex, the shallow from the profound, or the personal agenda from the common purpose. Eventually the table becomes burdened and confused with so many ideas. People begin arguing with one another. Factions form. A vote is taken. The majority opinion is still not accepted—and indeed it may not even be wise. Finally, there is mediation and a compromise. Brainstorming always ends in compromise, and planning based on dozens of compromises never works.

The second mistake is to do a SWOT analysis (i.e., a brief summary of strengths, weaknesses, opportunities, and threats to the organization). This not only provides insufficient data to make wise decisions, but makes strategic planning either reactionary or opportunistic. Churches tend to lurch between defense and offense without any real balance or discernment. Planning tends to be driven by panic or crisis, on the one hand, or by indulgence or dreaming on the other. The worst thing about a SWOT analysis as a substitute for strategic planning is that it burns out volunteers and sends professional pastors to disability. Then a new pastor arrives, and it all starts over again.

The third mistake is to send everyone on the vision team or core management team on a wild search for "best practices." Instead of looking for real leverage points to gain momentum, the church hopes to discover a magic program that will make everything better. The assumption is that what works there must work here. But this both ignores contextual realities regarding very different demographics and lifestyles and bypasses prayerful discernment to see what the Holy Spirit has in store for a different church, in a different place, with different gifts. In many ways, this is just an attempt to revive the old Christendom denominational franchise model for standardization.

The best strategic planning is simple, logical, and repeatable over and over again. This is particularly true for a merger. Mergers are both complicated and stressful, and the more strategic planning can simply be built into the routine of a church, the more leaders can experiment, fail, evaluate, improve, and try again until they get it right.

Table 18.1 provides a strategic planning template that is indeed simple, logical, and repeatable. It does not display the strategic plans for the two mergers in our story, because that would require too much detail. Such a display would also be counterproductive, because it would tempt the reader to *imitate* rather than *create*, and impose a top-down plan rather than develop a plan bottom up. The template reflects the overall process of strategic planning in all six steps of discipleship—but it also reflects the very same planning process within any given ministry area.

The core team begins by listing current programs and creative ideas in any given ministry area. The template can be formally or informally used to look at any strategy. It is particularly helpful to evaluate any program that is important but weak, or to start any creative idea. In the template, proceed from the top down, and then go left to right. Detailed instructions include:

1. Always begin by identifying the lifestyle group(s) or segment(s) that the program is intended to reach.
2. Always start by answering the first set of questions:
   a. *Why would we do this?* (Show how it connects with the mission.)

Table 18.1. Strategic Planning Template

Program or Creative Idea Connects with Top Ten Major Leveraging Strategies		Major Cost Centers (High, Medium, Low)	Coming Stress Points
The Point	**The Tactics**		
Why:	**When?** Begin? Schedule? Evaluation?	**Tradition:** / **Attitude:**	**Personal Growth:**
Who:	Closure?	**Leadership:**	**Accountability:**
	How? Training? Technology? Expertise?	**Organization:**	
Anticipated Results:	**Where?** Environment? Accessibility? Relationships?	**Property:** / **Technology:**	**Mission Sensitivity:**
		Finance:	**Lifestyle Adjustments:**
Acceleration:		**Impact:**	**Total Score:**
Delegation: Leader(s) to take authority & responsibility for implementation			**Termination?**

  b. *Who will do it?* (Always identify a team of at least two people.)

  c. *What should result from it?* (Choose the outcomes to be measured to evaluate success.)

3. If any of these first three questions cannot be adequately answered, don't waste any more time thinking about the program. Set it aside for further prayer. Move on to the programs for which you *can* say why you will do it, who will lead it, and what should result.

4. The first tactical question is *when to do it,* because *time* is the most valuable resource we have. Any given ministry team can figure out the details. For the purposes of strategic planning, the core team needs to know when it will begin and end, the basic schedule, and the time to evaluate progress.

5. The second tactical question is *how to do it,* because *relevance and excellence* are the two most important keys to success. Again, any given ministry team can figure out the details. The core team just needs to know what training, technologies, or paid expertise will be required to get the job done well.

6. The third tactical question is *where to do it,* because *mobility* is the key reality of life today. Any given ministry team can figure out the details, but the core team needs to know if the environment is usable, safe, and readily accessible physically or online; and if quality relationships can be fostered in it.

The core team can then evaluate the program or new idea on a scale of one (poor) to ten (excellent) in each category of *acceleration* and *impact.* Anything that scores between eight and ten can probably be continued or initiated with only a few tweaks and adjustments that can be left up to any given ministry team. Anything that scores four through seven requires some more significant change to program design or leadership, which will be on the agenda of the core team. And anything that scores under three needs to be either completely overhauled or terminated.

Obviously, the strategic plan tries to balance programs and ideas for acceleration and impact. Some programs and ideas are better suited to one or the other, and occasionally some accomplish both well. Similarly, some programs are better at developing *traction,* while others are better at focusing *steering;* and occasionally some do both at the same time. This is the art of strategic planning.

In our story, for example, the core teams for Church of the Good Shepherd and Faith Community Church reviewed both ongoing programs and new ideas from each church. This helped them understand how effectively parallel programs could be merged; how urgently new ideas needed to be implemented; and how critical it would be to terminate some programs to recycle resources.

For example, strategic planning led both merger teams to consider existing and future fellowship groups. These groups could be significant for two steps in the disciple-making process: hospitality (as doorways for newcomers to "meet Jesus" and connect with the church) and education (as vehicles to "learn faith" and mature as Christians).

Church of the Good Shepherd realized that the former Wesley and Asbury churches had very different approaches to fellowship groups. Wesley sustained a closely knit couples club that mainly included veterans of the church and their protégés. Asbury relied on large youth groups and small Bible study (curriculum-based) groups. The Wesley couples club was not clear how its purpose as a group aligned with the mission of the church, and indeed, some active couples maintained membership in the church but rarely attended worship. The group scored a "one" for acceleration, since it really didn't help the church get traction for growth spiritually, numerically, or in any other way. They scored a "three" for impact, but only because the club periodically sponsored housing projects for homeless families. The youth group and curriculum-based Bible study strategy worked well in the '80s, but not anymore. The youth group had plateaued at thirty participants, and Bible study attendance tended to go down as groups failed to sustain themselves.

The core team planned the following adjustments. The mission of the church and the lifestyle segments they wanted to reach demanded a strategy of multiple youth groups that could more broadly appeal to the real diversity of youth. The Bible study strategy needed to adjust to a world in which adults (as well as youth) required more visual tools and opportunities for dialogue. The new strategy for Church of the Good Shepherd would be to train the youth pastor in small-group ministry and to use more video and internet resources rather than print, for Bible study.

The former Faith Temple and Pine Street had traditionally relied on gender-based large groups for women and men. When the core team used the template for evaluation and planning, it became clear that these ministries were relevant to the lifestyle segments they aimed to reach, but that they were not completely effective. The women's group at Faith Temple was better at hospitality than education. It was a doorway for many single parents to connect with the church and make friends, but it didn't do much to nurture faith. The women's group at Pine Street was better at education than hospitality. It always studied and discussed some curriculum, but remained small and in-grown. Faith Temple scored about a "six" for acceleration, but only a "two" for impact. Pine Street scored a "two" for acceleration and, since its choice of curricula was based on personal curiosity rather than spiritual discipline, it scored a "four" for impact. A closer study revealed that both churches were vague about the purpose of the groups, and that Faith Temple was struggling to recruit group leaders. The tactics for when, how, and where groups functioned varied.

The core team planned the following adjustments. A women's group would continue, but its purpose would be solely focused on hospitality and serve as an opportunity for visitors and members to build and deepen friendships. They would always meet monthly in the church hall—over a supper prepared and served *by caterers* paid by the church—and provide quality, paid childcare. The leaders would be appointed by the core team rather than elected from the body. Success would be measured twice a year, and the goal would be that 15% of the participants in any given dinner would be first- or second-time visitors.

Another example might be useful. The core leadership teams for each merger also examined outreach. Outreach programs for each church were significant for mission impact, but they also could become part of serious spiritual disciplines of prayer, work, and reflection that would help members discern calling.

Church of the Good Shepherd realized that the former Wesley church sponsored a potpourri of small outreach projects mainly through charitable contributions, associating mission with money. Only a few people were personally involved in these projects, and the "outreach committee" was small and tired. The small amounts of money divided among multiple charities was not enough for any of them to make a big difference. Worship and outreach tended to diverge. Few of the people connected with outreach attended worship regularly; and worship rarely recognized or celebrated the outreach projects and volunteers they claimed to support. So they scored about a "one" for acceleration and about a "five" for impact.

The former Asbury church focused its energy almost entirely on hands-on projects to improve the quality of life in their neighborhoods and the world. Worship was outreach; and outreach was worship. Members were highly involved in the outreach ministries, but mainly as "doers" rather than "leaders." And because the members tended to be poorer, their outreach ministries were dependent on unpredictable grants and sporadic donors, and so they were chronically underfunded. They would have scored high for acceleration and impact, but lack of leadership and an inability to link personal transformation with more profound faith formation limited results.

The new strategic plan for Good Shepherd embraced both youth ministries and recovery ministries as signature outreach ministries of the church. These would involve both hands-on volunteering and financial support. All the small financial contributions to multiple charities would be canceled, and all the outreach funds pooled to develop these two ministries. Former Asbury people would continue to volunteer as "doers," but former Wesley people could step forward as planners and fundraisers. The Church of the Good Shepherd would reposition its outreach visibility in the community.

Meanwhile, Faith Community Church (formerly Faith Temple and Pine Street) also investigated outreach. Faith Temple had once clearly supported major educational outreach with its charter school. Many members were involved in it as teachers or teaching assistants. Many families connected with the church through the school. However, the increasingly burdensome state and federal requirements for educational institutions was a huge burden for the board. The school was ever more dependent on state and federal funding because the expense was beyond the means of the church and tuitions could not be raised. It scored very high for acceleration and impact, but it could do even better with skilled administration and a more effective fundraising strategy.

Pine Street had given small amounts of money to various outreach projects. Its biggest financial investment was in its music program. The salaried staff person developed an excellent vocal and instrumental program that not only blessed the church with great music, but also blessed schools, hospitals, and the general public with inspiration and hope. However, only a limited number of relatively skilled vocalists and musicians could really contribute to the program. Despite the quality of the program, members worried that the results in church growth and mission impact did not justify the rapidly increasing expense.

The newly merged Faith Community Church developed a strategic plan for the future that could make these two outreach ministries mutually supportive. It planned to introduce music and the arts into the charter school as a special and unique program. It could maximize impact by collecting, refurbishing, and donating unused musical instruments to kids, and create children's choirs and youth orchestrations through the school. This would open up more opportunities for professional musicians and generate more funding opportunities. The church also realized that their council governance model would be less effective managing outreach, and decided to merge the school and the music ministry into a separately incorporated nonprofit. The majority of the nonprofit board would be made up of church members; salaries for both school administrator and music developer would be funded through the nonprofit (to which the church could make contributions). The nonprofit school would essentially rent space from the church; and the church would essentially contract music leadership from the nonprofit.

In the normal process of strategic planning, the leadership team would now address the last two columns in the strategic planning template above. They had assessed and prioritized *why* they would do it, *who* would lead it, and *what measurable outcomes* would result. Then they studied *when, how, and where* to do any program. No strategic planning process is complete, however, until the team has discerned the true *cost of discipleship* in seven distinct cost centers, and developed a strategy for stress management if any of those cost centers is exceptionally high. (This piece of the planning process was described in chapter 5 when it was used to assess the cost of merger in general. Now it would be used to assess the cost of program development in particular.)

Similar strategic thinking was applied to all ministry areas in each new church. Church of the Good Shepherd and Faith Community Church evaluated the previous programs of each church. Some could simply be merged without much change. Others needed significant change in focus, leadership, and design in order to be more effective. And some were simply terminated because what was effective in the past would no longer work. The strategic plan for the future was a clear break with the past, but it had clearly learned from the past. Former members from each previous church could still celebrate the work that had been done before the merger and trace their progress after the merger.

Once church planners have discerned the true cost of discipleship, they can anticipate coming stress. This stage is often ignored. Leaders can become so enthusiastic about the plan that they fail to anticipate "coming stress points" and to plan ahead to address them. Leaders are tempted to respond with promises to "phase in" the changes, but these rarely work. This merely postpones the cost of discipleship, entrenches ineffective ministries, and makes change even more difficult.

The cost of change in any program around tradition and attitude is particularly high in the first couple years of a merger. The best way to address it is with tactics for personal or spiritual growth. This helps members understand the Realm of God and God's purpose to bless the world, the person and work of Jesus Christ, and the contemporary power and guidance of the Holy Spirit. They are able to rise above self-interest, and even above personal needs, to see the bigger picture and have broader compassion for the public.

The cost of change in any program around leadership and organization is often high because a merged church has redeveloped organizational structure and redeployed a core leadership team. Committee mandates and staff job descriptions change. These changes can challenge the depth of trust among church members. The best way to address these stress points is with tactics to share and model accountability. The foundation of trust, policies, decision-making habits, and spiritual practices of the merged church must be clear and widely understood.

The cost of change in any program around property or technology is often high because the merged church has sold, acquired, renovated, and updated facilities. The best way to address these stress points is to encourage mission sensitivity. The more members understand the different ministry expectations of lifestyle segments within their mission field, the more they understand the rationale of structural and technical change. Different publics relate better to certain kinds of architectures, facilities, internal and external symbols, and communication technologies than others.

Finally, the cost of change in any program around money is often high because merger churches are often concerned about stewardship expectations, debt management, and the use of reserve funds. The best response is not simply a fundraising strategy. Charitable giving is essentially a *lifestyle* choice. Members need to be coached to develop an overall Christian household financial plan that sees all aspects of a personal or family budget in the light of God's mission and Christian faithfulness.

Once leaders know how to anticipate stress, they are finally ready to evaluate every change for *acceleration* and *impact*. They can prioritize what is most effective; find the resources to meet the true cost of discipleship; and manage any future stress. They can delegate responsibility and authority to the right leader or team. Once strategic planning becomes a congregational habit, programs can be routinely evaluated and outcomes measured for success.

A New Beginning 19
Seven Years Later

So what happened? Church of the Good Shepherd and Faith Community Church did succeed. Each was able to combine the spirituality, volunteer energy, and physical resources of the former churches to sustain *critical mass* and *critical momentum*. Each church did grow spiritually, numerically, financially, and missionally.

The relative peace and unity of the churches were notable during their respective annual meetings in the years to come. Occasionally there were tense and heated discussions, and as always there were concerns and complaints. Overall, however, the meetings were calm and respectful, and the discussions were intelligent and faithful. Each new church had done well in embedding its core values, bedrock beliefs, vision, and mission. The unity of the church no longer depended on former properties, separate histories, or tribal "sacred cows."

The lay leadership had shifted. Church of the Good Shepherd had chosen a nine-person board model, with three leaders elected each year for three-year terms. Therefore, after three years, only a few board members had played similar roles in the former churches. Faith Community Church had chosen a council model. Since representatives from committees to the council tended to change more often, after seven years no one on the council had played a similar role in the former churches. Some volunteers who had been very active five years earlier had stepped away; some volunteers who had never been very active had stepped up; some new members had stepped forward.

The staff leadership had evolved. Church of the Good Shepherd was still a Methodist church, and the ordained minister who had been appointed to the newly merged church was in due course replaced. This time, however, the appointment was just as sensitive to the needs of the mission field as to the wishes of the membership. The church was so much more articulate about its core values, beliefs, vision, and mission as to ensure that a newly appointed pastor would be appropriate for a bi-racial, multicultural congregation.

Faith Community Church still maintained its ties to the Presbyterian Church, and would follow Presbyterian procedures regarding the call or dismissal of ordered ministers. That hadn't been an issue yet, because the pastor who was called to the new church continued as the leader and planned a long-term ministry. Other staff had changed, but those transitions were much smoother and less stressful than many members remembered from their former churches. This was because the identity and purpose of the church were now transparent and accountable, and programs were not dominated by controlling personalities.

The cultures of the churches had morphed. Church of the Good Shepherd had lost a number of people from lifestyle segments that were middle-class baby boomers. A few were angry about the change, but most respected the change and chose this moment to move their membership to churches closer to home. Still, Good Shepherd gained more people than it lost. Those it gained tended to be multicultural and included quite a few singles, couples, and single parents. Interestingly, almost all of the seniors over sixty-five, and more affluent members stayed—and with great enthusiasm.

Faith Community Church still attracted lifestyle segments with strong priorities for Bible-based education and strong support for the arts. The influx of younger families via the charter school and new music programs had lowered the median age of the church. This meant that more contemporary learning methodologies, and additional computer, video, and audio technologies, were being introduced into the worship and educational life of the church. It no longer had a reputation for being "boring," but it still had a reputation for being "profound."

The theology of the churches had morphed. Church of the Good Shepherd was still Methodist but with strong seeker-sensitive characteristics and a rather independent frame of mind. This made some of its relationships in the conference a bit troubled, but the sensitive support of the bishop helped. The church sustained a strong sacramental focus, albeit manifested in different ways. Faith Community Church gradually drifted toward congregational independence. Members and leaders grew more and more troubled by top-down theological changes and public policies from denominations, and their relationships with both Baptist federations and Presbyterian denominations waned. On the other hand, the church sustained a strong sense of "classic Christianity" that was biblically literate, led by an eldership, and that functioned by consensus. Their Presbyterian ways kept them in the Presbyterian fold.

The reputations of both churches grew. Faith Community Church was known for its charter school, educational ministries, and reformation ideals. Partnerships strengthened with the education, long-term health care, and arts sectors. Church of the Good Shepherd was known for its addiction-intervention ministries. Partnerships strengthened with urban core non-profits, health clinics, government family service agencies, and counseling centers.

Nothing is perfect. Neither church will become—nor did either ever expect to become—a megachurch, although both churches are considering expansion to multiple sites. There are still breakdowns in critical momentum, most notably in the disciple-making step for discerning call, but radical hospitality, life-shaping worship, and social service have clearly improved. Financial resources are still a challenge. Both churches still face high utility costs, and both churches have added paid staff. However, they are managing assets with an eye to mission rather than maintenance, and have slowly introduced annual fundraising strategies.

It's all good—especially when the church leaders look around and see that several other churches in their community have actually closed over the last seven years. No doubt the future will bring many surprises and challenges, but both churches are more confident that they will not only survive, but thrive.

Even if mergers are as successful as in our story, there is always a danger (especially in the first seven years) that the merged church will fall back into old ways and bad habits. Leaders should bear in mind Jesus's stern warning: "No one who puts a hand to the plow and looks back is fit for the kingdom of God" (Luke 9:62). So it is well to caution leaders that there are seven struggles that lie ahead.

1. Old Times versus New Visions

Churches can lose the energy for mission and revert to a maintenance mentality. This usually happens because the new church is not intentional enough about nomination processes to a board or council, and hiring practices by a leadership team. Leaders who are simply chosen for their *skills* or simply because they are *available to fill a position*, do not necessarily have the spiritual discipline required to sustain the new vision of the church.

It is essential that a newly merged church's governance and leadership teams, committee chairpersons, and ministry team leaders, are held accountable to core spiritual practices. These include regular weekly worship, daily prayer and Bible reading, theological reflection, personal service, and other strategies that not only take them deeper into faith, but awaken their heartburst for mission. *Every* leader must be trained and accountable to model and articulate the core values, beliefs, vision, and mission of the church. It only takes one or two leaders who intentionally or accidentally undermine, ignore, or confuse the DNA of the church to send ripples of self-centeredness through the church. The DNA of the church begins to be replaced by the personal agendas of individuals.

2. Power Struggles versus Power Sharing

The former competitiveness and prejudice of church leaders can also sabotage a merger. Factions representing the old priorities of the former institutions quarrel with those who uphold the new priorities of the merged church. Leaders who are chosen because they *represent* former groups (e.g., women's, men's, or youth groups; couples' clubs, retirees, outreach committees, and many other special interest groups) always lead the church into conflict. Their primary allegiance is not to the new church, but to old constituencies. Many of these leaders were in conflict with their *former* churches and carry that conflict over into the new church.

It is essential for leaders of a newly merged church to be chosen from the new, united organization, and represent only the new, united organization. In the amalgamation of a women's group, for example, the executive committee should be chosen by the entire group, using criteria formulated by the new church. In a Sunday school, the teachers are chosen from the new constituency of the new church and do not represent the program of the old church. Such power sharing not only creates harmony in those groups, but it establishes precedence for future groups.

3. Staffing to Build the Future versus Staffing to Preserve the Past

The love and allegiance church members feel for pastors, program, and support staff often prevents the merged church from developing the right staff for the future of the church. Unable to let staff go, they continue them in their old roles and with the same expectations. They tend to resist training, excuse themselves from evaluation, often perpetuate bad habits, or use old tactics no longer suitable for the new church. This not only reduces effectiveness for critical momentum, but it frustrates volunteers, disappoints newcomers, and eventually undermines critical mass. The longer ineffective staff are allowed to continue, the harder and harder it becomes to fire them.

It is essential that brand new job descriptions are developed for all staff positions (pastoral, program, and support; full-time, part-time, and volunteer) in a newly merged church. The new job descriptions should match the policy governance of the new church and not just repeat the task management of the old church. Instead of simply listing jobs to be performed, the new job descriptions should explicitly focus the mission of the position, the measurable outcomes for which the staff person will be held accountable, the boundaries of behavior and action they must honor, and the priorities they must follow. It is possible for previous staff persons to join the staff of a new church, but only if they are suitable for the new job descriptions.

4. Harmony versus Effectiveness

Church mergers bring together diverse people, some of whom we know and some we don't, some we instinctively like and some we instinctively dislike. It is natural and correct to build healthy relationships, multiply friendships, deepen fellowship, and promote unity. However, this can perpetuate an *obsession* over harmony that might have caused the former churches to decline and could cause the newly merged church to turn inward. Obsession about harmony encourages self-centeredness. The church must remain externally focused to grow, and be willing to risk harmony for the sake of mission effectiveness.

It is essential that the newly merged church resist codependencies, intervention with unhealthy personalities, and empowerment of dysfunctional members. This is all part of the "culture of accountability" that makes a church safe for newcomers and effective in mission. The members cannot be the mission. The mission lies out in the community. Effective organizations must always have the courage to disappoint a few in order to bless many. They must never obsess over whom they might lose; they need to focus instead on how many they might gain.

5. Fear of Growing versus
Readiness to Take Risks

Fear of church growth is always rooted in fear of personal growth. Church growth forces personal spiritual growth. Personal spiritual growth encourages church growth. The trouble is that church members often import their sense of personal complacency to the new church. Adults are unwilling to participate in Sunday schools, midweek small groups, mentoring relationships, or any other process that encourages deeper learning, expanded relationships, or daring outreach. Ancient Christians called it "sloth" and included it among the seven deadly sins. It blocks innovation and initiative, and causes mission impact to plateau.

It is essential that the newly merged church encourage strategies for adult spiritual growth and faith formation. There are two good ways to do this. The first is to proliferate midweek small groups. They should be a mix of affinity and curriculum-based groups, with designated or rotated leaders, who have training not only in building relationships but in deepening spirituality. The second is to encourage risk by universalizing protocols to learn from mistakes. Leaders become more confident about risk when they no longer fear failure, but learn to grow through failure.

6. Annual Meetings versus Congregational Celebrations

One bad administrative habit carried over from declining churches is that annual congregational gatherings are devoted to micromanagement. Meetings approve tedious reports, review even the smallest decisions, and debate every budget line. The problem is not just that this deenergizes volunteers. It distracts annual congregational gatherings from the one thing that is most important: to define, refine, and celebrate the identity and purpose of the church. This DNA is the essential consensus of the church. There are state and denominational rules requiring the election of trustees, approval of budgets, and major decisions like clergy pastoral relations or sale of property. Beyond this, wasting time doing consensus management is a tacit vote of nonconfidence in a board or council and leadership team.

It is essential that the newly merged church avoid redundant management. Congregational meetings are really celebrations of identity and purpose. From time to time, core values may need to evolve; bedrock beliefs may need to be clarified; vision and mission may need to be refocused. The primary responsibility and authority for this is the body of Christ as a whole. When responsibility and authority are undermined, the church suffers loss of both focus and accountability, and gets easily sidetracked by outside agendas or internal politics.

7. Sacred Cows versus Sacred Mission

It is remarkable how quickly "sacred cows" reemerge in the life of a church. Within months of building new facilities, acquiring new technologies, adopting new curricula or hymnbooks, and consecrating new leaders, a whole new mythology forms around these supposedly sacred objects, processes, and people. Jesus cautioned us with the parable of the man who empties his house of one demon, and through his subsequent complacency and inattention seven other demons make his life even worse than before (Matthew 12:43–44).

It is essential that newly merged churches emphasize that the only things that are "sacred" are relationship with Jesus Christ and participation in Christ's mission. Everything else is tactical. In order to reinforce this, the merged church should include timely termination of ineffective tactics into every annual strategic planning process. Whenever you start something, terminate something else. This is good stewardship of volunteer energies, and it reminds people that the only thing that is forever is God's grace.

Even the church merger itself is ultimately just a tactic. God will start a church, grow a church, and, when the mission demands it, close a church. Ultimately, the church is not an end in itself, but a means to an end. We do not sustain institutions. We anticipate the Realm of God.

Basics for a Successful Merger   **20**

Healthy, missional mergers are necessary so that the Christian movement can both survive and thrive in the postmodern world. We hope that our annotated story lines have demonstrated that healthy, missional mergers are possible. Merger may sometimes be hard and/or complicated, but *we can do this!*

The stories we have followed briefly revealed insights into the process of merger. There is a great deal of needless mystery about how to do them. The next chapters recap essential information to help leaders dispel the mystery and overcome subjectivity, that is, to understand objectively how mergers are accomplished and what mergers achieve.

At the beginning of any merger discussion, most people ask the wrong question. They ask: *What is the critical mass necessary for an effective church?* Immediately the merger discussion is sidetracked by arguments among different denominational traditions, community cultures, and individual biases about what it means to be a "church" and what it takes to be "effective." As such, merger not only becomes a matter of personal preferences for material things, but it focuses on institutional preservation rather than spiritual depth and missional impact. If you begin with the question about critical mass, you end up quarreling among yourselves. You then take action only when it is too late.

Healthy, missional mergers start with a different question: *What is the critical momentum for an effective church?* Immediately the merger conversation focuses on going deeper and further with Christ. Merger is really about people, not property; about discipleship, not money; and about following Christ to bless the world, rather than gathering in a building to bless ourselves. Once the preliminary question focuses on *critical momentum*, it's amazing how the subsequent merger conversation becomes so much clearer. The ecclesiological questions become secondary to the missional urgency.

To be sure, the question about *critical mass* is still important. But it should be the *second* question. And it will be easier to answer after leaders have addressed the first question.

After all, the reason that churches lose *critical mass* is that they have already lost *critical momentum*. Somehow the process of growing disciples has been interrupted with dire consequences to membership integrity and adaptability, volunteerism and program quality, and technology upgrades and financial giving. In many cases, it takes years of defective *critical momentum* before *critical mass* of a church is in jeopardy. The problem may go unnoticed (or at least unrecognized) until a disaster strikes, committees crumble, or a key benefactor dies.

In order to regain effectiveness, however, more will be required than an emergency capital campaign, or a downsized organizational model, or a series of opportune bequests. That recognition is what gives urgency to the conversation about merger. A church will only sustain *critical mass* if once again it can gain *critical momentum*. The point of a merger is not to enable the church to survive for a few more years, but to thrive for decades into the future.

Once critical momentum, and then critical mass, have been addressed, then the next set of questions becomes equally clear: *How do we get traction? How do we maintain direction?* Once again, the order of such questions is important.

Many merger conversations stall because leaders, again, ask the second of these questions *first!* This misstep is encouraged in postmodern culture because we are overly obsessed with visioning. We risk becoming like passengers in a car that is stuck in the ditch, who are quarreling with each other about which destination they should reach *before* actually getting the car back onto the road. For most merger conversations, the first challenge is not to decide what direction to take, but to get the church moving again. Indeed, once the church gets moving again, it is often remarkable how the destination becomes surprisingly clear. God's voice is better heard on the road than in the ditch.

Finally, it is essential for church leaders and members to know that mergers are *never* perfect. All problems will *not* be solved. All theological questions will *not* be answered. Occasional deficits will *not* disappear. All stressors will *not* be resolved. A church merger will *not* achieve the Realm of God on earth. It is simply a merger. It is profoundly a merger. It is a fresh opportunity to follow Christ in a world that is still as troubled as it was before.

Critical Momentum   **21**

The goal of a merger is to create a synergy of personal growth that transforms seekers into disciples.

Critical momentum does not depend on any particular set of tactics or programs. It depends on healthy systems. After all, there are many ways to *do* church, but there is really only one way to *be* church—the same system established in New Testament times and preserved in the earliest church. And although it has been done in different ways through history, it is essentially the same system that keeps churches vital today.

Once we understand that church vitality does not depend on an assortment of *programs*, but on the unity of a *system*, we can design a successful merger. We no longer try to simply coordinate programs to maintain an institution. Instead, we try to fill in the gaps between programs to create a dynamic system that transforms seekers into disciples.

Critical momentum can be more concretely understood as "hand-offs" from one program area or subsystem to another. Churches sustain vitality when people *move* from one ministry area to another, growing all the time. They enter the momentum of the church as seekers who have yet to experience the fullness of Christ, understand the significance of Christ, or participate in the mission of Christ. Leaders in each ministry area of the church "hand off" participants to the next ministry of the church. The seekers experience grace, understand faith, find their place in mission, and emerge from the process as disciples to bless the world. (See the juggler in figure 21.1.)

Critical Momentum

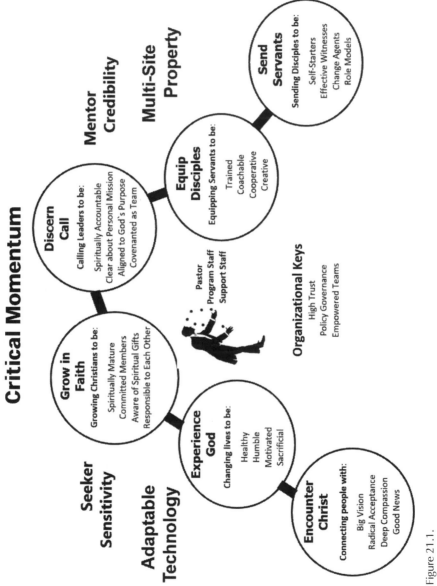

Discern Call

Calling Leaders to be:
Spiritually Accountable
Clear about Personal Mission
Aligned to God's Purpose
Covenanted as Team

Grow in Faith

Growing Christians to be:
Spiritually Mature
Committed Members
Aware of Spiritual Gifts
Responsible to Each Other

Equip Disciples

Equipping Servants to be:
Trained
Coachable
Cooperative
Creative

Send Servants

Sending Disciples to be:
Self-Starters
Effective Witnesses
Change Agents
Role Models

Experience God

Changing lives to be:
Healthy
Humble
Motivated
Sacrificial

Encounter Christ

Connecting people with:
Big Vision
Radical Acceptance
Deep Compassion
Good News

Pastor
Program Staff
Support Staff

Organizational Keys

High Trust
Policy Governance
Empowered Teams

Seeker
Sensitivity

Adaptable
Technology

Mentor
Credibility

Multi-Site
Property

Figure 21.1.

Critical momentum breaks down when the church allows participants to get "stuck" at one stage of the process and fails to move them forward into the next. If a church connects with newcomers, but fails to change their lives, then the church becomes a club. If a church connects with newcomers and changes lives, but fails to grow relationships and faith, then the church becomes a revolving door as people appear and then disappear. If a church makes connections, changes lives, grows relationships and faith, but fails to help people discern their personal calling into God's mission, then the church becomes a center for continuing education and no more. If a church makes connections, changes, grows, and calls people into mission, but fails to resource its efforts effectively, then volunteers burn out and drop out. And if the church does everything else right, but fails to send gifted, called, and equipped servants to bless the world and do outreach, then the mission is unsustainable and the public fails to connect with the church.

In practice, critical momentum requires the integration of traditional program areas (subsystems) of the church. These programs are not independent of one another. They are designed to deliberately "move people along" from one program area to another. The mistake of many churches is that they allow people to "stay put" forever in a particular committee, program, or activity. Their personal, spiritual, and missional growth effectively stops. The church as a whole loses momentum.

- The ability of a church to *connect* with the public is associated with programs of *hospitality*. The best hospitality welcomes and accepts people as they are, introduces and builds meaningful relationships, and follows up with assurance and support. As a subsystem of a discipling process, however, the ability of a church to connect with the public is more than just greeters and good coffee. It is the combined power of every leader and member to help seekers *encounter Christ*. Church people reveal in their spontaneous deeds and unrehearsed words the big vision, radical acceptance, deep compassion, and compelling hope that marked the behavior of Jesus.
- The ability of a church to *change lives* is usually associated with services of *worship*. Lives are changed when people experience grace in ways that are uniquely relevant to their lifestyle anxieties. Worship engages their attention. It is immediately useful, as participants "take away" insights or experiences that can be applied to daily living. And it strongly motivates participants to explore, discover, and discern more about God, themselves, and each other. As a subsystem of a

discipling process, however, the ability of a church to change lives is more than just worship services. It is the work of the people of faith to help people experience God in intimate, life-changing, and lifestyle-shaping ways. Worship is any experience of the Holy that changes lives to be healthy, humble, sacrificial, and motivated to follow Christ.

- The ability of a church to *grow* people in faith is usually associated with processes for *education*. Modern churches tended to rely on Sunday schools and retreats, and postmodern churches tend to rely on midweek small groups and mentoring covenants Churches are intentional about membership training and guide people to customize disciplines or habits for a spiritual life. As a subsystem of a discipling process, however, faith formation is more than information. It is the example, of leaders and members, that models maturity, demonstrates commitment, uses spiritual gifts, and (like Jesus) uses any ordinary thing or event as a means to mature faith.

- The ability of a church to *call* Christians into ministries is usually associated with processes of *volunteer empowerment*. Mature church leaders mentor emerging leaders to discern personal mission. They embed the core values, beliefs, vision, and mission. They help people discover their place in God's plan, and demonstrate or model teamwork. As a subsystem of a discipling process, however, discernment of call is more than holding an office or joining a committee. It is the kind of mentoring that Jesus did with each of the twelve disciples. Leaders and members align their entire lives with God's mission, and hold one another accountable to exercise their gifts and contribute to the Realm of God.

- The ability of a church to *equip* disciples is usually associated with *training* and *stewardship* (or processes to encourage expertise and extravagant generosity). Churches provide basic training and continuous coaching for volunteers. They resource their volunteers with effective facilities, updated technologies, and funding. They do capital campaigns for the sake of mission rather than maintenance. They coach volunteers to reduce personal debt so they can maximize personal generosity. As a subsystem of a discipling process, however, equipping involves more than tools and equipment. It is the ability to prepare disciples like Jesus did, to confidently, collaboratively, and creatively anticipate and overcome the difficulties of life and the challenges of ministry.

- The ability of a church to *send* servants is usually associated with *relevant outreach*. The church organizes volunteers into entrepreneurial teams and trains them to simultaneously do good and share faith. They innovate action plans that get mission results, become role models for peace and justice, and develop partnerships or networks with other churches, agencies, and organizations. As a subsystem of a discipling process, however, the ability of a church to send teams reveals its urgency to proclaim hope and change the world one lifestyle segment at a time.

Critical momentum is managed, monitored, and sustained by the pastor and core leadership team. Think of them as our juggler in figure 21.1, constantly rotating a set of balls in the air. If the pastor and leadership team "drop the ball," then critical momentum stops. The flow of Christian growth is interrupted. Seekers don't find what they're looking for. Christians don't fulfill themselves in mission. The community and world remain unchanged. The pastor and core leaders are less likely to drop the ball, and more likely to keep all the balls moving, if their feet are planted on a solid foundation. This foundation is the high trust of the church based on core values and beliefs, the alignment of the church with a motivational vision and heartbursts to bless particular lifestyle groups in the mission field, and commitment to high standards of accountability for leaders and members. This helps them achieve the measurable outcomes in each stage of the disciple-making process.

For example, irreversible church decline often results from failure to succeed in the first, fourth, and sixth areas listed above. Churches consistently fail to *connect* with the public through radical hospitality. Since new people are not added, the increasing homogeneity undermines the church as it becomes progressively inward, aged, and privileged. Although they may have high quality worship and excellent Sunday schools to *change* and *grow* participants, they consistently fail to mentor members and volunteers to discern *call*. Although their stewardship strategy raises money and builds huge capital reserves, they consistently fail to *train*, deploy, and hold staff accountable for their attitude, integrity, competency, and teamwork. The behavior of a custodian, organist, or secretary may contradict the core values of the church; the skepticism of the pastor or board may contradict the beliefs of the church; staff or volunteer mediocrity and unwillingness to learn new things may render church programs ineffective; or the personality conflicts and differing agendas of staff may undermine team cooperation, so that the team can actually *send* only a few people in a small committee to do *outreach*.

Mergers fail if they only try to merge the existing program units of each participating church. They succeed if they are able to intentionally link each ministry to create a flow of personal and spiritual growth. Each ministry addresses a stage in disciple development, and then moves each person forward into the next stage of development. This is why mergers should motivate every member or leader to evaluate where they are in the process. It may be time for a member who has long participated in one ministry area to move on to a different ministry area. For example, it may be time for a veteran choir member to seize the opportunity to transition from the choir to some other form of small group or outreach for the sake of his or her own spiritual growth.

The movement from one ministry area to another for the sake of personal growth rarely happens automatically, although occasionally it happens by accident. The successful merger process demands that this self-assessment happen consistently and uniformly across the leadership and membership of each participating church. We describe this as the *mentoring moment*. The mentoring moment occurs when a ministry area leader takes a participant aside for one-on-one conversation, and it is characterized as follows:

- It is usually informal (over coffee or dessert), so that it is a *conversation* and not a *directive*.
- It is usually in a neutral place, outside the church building and away from any particular room or space that is the habitual environment for past participation. This change of location will help a mentee to feel free from lingering guilt, obligation, or sense of duty, in order to imagine something more.
- It is *always* intentional. There is no trickery. A participant is not surprised by the conversation, but knows in advance that the conversation will be about personal spiritual growth and ministry vocation.

In the end, people are never forced to move on to a different step of discipleship. However, they understand that this same mentoring moment will occur on a regular basis. They are reminded that church participation is about growing as a disciple, and not just doing tasks. Mentors are asked to be gentle—but be persistent.

When three of six steps in the discipling system consistently fail, the church is not just in trouble. It is broken. The routine interventions that might work if the church was only failing in one or two steps of discipling won't solve the problem. Strategies for continuing education, introduction of new curriculums, staff changes, interim ministries, relocation, and other solutions won't work. "Drastic action" is required.

Church leaders always ask: *Why three out of six? Why is the dysfunction of* three *out of six discipling subsystems the "tipping point" toward drastic action?* The "tipping point" is fixed by the speed of change in the cultural context in which the church exists. Cultural change is occurring faster and faster, and the church simply does not have time to fix all its problems and keep up with the mission field. We are in a race not just with other religions and spiritualities, but with cultural forms of all kinds that vie for the attention and allegiance of the public. There are currently seventy-one distinct lifestyle segments in the United States alone, and the competition of political parties, ideological perspectives, entertainment venues, nonprofit institutions, and corporate marketers to influence their lives is fierce. Imagine that this race is like a regatta of sailing ships. If our boat has one leak, we can still fix it on the fly and compete. If our boat has two leaks, we may fall behind, but if we strain every muscle and muster all hands, we can fix both leaks and catch up. But if our boat has *three* leaks, we are out of the race unless we take drastic action. We can "shift our flag" to another boat, unite the crews, and keep going; or enter dry dock for radical repairs; or sink.

The actual time it takes to renew a church is notoriously contextual. One church, in a rural region, may take seven years; another church, in a small Midwestern town, may take three years; and churches in very fast-growing megalopolis regions may take just one year to sustain relevance or be rendered obsolete. However, as a rule of thumb, it takes *one year* to fix each dysfunctional system of a church. For example, if the church consistently fails to help seekers "encounter Christ," it takes one year of training and accountability to improve hospitality to fix the problem. The subsystem for "experiencing God" involves worship, and we all know that one year is often not enough to fix a problem. If "growing mature Christians" is dysfunctional, it takes one year with a new curriculum and retrained teachers to fix the problem. The point is that *three* dysfunctional systems out of six means that it will take at least *three years* to fix the problems—and most churches in North America today don't have that much time.

In order to assess the critical momentum of a congregation, church leaders need to focus on *results* rather than *tasks*. Churches lose momentum, decline in growth and impact, and eventually stop and stagnate, because they micromanage tasks without measuring success. They seem to be implementing all the right programs (hospitality, worship, Sunday school, midweek groups, outreach, stewardship, and maintenance); but they are not really getting the results that will forward people along the path of discipleship.

It is interesting to note that the churches most in need of revitalization, and who most urgently should consider merger, are precisely the same churches that resist and even resent measuring success. As long as the programs survive, reluctant people can still be recruited to hold offices, and volunteers only have to try, the church assumes that it is faithful. However, churches that encourage a culture of acceptable mediocrity are not faithful by any biblical standard. Churches that are faithful hold themselves accountable for getting results. The results may be onefold, threefold, or tenfold of their investment of energy, but the last thing faithful churches do is allow themselves to bury their talents in the ground and accomplish nothing.

Measurable outcomes are sometimes called *ends policies*. These define the *end game* or final results that actually gauge how effectively any organization has lived up to its mission statement. A mission statement without clear measurable outcomes is like an airplane without landing gear. It looks nice on the tarmac and may even attract a lot of admirers, but it is unable to take off and land. It is like a balloon without ballast: filled with hot air, a thrilling ride in the clouds with a grand view of the landscape, but helpless before the winds. What good is it to fly high if you can't make a difference down below?

There are *six sets of* ends policies that are necessary for a church to measure success. These correspond to the six steps of discipleship. A church that consistently fails to succeed in three or more outcomes must go beyond tactical adjustments and consider drastic action. Each ends policy defines the single, essential outcome in the steps of the discipling process that connect seekers with grace, change their lives, grow them up, focus their calling, equip them for ministries, and send them into service.

Find the two essential things that *must* occur in each step of the discipling process that will allow the congregation to fulfill its mission. One ends policy relates to leadership development; and the other relates to program development. These essential things can be observed, tracked, and regularly evaluated. If they occur, the system gains momentum. If they do not occur, then the system loses momentum.

1. **Connect:** The essential outcomes of all our efforts to help seekers encounter Christ and connect the church with the general public. For example, the leadership development goal might be: *All greeters, ushers, servers, receptionists, and custodial staff will receive basic training to*

naturally, confidently, and gently share their own experience with Christ. The program development goal might be: *Two hundred new people (visitors, inquirers, website registrations, etc.) will contact the church, and receive an intentional, personal response from the church, every year.*

2. **Change:** The essential outcomes of all our efforts to help people experience God, and change the lives and lifestyles of people participating in all ministries of the church, motivating them to go deeper and further in Christ. For example, the leadership development goal might be: *The musicians and lay leaders in worship will be deployed as the "front line" of evangelism to interact with visitors before and after worship.* The program development goal might be: *Among worshippers in every service, 15% will be first- or second-time visitors who are "checking us out" because of the wonderful stories they have heard about blessings received in worship.*

3. **Grow:** The essential outcomes of all our efforts to help people grow in faith, and mature as church members in Christian faith and values. For example, the leadership development goal might be: *Designated small group leaders will have coaching available to them 24/7 to help them overcome any obstacles in building healthy relationships and understanding scripture.* The program development goal might be: *Adult participation in Christian education classes and midweek small groups will increase 10% each year, with an annual net growth of three small groups each year.*

4. **Call:** The essential outcomes of all our efforts to help Christians discern their personal mission, so that they experience personal fulfillment and never burn out. For example, the leadership development goal might be: *Every staff and board leader will mentor at least six different church members in spiritual life and vocational discernment every year.* The program development goal might be: *Every new program initiative must have at least two volunteers who are passionate about the idea and ready to take responsibility and authority to build a team and pursue the dream.*

5. **Equip:** The essential outcomes of all our efforts to provide training and resources to ensure the quality and effectiveness of all our ministries. For example, the leadership development goal might be: *The annual budget for volunteer leadership will be at least 40% higher than the budget for professional staff development.* The program development goal might be: *No technology used in worship will be over seven years old.*

6. **Send:** The essential outcome of all our efforts to deploy volunteers and teams for outreach into the community, so that we simultaneously do good stuff and share faith motivation for doing it. For example,

the leadership development goal might be: *The staff position for our signature outreach ministry will become full time within two years.* The program development goal might be: *We will sustain one major outreach ministry to a lifestyle segment underrepresented in our church, in which at least 20% of our membership is personally involved as volunteers on a regular basis.*

A "disciple" is someone who is connected with Christ, changed by Christ, matured to know Christ, committed to follow Christ, equipped to do ministry with excellence, and deployed to serve in Christ's name. The more disciples are deployed to serve in Christ's name, the more strangers to grace are drawn to the experience of Christ, and the more the church grows. An ends policy or measurable outcome is the way the church measures success in each step. If a church is consistently unable to succeed in three or more of these outcomes, a merger or some other "drastic action" is in order.

"Drastic Action" can mean many things, including closure of a congregation and the redistribution of assets to healthier churches ready to grow; closure of a congregation and the reinvestment of assets to sustain a nonprofit social service; and merger. Many denominations have begun to follow a wiser, harder, more challenging strategy toward chronically dysfunctional churches.

If one or two subsystems for critical momentum are dysfunctional in the life of a church, so that the church's momentum for discipleship growth and mission impact have slowed down or stopped altogether, it is given a reasonable amount of time and expert advice to solve the problem. A church may be given three chances for renewal. However, if a church fails to renew itself after three attempts, denominational leaders conclude that systemic problems will not be resolved by program or leadership changes alone. If three or more of the church's systems are dysfunctional, the denomination will provide future personnel and/or financial support only if the church pursues some kind of merger. This way of proceeding has sometimes been described with a term borrowed from the emergency health care field: *triage.*

Momentum is essential for organizational viability. Organizations simply cannot be allowed to stop progress altogether. This is certainly true of the church. Several metaphors come to mind.

- A ship that loses momentum also loses steerage, and begins to "box the compass," driven by waves, tides, winds, and other exterior forces beyond its control. This is why momentum is often associated with the vision and mission of a church. A church that is not going somewhere soon fails to get anywhere. The whims of influential members and the pressures of outside issues and organizations drive the church.

- A car that loses forward momentum starts to roll backward, and it requires more and more passengers leaping out to push the car just to keep it still. This is why momentum is often associated with membership. A church that stays the same and resists all change begins to age and decline. It burns out more and more leaders and volunteers to have to expend enormous energy simply to maintain the status quo.

- A train that loses momentum becomes a huge mass of inert steel that rusts to the rails and requires ten times as much energy to start up again. Even the slightest forward progress provides steerage, less physical labor, and a small surplus for a burst of energy in an emergency. This is why momentum is often associated with finances. A church that stops measuring success and accomplishing goals is soon overwhelmed by the weight and cost of property and debt, and requires an enormous infusion of new investment to start up again.

Once a church loses critical momentum and is unable to regain it, the church will inevitably begin losing *critical mass*. And the analysis of *critical mass* often reveals why and how the church is losing critical momentum.

Critical Mass **22**

> *The goal of a merger is to achieve and sustain critical mass for the life and mission of the church.*

In the previous chapter, we explored how a core leadership team must sustain critical momentum for the church to thrive. This involved six steps in a discipling system, measurable outcomes to evaluate success, resources for leadership and program development, credible leadership to motivate and mentor people through the process, and a foundation of trust to nurture accountability. When critical momentum breaks down, the church begins to lose critical mass.

Critical mass for an established church comprises whatever it takes to sustain one full-time minister (usually with part-time, paid or unpaid, program and support staff, like a musician and secretary), relevant and meaningful worship, essential Christian education and membership assimilation programs, and essential facilities or technologies that make ministries effective. By "established church" we mean any faith community that was founded and grounded in the Christendom world prior to 1965 (the peak year for church membership for many denominations), or that was founded since 1965 on the Christendom assumption that Christianity was the religious choice of most people in Western culture.

A general description of critical mass is only a starting place for any particular local church. Much depends on the context of ministry and membership expectations of the church. For example, operational budgets can vary depending on the cost of living in the region. Staff costs may vary depending on denominational personnel policies. Churches that encourage tithing are able to sustain critical mass longer than churches that encourage percentage giving. Unique crises and unexpected blessings may shorten or lengthen the window of opportunity for change.

There are a couple other universal truths to consider with regard to critical mass. Local churches can "reality-test" each of the following points. But be advised: *Churches always exaggerate their strengths and underestimate their weaknesses.*

- Churches always assume there are hidden pockets of money when there are none. They always believe there will be generous volunteers that will suddenly appear from nowhere, and messianic pastors or priests who will work miracles to attract new members even though seminary enrollment is dramatically declining and the pool of clergy dramatically aging. They cling to fantasies about "pendulum swings" that will bring a returning influx of youth and young couples back to traditional institutions. They uncritically rely on ridiculously ambitious denominational programs to convert seekers, multiply members, or transform churches.
- Churches always minimize risks. They imagine they are still immune from municipal or state policies regarding fire safety, food preparation, accessibility, parking, hazardous materials, and child security, and will never be forced into expensive upgrades. They ignore urgent and expensive repairs. Alternatively, they tie up money in large reserve funds for a "rainy day" and expect that personnel and programs can function effectively with almost no funding. They overlook gross breaches in staff or membership behavior in order to maintain status quo, believing that they will never face litigation. They tolerate eccentric expressions of faith, bizarre spiritual fads, and extreme ideological positions, believing the public will still respect them and give them money.

By all means, test each point and make reasonable adjustments to suit your local church situation. On the other hand, stop living in "fantasy land"! Like it or not, the Western world is becoming increasingly indifferent or hostile to the established church. No denomination is immune to membership decline. Financial subsidies are disappearing. The critical mass required to sustain a church increases with each generation—*and will continue to rise.*

So here are benchmarks for critical mass for the mid-2010s: In order to sustain congregational independence (i.e., without merging or clustering), one full-time pastor (with volunteer or *very* part-time administrative and program staff), and essential programs for worship and membership development, the following usually need to be in place:

- Clarity and consensus around the vision, mission, core values, and bedrock beliefs of the congregation
- 4 to 7 board members respected as "spiritual leaders" of the church, who mentor emerging leaders and model core values
- 125 to 150 members (resident or active in congregational programs at least nine months out of the year)
- 100 to 125 people average, in weekly worship attendance
- 100 to 200 first- or second-time connections to worship made each year
- 1 worship service that is highly motivational and culturally relevant to 1 or more major lifestyle segments in the community
- 1 strong hospitality team, trained in seeker sensitivity and regularly in prayer for the community
- 60% of adult worshippers active in a midweek small group (fellowship plus accountable spiritual growth)
- 1/3 of adult members active as regular, hands-on volunteers in outreach specifically sponsored by the congregation
- 1 major, year-round outreach focus or signature outreach ministry for which the church has a public reputation
- Pledging by church leaders that is at least 3 to 5% *higher* than the average or median congregational pledge (whichever is higher)
- An intentional, year-round stewardship plan with multiple choices in giving, and optional coaching for personal and family Christian financial planning
- 1 regular, affordable, accessible location at which to gather

The goal of a merger is to achieve and sustain all these criteria for critical mass for a church. This is the only way to ensure that the merged church is in fact more than the combined total of former members, programs, and resources of each of the former churches. Many mergers fail to achieve such critical mass. The final merger is in fact less than the combined membership, programs, and resources of the total of previous churches. When this happens, the merged church revives for a time, but then returns to inevitable decline. However, when the merger achieves critical mass, the new church can thrive and grow.

Clarity and Consensus about Values, Beliefs, Vision, and Mission

The goal of a merger is to achieve and sustain clear consensus for the overarching vision and mission of the church, and the underlying values and beliefs for which members and leaders will be held accountable.

You might call this "critical *quality*" rather than "critical *quantity*." The truth is that authenticity and credibility are much more important to critical mass than perfection or performance. A church can have mediocre preaching, amateur music, simple surroundings, somewhat dated technologies, and recycled curricula and still thrive—*provided that members are clear and united about values, beliefs, vision, and mission.* This is what we have been calling congregational DNA, a term likely coined by church growth specialists. It refers to the high integrity of a church that is revealed in every member and program of the body of Christ. It is consistently and regularly used to measure success and protect accountability. It is what makes the church credible to the general public and worthy of respect. It is the foundation of trust.[1]

The problem is that most churches don't have it! Pastors, boards, denominations, and consultants have invested considerable time and effort in the last ten to twenty years trying to build or restore it. It has been difficult: It usually takes three to five years of hard work, intentional practice, and stress management to achieve congregational DNA, and it can be easily lost again with the next change in pastoral relationship, board membership, or volunteer leadership. It is one of those crucial but precarious things every effective organization must sustain. Without it, the rest of the benchmarks for critical mass may not even be achievable. With it, these minimal benchmarks can be maintained and even exceeded.

Consider a typical church in a small town. It has a welcome sign outside with the denominational logo, worship times, and the claim to be a friendly, Bible-believing church. Inside it has a long, generic mission statement that nobody remembers carved in oak and mounted on the wall of the narthex. The greeters spend most of the time gossiping with friends and seem tongue-tied when welcoming strangers. The Bible is quoted occasionally, but the *fruits of the Spirit* are not very apparent. There is more passion around plans for the potluck supper than around recent experiences of Jesus Christ. It is a matter of perception, to be sure, but visitors size up a church within thirty seconds of entering. Credibility and trust are absolutely foundational to critical mass.

The goal of a merger is to create a new consensus of vision and mission to which all programs and resources will be resolutely aligned, and a new consensus of values and beliefs for which all leaders and members will be held accountable. The problem is that most declining churches are unclear about this DNA in the first place, making a consensus for a merged church difficult and undermining the trust required for serious negotiation. It may take months, and even years, for such consensus to be achieved, but it is the first step in the merger conversation. Don't wait! Start now!

A Board of 4–7 Spiritual Leaders

The goal of a merger is to create a small, compact, dedicated board of spiritual leaders, who model and mentor the values, beliefs, vision, and mission, that is the consensus of the new church.

Most churches wrongly assume that critical mass depends on the energy, creativity, and professionalism of the pastor or priest. This is no longer true. Yes, the minister is important. He or she must be a role model for the core values and beliefs of the church; and must be a leader who can keep members and programs aligned to the vision and mission of the church. It helps a lot if the minister is competent in at least some key areas of ministry like preaching, pastoral care, and the celebration of the sacraments. Yet when it comes to critical mass and the basic necessities of life for the body of Christ, the minister is surprisingly less important.

The board is the key to critical mass—not the pastor. The board does not need to be large. Our estimate of four to seven may be unnecessarily large in some circumstances. The important thing is that the board members are nominated and elected because they are perceived to be models and mentors of the DNA of the church. They are credible spiritual leaders who practice intentional spiritual habits (including daily prayer and meditation, weekly worship and/or sacramental participation, monthly hands-on service, and personal witness). They need not be theologians and scholars, but they know and affirm the faith, read and learn from scripture, and readily talk about it with joy. They hold themselves accountable to a mission attitude, high standard of integrity, continuous learning, and commitment to teamwork.[2]

The problem, of course, is that most churches don't have such a board. The typical board of a struggling institutional church has been nominated to fill a vacuum and elected because the members have skills in accounting, construction, education, or other jobs. They tend to represent a faction rather than articulate a mission. They are not expected to practice any spiritual habits and may even be inconsistent in weekly worship attendance. They are bashful and inarticulate about faith. Their meetings are all business. They are motivated by duty rather than joy. They are dedicated to "keeping the doors open" rather than "opening new doors." When a board listens to factions and is inwardly focused on survival alone, the church will struggle all the harder to maintain critical mass. But when a board listens to the Holy Spirit and is outwardly focused on mission above all, anything is possible.

Consider a typical church in the urban core. Its board members are chosen from a limited pool of volunteers. This is understandable, since the congregation is quite elderly or made up of people whose personal issues or job complications inhibit their leadership potential. They are very dependent on a professional pastor to perform all the duties of Word, sacrament, and pastoral care; represent them in the community; and lobby for their interests with the denomination. There is no expectation that the board be long-term planners, mentors to emerging leaders, role models of integrity in the community, and committed to spiritual growth—nor is there any available training toward those ends. The board tends to focus on money and property management, and it relays complaints to the pastor. The more it concentrates on maintaining a happy status quo, the more it encourages unhappy decline. If this is your church, then you no longer have critical mass.

Again, the goal of a merger is not to combine multiple boards, but to create a new board. The board members do not represent the special interests of each church, but embody the values, beliefs, vision, and mission of the new church. They develop new policies, processes, and executive limitations for an entirely new organization. Imagine that you are building a brand new ship in dry dock. You do not borrow and patch together the old parts from old ships. And when you are ready to smash a champagne bottle on your new ship's prow and launch the ship, you immediately take all the old hulks out of the water. It may take a "shakedown cruise" of a year to plug all the minor leaks, but eventually you set sail and never look back.

125–150 Resident, Active Members

The goal of a merger is to consolidate a critical mass of resident, active members who will celebrate the new DNA and follow the new core leadership in whatever new directions God calls them to go.

Many churches struggling with critical mass pare down their membership rolls. This is a good thing that is often done for the wrong reasons. Churches do it because the denomination taxes them based on membership, and they are trying to save money. This is a stressful thing because extended families like to claim membership for free services (occasional weddings, baptisms, funerals, or hospice care) and because pastors want to protect their careers and enhance potential promotions. All this has led to a morass of subtle membership distinctions that are completely irrelevant to critical mass.

The right reason to pare down membership rolls is to identify who is *really* active in the church and who is not. This is actually not very hard to figure out. An "active" member is someone who regularly participates in some program specifically related to the faith community of the church for at least nine months of the year. For many, this means regular participation in worship at least forty out of fifty-two weeks a year. In our mobile world today participation may be digital, and occasionally it may be on the road and in another church, but it is always *trackable*. The pastor or the board member *inquires*—and holds members accountable to worship.

However, participation for some may be through some other program of the church (e.g., small group, Bible study class, outreach ministry, a counseling relationship, etc.). Elderly, disabled, and otherwise limited members may not be able to worship regularly, and some jobs limit the presence of members on Sunday morning. Yet their participation is clearly and directly with the faith community, not with some related chaplaincy, agency, or other body not directly monitored by the board. Again, the church is able to *track* participation.

The word "active" means "not passive." Therefore, you do not simply count *donors* or people who use institutional church donation envelopes or who preauthorize money to be withdrawn from their accounts by the church. Donors are not necessarily participants, and the future of your church cannot be based on philanthropy. Those passive philanthropists who do not participate but give money either because they like you or need a tax receipt are at best "fair weather friends." They may *stop* liking you because of some policy or practice that they find offensive; or they may die, and their executors no longer care about the church; or they may find some other charity that captures their interest. At worst, they hold the church hostage and limit creativity, or rein in the faithfulness for Christian mission. When the future of the church depends on people who are *not there*, the church will perish sooner or later. When the future of the church depends on people who *are present and accounted for*, the church can thrive against all odds.

Let's consider an exurban church on the fringe of a city. The demographic wave of young families that grew the Sunday school in the past has now driven past, en route to the suburbs. Once the church excludes a long list of nonresident members who occasionally send money and another list of extended family members who occasionally return for weddings and special worship services, their actual active membership consists of eighty-five people, most of whom are over sixty. This means that the available volunteer pool is quite small. Members wear multiple "hats" to serve offices and frequently complain that they are exhausted. Even two or three new able-bodied members could make a difference, and so the members tend to pounce on visitors with the hope of recruiting them into the service of the institution. If this is your church, then you no longer have critical mass.

The goal of a merger is to gather and unite at least 125 to 150 members in a new church entity. There may be additional members who are nonresident or who (for various reasons of age or health) may be inactive. The church needs to bless them, but it cannot depend on them. Active members are expected to worship regularly, participate in programs, and support the church with time, talent, and money.

100–125 Weekly Participants in Worship

The goal of a merger is to assemble a critical mass of weekly worshippers, including members, adherents, and visitors.

The benchmark for active membership usually implies about 100 to 125 members in worship each week. That statistic is immediately intimidating to many churches, because research suggests that about 80% of the established churches in North America count fewer than one hundred people in their congregations. So well over two-thirds of the churches in North America are already below critical mass! They need to do something quickly, but unfortunately many of them choose to do something slowly or not at all.

Here is the best way to get an accurate picture of regular worship attendance. First, be sure to *include only* Sunday morning services, and *exclude* special services like Christmas Eve, Easter Sunrise, and other events. These are often seeker-sensitive or draw occasional members and their extended families, but they are not reliable for consistent participation or financial support. Second, *exclude* from the calculation the three Sundays with the *highest* attendance and the three Sundays with the *lowest* attendance. Average the remaining forty-six Sundays.

Another method is to only average the Sundays from October, November, February, and March. However, this method tacitly accepts a sharply abbreviated "church year" as normative for church membership. It suggests that it is acceptable for church members to disappear in summer and winter for holidays or seasonal homes, and focus only on high holy days like Christmas and Easter. Worship attendance with extreme peaks and valleys cannot sustain an established church in the post-Christendom era.

Worship is the engine that drives the critical momentum of discipleship. Think of it as a pump that circulates water (i.e., Christians) through a spiritual life that includes spiritual growth, discernment of call, service to the community, witness to seekers, and then returns to worship to be energized all over again. There may be many reasons why church members and other seekers drop out of worship, but the end result is that they eventually drop out of discipleship. Spiritual growth stops or gets sidetracked (*I'm too busy!*). Discernment of call is forgotten (*I'm too unimportant!*). Service to the community becomes sporadic (*I'm too tired!*). Christian witness is avoided (*I don't know what to say or do!*). Worship motivates, inspires, heals, instructs, and generally drives discipleship.

When worship participation in an established church drops below one hundred, the congregation ceases to be a faith community and becomes a support group, clubhouse, or family chapel. Worship no longer drives discipleship. Support groups are good ministries, but they cannot sustain an established church without significant financial subsidies that are unavailable today. Clubs are good fellowship meetings, but the church cannot compete with other organizations that do it better for less cost. Family chapels are good, but there are few families that are large enough and wealthy enough to pay for what has become a luxury of privilege rather than a necessity of life.

Consider a typical church in the country. It was founded either in the late 1800s or early 1900s in a small village, and multigenerational families used to travel several miles from their farms to attend worship. Indeed, they spent the whole Sunday in worship, child and adult Sunday schools, fellowship dinners, and mission planning. Worship "pumped them up," and they had an impact locally, regionally, and even globally out of all proportion to their size. Today it's very different. Once you factor out the highest and lowest attended Sundays, the church averages about fifty regular worshippers. They are over sixty years old and occasionally bring grandchildren. They greet each other warmly, catch up on news, support one another in adversity, chuckle at the little children's story, and remind the pastor of all the work he or she has to do that week. If that is your church, you are below critical mass.

The goal of a merger is to gather a critical mass of worshippers. Most members return again and again because they enjoy strong singing, demographically diverse fellowship, and enthusiastic participation. Most visitors prefer to blend in, avoid pressure, and choose the manner and extent of their participation. It takes a minimum of about 100 to 125 people in an area that seats about 200 to 250 to make that happen.

100–200 First- or Second-Time New and "Trackable" Connections Each Year

The goal of a merger is to connect and follow up with a significant number of newcomers, visitors, or seekers of Sunday worship and special worship services through the year.

This benchmark for critical mass is even more challenging than the previous benchmarks for membership and average worship attendance. The fact is that for good and bad reasons all the members do not worship regularly. It would be nice if 125 to 150 members translated into 100 to 125 average worship attendance. In an ideal world, 80% of the members would worship regularly (with the remaining 20% unable to do so for reasons of health, work, or other obligations beyond their control). That still means that churches of 125 to 150 members can only ideally expect 90 to 120 worshippers—barely enough to sustain an established church. That's why it only takes the departure of a single family transferred out of state, or the smallest controversy that alienates a few, to push the church below critical mass. Most churches, of course, experience less than a 50% rate of regular attendance by members. Churches can only sustain worship attendance if there are visitors coming or returning all the time.

The more compelling reason to track visitors, of course, is that worship should be a blessing to more and more people. Broken, lost, lonely, dying, abused, addicted, or discarded people are compelled by their anxieties to seek worship that is relevant to their needs; and worship can heal, guide, befriend, inspire, vindicate, liberate, and accept them through experiences of the real presence of Christ. Visitors in worship are a sign that a church is vital and effective.

A target of one hundred to two hundred first- or second-time visitors to worship translates to about two to four visitors each week. This might mean two individuals, or one couple, or one family. Visitors are more likely to come through the personal invitation of friends who accompany them to church than through advertisements; the era of "church shopping" is over in most parts of the country. Visitors are more likely to come because of the reputation of the church for outreach in the community and the stories of positive change they have heard from others, than out of loyalty to a denomination or curiosity about a pastor.

In this calculation, churches should *include* all of the special services celebrated morning or evening during the year. Christmas Eve, for example, should be included because this is one of the most common ways seekers connect or reconnect with a church. Small churches may not have visitors every week, but they can make up for that by special efforts to bless nonmembers on major holy days and holidays. The key, of course, is for visitors or visits to be *tracked*. The church gets their name and contact information (email, phone number, address). Alternatively, the church makes sure that a special gift is given each visitor with the website, mission statement, and contact information of the church. They follow up to communicate with visitors; or do their best to encourage visitors to follow up with them. Either way, they are able to actually count the visitors in a year.

The problem of course, is that so many churches do not encourage visitors, or they ignore them if they come. Consider that typical church in the city. The few visitors that come as a result of newspaper advertisements and the faded denominational sign outside remain anonymous. The greeters pay more attention to friends than strangers. They fail to get names and contact information, and they are satisfied if the visitor remembers to take the worship bulletin home. Christmas Eve welcomes strangers, but most of the choir is away visiting family, and the church operates with a handful of volunteers. There is no actual count of first- or second-time visitors, which leads many members to think that no one ever visits. Eventually perception becomes reality, because despite the love members have for one another, the general public thinks the church is unfriendly and irrelevant to their needs. If this is your church, then you are falling below critical mass.

The goal of a merger is to attract and track a significant number of visitors to worship each year. The churches that merge not only pool their technologies and talents for more engaging and relevant worship, but the very size of and diversity of worship of the merged church helps visitors fit in and find ways to personally connect with church members and leaders. The merged church deploys more volunteers, and provides more communication options, to follow up with visitors and answer questions or guide their interests.

1 Worship Service That Is Highly Motivational and Culturally Relevant to One or More Major Lifestyle Segments in the Community

The goal of a merger is to design at least one motivational, relevant worship experience that blesses major lifestyle segments in the immediate mission field.

Critical mass is not only determined by the number of worshippers or visitors on Sunday morning. It is also determined by the intentionality of worship or "mission focus." Classically trained clergy and veteran church members may balk at this, because for them worship emerges from a context of theological sophistication and a strong sense of duty: *Worship is something you learn to understand and perform and it is compelled by a strong sense of duty to God, country, and tradition.*

This is less and less true as the postmodern world evolves. Worship is something that grasps amateur seekers with indescribable grace. Ordinary people are compelled to return to worship by fundamental anxieties about life.[3] In order to sustain numbers of worship attendees and visitors, worship must be truly extraordinary. This does not necessarily mean exceptional performance quality. It means extraordinary authenticity (i.e., a combination of absolute sincerity on the part of worship leaders and immediate transparency to the blessing of God that seekers seek). The urgency of human need meets the availability of God's grace.

Critical mass is gained when worship designers pay more attention to demographic research than dogmatic theology. They seek to adapt worship to bless diverse people, rather than expecting all people to adapt themselves to appreciate worship. This is possible even for those Eucharistic traditions for which prescribed words and rituals are important. The sincerity of leaders and the cultural sensitivity of liturgies are what motivate worshippers to not only return again and again, but to participate in midweek groups or educational opportunities following worship.

Here is the problem with so many declining established churches: Their worship options are neither motivational nor relevant. The most common responses to worship are that worship is boring and unhelpful. Worship assumes a theological sophistication that attendees no longer possess, is led by clergy following a perfunctory routine or artificial performance, and only motivates worshippers to go home to lunch.

Critical mass requires that worship address the specific existential anxieties that compel distinct lifestyle segments to search for God. Worship is fundamentally an experience of *the real presence of Christ.* Worship offers a relevant opportunity to "meet Jesus" in whatever manner is most significant to the worshipper:

- People who are lost experience Christ as Spiritual Guide.
- People who are broken experience Christ as Healer.
- People who are lonely experience Christ as Perfect Companion.
- People who are dying experience Christ as Promise Keeper.
- People who are abused or suffering injustice experience Christ as Vindicator.
- People who are discarded and forgotten experience Christ as Shepherd.
- People who are trapped or addicted experience Christ as Higher Power.

This is why traditional attempts at "blended worship" actually block a church from achieving and sustaining critical mass. Blended worship tries to be all things to all people, and succeeds in being nothing to anyone. It is better to target a distinct lifestyle segment for a heartburst of outreach, and design worship for that lifestyle segment, than try to bless the whole diversity of the community with one single option of worship.

The goal of a merger is to gather sufficient talent and resources to design an engaging and relevant weekly worship service. Larger and more diverse worship leadership can better mirror the proportionate lifestyle-segment diversity of the mission field. They have the ability to empathize with their needs and expectations, and shape an encounter with God that motivates 24/7 spiritual growth at church, home, work, and play. The combined talent and resources eventually allow the merged churches to create yet another worship option, designed differently, to be relevant to a different public, driven by different needs.

1 Strong Hospitality Team, Trained in Seeker Sensitivity and Regularly in Prayer for the Community

The goal of a merger is to gather and deploy volunteers to create an experience of radical hospitality on Sunday morning.

Critical mass requires more sensitivity to the diverse publics of the community than ever before. The people who have grown up in the church are fewer and fewer, and even those never received (or have forgotten) much of the theological and ecclesiastical training that was common earlier in the twentieth century. A casual greeting and a friendly handshake won't help a church sustain critical mass no matter how "friendly" the congregation thinks it is.

The low priority of hospitality for many declining churches is revealed by the fact that responsibilities for various aspects of hospitality are divided among several committees that are not intentionally coordinated. As a result, pre- and post-worship greeting, visitor welcome centers, ushering, assistance for seniors and young families, refreshment services, and other ministries to special needs are inconsistent or missing. Moreover, training to equip volunteers with culturally sensitive and relevant skills to encounter the diversity of the public is almost always missing. Volunteers are often inapt or inept, alienating visitors and only really connecting with a handful of friends or privileged members.

Critical mass is sustained when there is one united hospitality team that divides and coordinates all the different hospitality tasks. They understand hospitality as a ministry of crucial importance that sets the context for the coming worship service and also supports the opportunities for midweek spiritual growth, Christian education, and social service following worship. The hospitality team is omnipresent before, during, and after worship. Their real goal is not just to greet people, but to engage people with significant conversation about faith and life.

This high priority for hospitality is revealed by intentional training. The team is trained to understand the diversity of lifestyle segments that are in proximate community with the church. Team members are chosen because of their heart for mission, equipped with relevant skills in communication and personal support, and held accountable for their ability not only to make people "feel at home" but also to engage people in significant conversation. These are volunteers who are radically inclusive, totally respectful, passionate about God, and capable of talking about values and beliefs instead of the weather.

One of the most outstanding signs of a strong hospitality ministry that sustains critical mass is that the hospitality team (as individuals and as a group) follows a regular discipline of prayer for visitors and members who attend worship on any given occasion. Indeed, they are held accountable by the church for intercessory prayer, just as they are accountable for skills and coordinate as a team.

The goal of a merger is to provide the necessary volunteers, with adequate training, and sufficient resources, who can design a strategy for hospitality "from entry to exit." The welcome, personal support, refreshments, significant conversations, and even the wave goodbye must be sensitive, authentic, and enthusiastic. Put another way, the greeting must be sincere, the interest must be genuine, the food must be opulent, the conversation must be rich, and the farewell must be filled with promise.

60% of Adult Worshippers Active in Midweek Small Groups

The goal of a merger is to connect members and visitors with a greater variety of interesting, relevant, and helpful midweek small groups.

A small group is a regular gathering of three to twelve people that meets to deepen friendships and spiritual life at the same time. There can be extraordinary diversity within small groups. They may gather around a curriculum to study or around some affinity that is a shared enthusiasm or concern. They may meet inside or beyond the church building. They may rely on a trained facilitator, host, or leader; or they may rotate leadership for each gathering among the participants. They may meet for three weeks or three years. They are, however, consistent in attendance and serious about high trust and deep spirituality.

The small-group strategy is replacing Sunday school as the primary tactic for youth and adult education, and the principles of small-group organization are also replacing committees and task groups as the most effective tactic for both social service and administration. Churches no longer *use* volunteers to get institutional tasks done. They *empower* volunteers with benefits in deeper friendships, personal growth, and spiritual life—and then turn them loose to do whatever God calls them to accomplish. Volunteer burnout is reduced. More ministries get done. Adults mature in the faith through both action and reflection.

Adult faith formation is the pivot on which church growth turns. The problem is that for many declining established churches, less than 10% of the adults worshipping on Sunday morning will participate in such a small group during the week. This leads to all kinds of problems. The core group of spiritually mature members shrinks. It is difficult to nominate people to fill offices or select board members. Volunteers burn out, and visitors are afraid to volunteer. Financial generosity declines. Members are increasingly hesitant and inarticulate about faith when they are talking to visitors, or among neighbors, colleagues, and extended family.

A rule of thumb is that critical mass requires 60% of worshippers to participate in small groups (including members, adherents, and visitors). Since groups are starting and stopping all the time, last for different lengths of time, and meet outside the church building, church leaders must work harder to estimate participation. Even if the church does not use specialized software or reporting systems, the board members of a small church can provide a close estimate.

The important thing is to only count *true* small groups. Many churches have a variety of fellowship groups or clubs (e.g., couples' clubs, craft groups, etc.) that are strong on fellowship but undisciplined about spiritual growth. Conversely, they have a few task groups and classes (e.g., service committees or Bible studies) that are intentional about outreach or education (but fail to deepen intimacy). In the end, many superficially "active" churches actually fail to deepen intimacy and grow friendships, and fail to deepen faith and grow spiritual life.

Most churches discover that the goal of 60% is exceedingly ambitious.[4] Members often believe they are privileged and do not need any further adult faith formation once they are baptized or confirmed. Visitors are often consumers who feel no urgency to grow once their immediate need has been met. Critical mass requires a church to create an organizational culture that values high trust and constant spiritual growth. The process begins with the core leadership. Once the staff, board, worship, and hospitality teams lead the way, other members follow.

The goal of a merger is to multiply the number of small-group options. The merged church has more volunteers to be trained as small-group leaders. It offers more choices for topics, timelines, meeting places, expertise, and customized spiritual growth. The real leverage for growth in a church merger is not the perpetuation of former Sunday schools or even a larger youth group. It is the participation of adults in small groups that build relationships and deepen faith.

1/3 of Adult Members Participate Regularly as Hands-On Volunteers in Congregational Outreach

The goal of a merger is to support and sustain a single, major outreach ministry that blesses nonmembers or strangers to grace.

The primary purpose of outreach is to bless the community. However, volunteering in general benefits the church. Too many churches rely on paid professionals (pastor and other staff) to do the work of outreach, supported by only a committee or a handful of volunteers. In the short term, professional expertise allows the church to have greater impact on positive change in the community. But in the long term, dependence on paid staff to do outreach encourages church decline. Churches sustain health and growth when about one-third of the adult members regularly participate in hands-on outreach.

Volunteering accelerates spiritual growth for the members. There is nothing more powerful than an ongoing process of action, reflection, and prayer. Personal participation in outreach challenges members to empathize with the public, wrestle with ethical dilemmas and theological questions, and put their hearts into intercessory prayer. Service is as important to spiritual discipline as Bible study.

Volunteering stimulates the relevance of worship. The more volunteers interact with the public, the more they will expect worship to relate to local, regional, and global situations. It is easier to design worship once the members set aside personal preferences; stop arguing about theories, tastes, and traditions; and focus on what attracts and blesses strangers to grace.

Volunteering generates a positive reputation in the community. The public judges a church more by the behavior of volunteers than the behavior of paid staff. Volunteers are the true "face" of the congregation. The more volunteers visibly labor for the benefit of their neighbors, the higher the respect for the congregation. This not only generates membership growth, but multiplies valuable networks across sectors.

Volunteering stimulates financial generosity. When members are personally involved in volunteering, they almost always increase their financial giving to the church. This is not just giving toward mission. It is also giving toward the overhead costs of salaries, programs, and properties. They feel so good about what the church is doing, that they increase their giving to sustain the church's existence.

Notice that critical mass depends on volunteering for *congregational mission*. Many members may be volunteering for other agencies. If the church is not actively deploying volunteers in mission, however, these members will drift away from regular worship and the church as a whole in order to be fulfilled in these other missions. There must be a direct link between the worship and educational life of the church and outreach.

There are different ways in which congregations engage in outreach. These include property rental to outside service agencies, raising money for outreach committee projects, giving grants to outreach agencies within or beyond the denomination, service on the boards of agencies, and hands-on participation. Property rental and fundraising do very little to sustain the vitality of the congregation. Members that serve on the boards of other agencies is a greater benefit, but it is still limited to a handful of people. The most effective way to sustain critical mass is to encourage members to "get their hands dirty" by directly volunteering their time, talent, and energy to mission.

The goal of a merger is to increase the pool of volunteers that participate in outreach ministries of the church. This is not about increasing financial giving to charitable causes, but about involving members personally in hands-on missions that bless the community. The expanded resources and expertise of the merged church provide better training, deeper friendships, and higher accountability, which are all necessary to motivate volunteers to step forward.

1 Major, Year-Round Outreach Focus or Signature Outreach Ministry for Which the Church Has a Public Reputation

The goal of a merger is to support and sustain a single, major outreach ministry that blesses nonmembers or strangers to grace.

Churches decline when they fritter away their money and energy on dozens of minor, short-term outreach projects; and they grow when they concentrate their money and energy on one major, ongoing outreach ministry.

Ironically, the more churches lose critical mass, the more they seem to diversify financial spending on various projects. They also tend to rent or donate their space to outside service agencies. They mistakenly believe this will increase their mission impact, when in fact it lessens impact and accelerates decline. These agencies soon learn that they cannot depend on the meager financial support of churches. They either take over the entire space in order to maintain it to their standards, or they move to more efficient space and leave the church empty once again. The church building may get a reputation as a community center, but the worshipping congregation ages and dies.

A signature outreach ministry emerges from the clarity of vision and mission purpose of the church. It is the one "big thing" for which the church is known. Just as your handwritten signature reveals your true personality, so also a signature outreach reveals the true personality of the church. It perfectly demonstrates the values and beliefs of the congregation. A large number of members participate in this signature outreach ministry in some way, at some time, every year.

The signature outreach ministry is a key to the public reputation of the church. People may not even know the church by name, but they know the outreach ministry: "Oh, *that's* the church that does that wonderful thing!" Sometimes this major outreach ministry becomes a separately incorporated nonprofit whose grants and public donations could benefit the church financially by offsetting overhead for staff, property, or technology housed in the church building.

The goal of a merger is to reduce the number of minor charities and limited projects and create instead a major ongoing outreach ministry that involves the enthusiastic participation of many members, deserves prayer and celebration in every worship service, and captures the attention and imagination of the public. More people connect with a church through outreach than by "church shopping" on Sunday morning. On the other hand, more visitors will return to worship again and again if they have been guided to participate in a significant outreach ministry that is highly beneficial and credible to their neighbors.

Pledging by Church Leaders That Is at Least 3 to 5% *Higher* Than the Average or Median Congregational Pledge

The goal of a merger is to gather core leaders who are willing to stake more on the church than the average member.

In order to sustain critical mass, the church must receive adequate financial support. In order to stimulate financial giving, the church must provide the right information. The trouble is that most churches provide *the wrong* information, which often includes a detailed financial statement, a detailed budget, a monthly or annual deficit, and a spreadsheet of actual percentage giving.

The truth is that none of this information answers the real question of church members. The real question they are asking is: *What are the leaders giving?* People will follow the leaders. The members won't increase their giving *some* unless the leaders increase their giving *more*. The members need to know what the leaders are ready to *stake* on the future of the church. They don't really need to know the details; they probably won't read them. And if they do read them, they probably won't understand them. They need to trust the leaders.

A church can be in serious financial straits, but, again, members will give more if the leaders give more. Conversely, a church can be financially well off, and the members will give less because the leaders give less. Leaders set the pace. If the leaders pledge 1%, many members will pledge less than 0.5% of the annual net income. If the leaders pledge 5% or 10% (a tithe), then members will pledge 3% or 6% (and will be willing to learn how to tithe).

It is not the *amount* that matters. It is the *risk* that matters. Affluent leaders may give large sums, but that represents very little personal risk. Poor leaders may give small sums, but that represents very high risks. Affluent leaders do not necessarily grow churches. In fact, less affluent leaders who are willing to stake larger percentages are more credible leaders. People follow credibility.

This does not mean that a church must publicize individual names, incomes, and percentages. It means that a church publicizes the average percentage giving of the leaders as a group. The rule of thumb is that leaders should pledge 3 to 5% higher than the average or median pledge of the congregation (whichever of these is higher). That sets the gold standard to which every member can compare his or her giving.

We already know that a goal of a merger is to gather a new board of spiritual leaders that are prepared to model and mentor the DNA of the new church. Commitment must be expanded to include staff (paid and unpaid, full-time and part-time, program staff and support staff) who are prepared to risk more for the sake of the church than the average member. A church merger takes work and sacrifice. Leaders need to believe in the church and work harder than ever to make the merger work. One practical and visible way to do that is to expect a higher than average financial commitment to the church.

An Intentional, Year-Round Stewardship Plan with Multiple Choices, and Optional Coaching for Christian Financial Planning

> *The goal of a merger is to develop an intentional stewardship strategy that will tap the real financial potential of the members and the community.*

There was a time when churches didn't really need a financial plan. Everybody went to church or thought the church was a good thing. The church was the most effective charitable organization in town, and church members all wanted a tax credit for their donations. All the church needed to do was disseminate information about annual expenses and projected budgets. The money would flow, and everyone would praise God on a Sunday. Done.

Those days are over, but it is surprising how many churches don't know it. Many churches don't really have a plan at all and are constantly surprised (and discouraged) by sudden shortfalls. Other churches have only a seasonal stewardship plan (usually in the fall) that sneaks up on them, precipitating a scramble to organize, preach, and communicate in a small window of opportunity squeezed between the close of summer vacation (which happens later and later) and the start of Christmas shopping (which starts earlier and earlier).

The stewardship plan needs to be intentional. A designated core of leaders gives it their complete attention, plans ahead for each stage, and prays for its success. The leaders understand that stewardship is really a spiritual discernment process that has a financial outcome.

The stewardship plan must be annual. It should actually begin in January with a leadership retreat that has personal risk management and strategic planning priorities and resource needs on the agenda, and probably a keynote speaker on Christian family financial planning. There may be seminars in the spring on family debt-relief and tithing, and a May fundraising campaign solely to support mission projects by asking the congregation to tithe tax refunds. The summer may begin with a special dinner for the top givers in the church, to update them on future ministry opportunities and needs; include a summer meditation guide on spiritual life and service; and maybe end with special fundraising events.

In an annual stewardship plan, handouts are photocopied, teams are trained, and sermon series are prepared *before* the busy time of September. The fall stewardship campaign begins with volunteer appreciation and includes advanced pledging by leaders to underwrite the budget. By the time members receive pledge cards or personal visits, they already know how much the leaders have risked, what opportunities and challenges lie ahead, and how effective the church is. All that's left is to celebrate in November, send thank you cards in December—and start all over again in January.

The stewardship plan must offer choices. Different people absorb financial information, and make financial commitments, in different ways. People need options to digest information, designate their giving, and make their payments. Some need data; others need stories. Some want to read about it; others want to talk about it. Some preauthorize giving; others send checks or cash.

Finally, any effective stewardship plan today must include optional coaching for Christian financial planning. Many lifestyle segments today are over their heads in debt and couldn't manage their way out of a cardboard box. They are certainly paralyzed when it comes to giving to the church. Before they can even think about giving 5% of their net income to the church, they have to figure out how to reduce interest payments that are 15% and higher. More and more resources are developed to help good people think clearly.

The goal of a merger is to develop and implement a realistic financial plan to sustain and grow the church. The first step will be to gather objective information on the giving potential of the community in order to dispel that "perception of poverty" that is prevalent in many aging, declining churches. Church people say that they are too poor to increase giving even though they have significant disposable income for extended vacations, entertainment, and other personal activities. Similarly, church people often generalize a perception of poverty onto the entire community, often because they are preoccupied with people below the poverty line and judgmental toward people who are wealthier than they are.

Nonprofit organizations set realistic fundraising targets because they have demographic information that reveals the true giving potential of a community. Churches must do the same.

1 Regular, Affordable, Accessible Location

The goal of a merger is to gather the members of several different churches at one location that is effective for mission.

The last thing to consider for critical mass is the location, affordability, and accessibility of the facility that will be the focal point of congregational gatherings and the launching pad for congregational ministries. Although the facility is important, notice that it is the *last* thing on the agenda for critical mass. Unfortunately, it is often the *first* thing on the agenda of a merger conversation. The truth is that if all the other criteria for critical mass are met, then the church can sustain itself in temporary, basic, or even broken-down space for long periods of time. If the other criteria are not met, the church will die inside a lovely mausoleum with a manicured front lawn.

In the short term, a church can sustain itself and grow in temporary, even changeable, facilities. In the long term, however, rental facilities do not sustain a church, for various reasons:

- First, members and potential new members need a stable place to meet, plan, and celebrate. The last thing you want is for potential visitors to wonder where you are located this month.
- Second, members will tire of setting up and taking down seating, technology, portable symbols, classrooms, and all the space and stuff needed for Sunday morning. Members will also grow tired of hosting or visiting private homes for all of the work and ministry, and members with physical limitations will hesitate to participate in programs that may or may not be accessible.
- Third (and perhaps most importantly), rented space makes the church vulnerable in the emerging secular world. The church is now a minority that is often treated with skepticism if not hostility. A church cannot afford to make its worship and mission hostage to a landlord who may not respect the values, beliefs, policies, and missions of the church, or who can get more money from quieter, more respectable tenants. Many school boards and other publicly owned facilities no longer rent to religious groups because it is just too controversial. A

church in the postmodern world must have control over its life and mission.

The location, floor plan, and technologies of a facility are entirely dependent on the needs and expectations of the mission field. They should not be dependent on the tastes, personal preferences, and sacred cows of church members. In a merger, the issue of critical mass and property is resolved by understanding the mission field, and not by negotiating compromises among participating churches.

The goal of a merger is to bring everyone together. The merger cannot spiritually sustain and cannot financially afford one congregation worshipping in multiple locations. Moreover, the facility must be evaluated for its effectiveness in reaching the surrounding mission field, and not for its effectiveness in preserving memories. Sometimes the merged church can use one of the properties of the former congregations, but often none of the old facilities will serve and the merged church will move to an entirely new facility.

Earlier, we pointed out that loss of critical momentum inevitably leads to loss of critical mass. However, once critical mass is explained, it should be apparent that understanding problems in critical mass provides clues to understanding gaps in critical momentum. Leaders start asking the right questions: *How do we regain critical mass? How do we get moving? How do we make a difference in the world?*

How to Get Traction   **23**

> *The goal of a merger is to regain the traction that gets the church moving.*

Imagine a bus that is stopped and stranded on the side of the road. The drivers of passing cars probably wonder what went wrong. Did the bus run out of gas? Is there a flat tire? Did the engine fail? In the same way, many institutional churches have stopped and are stranded beside the road of God's mission. The public walks by the deserted church building and the empty parking lot, and wonders what happened. Christians visit the church, observe the empty pews, the aging members, the diminishing volunteers, the disused rooms, and the growing budget deficits, and they wonder what happened.

It is true enough that we live in challenging times. Church leaders may use various criteria, but most would agree that active church members are now a minority in North America, along with many other religious minorities, and are surrounded by an indifferent or suspicious consumer public. However, using hard times as an excuse to stop working and cancel the journey of faith would be like a bus driver using bad roads as an excuse for cancelling the trip. Yes, the roads are bumpier than ever before, but other buses are finding a way to keep going. Yes, culture is more challenging than ever before, but other churches are finding a way to maintain forward movement.

Figure 23.1 captures the essentials of forward movement. Color the bus any denominational tint that you want. Let it be brand new with shiny paint or ancient with lots of rust. Let it be big or small. Maybe it

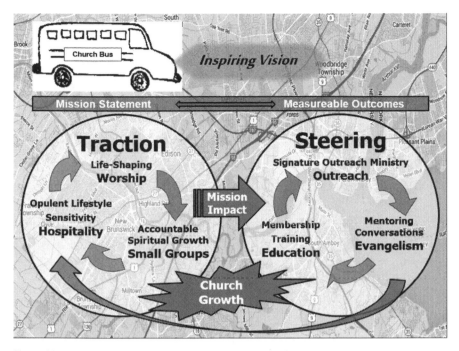

Figure 23.1.

is equipped with padded seats and all the latest technologies, or stripped down to the bare frame without air conditioning or heat. All that matters is that the bus moves forward.

A good mechanic will have diagrams for the various systems of a motor vehicle posted on the wall of his or her workshop. Not only will it help the mechanic remember which parts go where and how they are connected to each other, but it will keep the mechanic focused on the essential tasks that will get this vehicle on the road again. Faithful church leaders will have such a diagram on the wall of their office for the same reason. It will help them remember which parts go where, and how they are connected, and what should result if essential systems are working well together.

One of the first questions in a merger must be: *How will we get traction?* Eventually we will also have to consider where we're going, how we will sustain direction, and who will be driving. Yet it is a mistake to debate those questions first. If you can't get the wheels to grip the road to mission in the first place, all else is moot.

Traction is the action of the rear wheels of a bus (or any other motor vehicle) gripping the highway to move the vehicle forward. When the bus

Figure 23.2.

loses traction, the wheels may spin, but the bus doesn't go anywhere. At best, there is a lot of smoke and a bad smell of burning rubber.

Traction for a church is achieved by the actions of inclusivity, spirituality, and intimacy spinning around an axis (or "axle") of profound trust (see figure 23.2). If any of these activities are ineffective, or if the axis of trust breaks down, the wheels spin but produce no forward movement. At best there is a great deal of smoke arising from conflict, or there is a terrible stink of hypocrisy.

Inclusivity

Inclusivity means that the church aggressively and sensitively reaches out to include all the different lifestyle segments in its primary mission field (roughly defined by the average distance people in the region drive to work or shop).

Effective church mergers radicalize hospitality to welcome and include the demographic and lifestyle diversity of the surrounding communities.

Faithful churches in the Christendom era were shaped around homogeneity; but faithful churches in the post-Christendom world are shaped around heterogeneity. The church strives to mirror the demographic and lifestyle diversity of the mission field. The proportionate representation of lifestyle segments in the membership mirrors the proportionate representation of lifestyles in the surrounding neighborhoods.

Inclusivity is best revealed through *radical hospitality*. Proportionate lifestyle representation in the community determines how hospitality ministries in the church are trained and deployed. When lifestyle segments represented in the church are *disproportionately larger* than the representation in the community, then hospitality ministries favor insiders more than outsiders. Visitors may expect a hearty welcome and a gift, but members only offer a distant handshake and ask for money. People in the community may appreciate great coffee and a variety of excellent fresh food choices, but members settle for instant coffee and packaged cookies.

Yet hospitality is not just about tactics. And the real concern for "traction" is not about the specific tactics of greeting or food service, but the larger goal of inclusivity. Churches only "move forward" if they not only welcome newcomers with acceptance and respect, but also if they proactively go out to meet seekers where they are, with compassion and generosity. Inclusivity eliminates the barriers between "insiders" and "outsiders."

Paradoxically, churches often merge for reasons of exclusivity rather than inclusivity. They share a *selective dislike* for certain lifestyle segments, rather than a *general compassion* for all lifestyle segments. These mergers eventually fail for two reasons. First, they fail because they must continually expand their geographic reach in order to filter sufficient numbers of the *same kind of people* to sustain the institution—and every traffic light and gasoline pump increase defeat their purpose. Second, they fail because emerging generations value inclusivity, rather than exclusivity, as a sign of integrity. Exclusive churches, no matter how often they merge or how large they might become, are simply not respected.

Inclusivity is a much stronger foundation for a successful church merger. Two or more churches discover that their notions of radical hospitality are basically the same. Their ambitions to bless specific lifestyle segments are essentially compatible. Their merger enhances what each party is already striving to accomplish. The open door to public participation does not close. It does not even narrow. It opens even wider to invite new people.

Effective church mergers do whatever it takes to bring people into the life-changing presence of Jesus Christ.

Spirituality

These days the term *spirituality* can mean almost anything from the supernatural to the sentimental. The essence of spirituality, however, is "ecstasy," which literally means "standing outside yourself." The church helps people step away from their ordinary world of struggle and anxiety, and into a world of hope and joy. The former experience is "mundane" or "secular"; the latter experience is "special" and "sacred."

Ecstatic experience in the church only contributes to "traction," however, it empowers people to return to ordinary life with renewed hope. Spirituality is not really about weird and wonderful experiences, but about hope in everyday life. Every lifestyle segment, and indeed every human being, is beset by chronic and occasionally acute anxieties about emptiness, meaninglessness, fate, death, guilt, shame, and alienation. They may feel lost, lonely, trapped, dying, broken, abused, and discarded. Ecstatic experience lets them step out of life to find grace; and then to step back into life newly empowered.[1]

Spirituality (ecstatic experience) is best revealed in a church through worship. Inclusivity draws people to ecstasy. Radical hospitality draws people into worship. Each lifestyle segment or each person experiences grace and finds hope in unique ways. Worship can be designed to target unique anxieties, create opportunities to receive grace in a special way, and empower people to return to the world equipped for the struggle. Churches understand this as an experience of "incarnation" in which individuals encounter the real presence of Jesus Christ.

Traction is not gained simply by using different tactics in worship. It is gained by aligning tactics to deliver mission purpose. First the church must decide the *purpose* of worship that is most relevant to the particular publics they yearn to bless. Then the church initiates, develops, or perfects the tactics that will accomplish the mission. Everything about liturgy and preaching style, music and instrumentation, and media and décor will be decided based on mission effectiveness.

Paradoxically, churches often merge because church insiders have similar tastes for worship tactics, and not because they have similar mission goals for worship. The merger conversation is a prolonged negotiation about preferred liturgy, preaching styles, musical genres, seating, and artistic nuances that make worship comfortable and familiar for the largest number of current church members. These mergers eventually fail. They struggle for the same reason that any other entertainment venue struggles: because the church strives to please itself rather than bless strangers to grace.

Successful mergers focus on common goals for worship. Which lifestyle segments will participate? What chronic and acute anxieties will be addressed? What blessings will be most visible? Success does not depend on the favorite tactics people want to keep, but the urgent blessings people yearn to give away.

> **Effective church mergers help Christians build their spiritual lives around intimacy with each other and God.**

Intimacy

Intimacy means that people are going ever deeper in their trusted relationships with one another. People do not have to agree about every idea or public policy, but they do have to bond together in mutual support. Intimacy is achieved through a blend of humility, compassion, and conversation. The evolution of intimacy is guided by three personal affirmations:

- Life and faith are mysteries, and I don't have all the answers.
- I care deeply about others and want to help them live in health and hope.
- I will listen and learn before I speak and teach.

Genuine intimacy will not happen if you believe you already have all the answers, if you really don't care that others live healthy and hopeful lives, or if you are unprepared to listen and learn.

These three elements for intimacy are the same for the spiritual life: *humilitas, humanitas,* and *conversatio.* The spiritual life generates intimacy with God. The genuine seeker accepts the limitations of the human mind and experience, on the one hand, and the vast mystery of God and the universe that surrounds them and escapes total comprehension, on the other. The seeker practices mercy, forgiveness, and encouragement to live well as means to encounter the divine in other people. The seeker prioritizes silence over speech and is constantly learning and growing.

Ecstasy motivates intimacy. The church gains "traction" because worship motivates people into small groups. Small-group experience is different from modern Christian education because the focus is on intimacy rather than information. Small groups are intentionally designed for both "horizontal" intimacy with others, and "vertical" intimacy with God. A small group may gather around any number of affinities or activities, but the three principles of intimacy (humility, compassion, and conversation) provide the real structure of a small group. This is why the leader of a small group functions more as a host and spiritual guide than as a manager and teacher.

Paradoxically, most churches often merge in order to avoid intimacy rather than to nurture intimacy. They focus on *agreement* rather than intimacy. The conversation about merger is often dominated by debates over doctrinal interpretation, biblical authority, or public policy. Hundreds of years of failed ecumenical dialogue highlight the dangers of this confusion. Even churches of the same tradition or denomination find it difficult to gain intellectual agreement in theology or ethics.

Mergers may actually be based on agreement over a particular point of view about policy or dogma. Such mergers are incredibly fragile, because a church based on intellectual assent will inevitably encourage splits based on intellectual dissent.

Successful mergers are based on a quest for intimacy that goes far beyond the mere "friendliness" of which so many churches boast. Merger is not about preserving old friendship circles or providing comfortable space and time for people to catch up with one another or chat about common interests. It is really about readiness to make new friendships, explore new depths of vulnerability and support in old friendships, and forge bonds of respect with people who are outside our normal circles of acquaintance. This becomes the vehicle to experience God in fresh and unexpected ways.

Imagine the forward progress of a motor vehicle. The church is like a bus. Traction is gained as people spin round and round the cycle of inclusivity, ecstasy, and intimacy. We visualize this more practically in the church institution as the continuous movement of people from *radical hospitality*, to *life shaping worship*, and *healthy intimacy*—and back again to *radical hospitality*. The more you "rev up" this movement, the better the church grips the road to mission, and the faster it moves forward.

Effective church mergers hold members accountable to a high standard of trust.

The axle on which the wheel turns is a community of high trust. Every spoke of the wheel—and every member of the church—is linked to that axle. The foundation of trust is a combination of two things.[2]

First, there is general consensus about core values. These are not abstract ideals or public policies, but the positive behavior patterns expected in both the intentional and spontaneous behavior of church members in everyday living. Think of these as the *fruits of the Spirit* that make church people behave differently from secular society.

Second, there is a general consensus about bedrock beliefs. These are not dogmas or doctrines, but convictions to which church members can be expected to return for strength in times of trouble, confusion, or stress. Think of these as essential truths that guide decisions and ground perseverance in ambiguous situations or desperate times.

High trust occurs when the church generates a culture of accountability around core values and bedrock beliefs. Accountability permeates the organization among paid staff and volunteers, from the Sunday school and the choir to the finance committee and the ushers. Everyone models the values and beliefs. Every leader is routinely evaluated to live up to the values and beliefs. Since we are all human and make mistakes, everyone needs forgiveness but will resolve to behave better and live with more integrity in the future.

The culture of accountability is the exact opposite of a culture of judgment. Judgmental organizations emerge when the community of faith lives in a fog about core values and bedrock beliefs, and there is an absence of routine evaluation among staff and volunteers. The void is filled by intimidating personalities or egocentric individuals that impose their personal tastes, preferences, opinions, or priorities as the norm for everyone else. A culture of judgment shapes the church around a handful of controlling bullies. A culture of accountability frees the church from the power of bullies, and evaluates everyone based on mutual expectations of Christlike behavior and Christ-centered convictions.

This, then, is the "axle" or "hub" around which the "rear wheels" gain traction. Inclusivity, spirituality, and intimacy rotate around trust. Hospitality, worship, and small groups spin round and round this axis of accountability.

Paradoxically, many church mergers are the end result of breakdowns in trust, rather than high trust. These are often churches that have recently experienced conflict. Churches come to merger because broken trust has shattered pastoral relationships or split the church. The merger is often driven by controlling interests or intimidating personalities that are actually pursuing their personal agendas in the name of Christ. Yet two or more churches with low trust always generate a merged church with even lower trust, and the merger will ultimately fail.

In a successful merger, the individual parties are all clear about the core values and bedrock beliefs that form the foundation of trust in their unique faith community. They already try to generate a culture of accountability, and have already sustained a safe environment in which members and strangers can mingle with clear boundaries and no bullying. The merger expands and nuances the consensus of core values and beliefs as it continues the culture of accountability.

Torque

Traction generates "torque," which is the transfer of energy from the rear wheels to the front wheels. A TV commercial for heavy-duty trucks emphasizes torque, saying that if you only want a truck to carry a few people to deliver pizzas around the block, you don't need much torque. But if you want a truck to carry heavy loads a long distance over difficult terrain, then you need as much torque as you can get.

The same is true for churches—and church mergers. If you only expect the merger to support a few members—to preserve shared comfort zones for a few more years before they die—then you don't need much torque or traction. You only need a light-duty axle that won't be required to bear much stress. You can settle for exclusive hospitality and enjoyable worship that will powerfully motivate participants to go home to lunch. Any stress in congregational life can be resolved with a potluck supper.

But if you expect more from a merger, the plan is different. If you expect the merger to support a growing community of faith, shape lives and lifestyles through encounters with the Holy, and constantly deepen relationships with both friends and strangers in every stage and age of life, then you need lots of torque. You need major traction. You need a heavy-duty axle that will bear the weight of inevitable stress, and keep going despite disagreements.

Torque for the institutional church is what we call *mission impact*. Most churches focus on the *content* of faith and the *practice* of faith, but they ignore the vital issue of the *impact* of faith. They welcome people in hospitality, bless them in worship—and then sidetrack them into committees. The result is that church members understand their faith and serve the church, but they fail to change the world. *Impact* is that tangible, measurable force that pulls heavy loads, bears increasing stress, and *gets the job done.*

The obsession with the *content* and *practice* of faith, and general indifference to the *impact* of faith, is what causes church decline in the first place. Therefore, the conversation about church merger must focus primarily on the *impact* of faith and less on the *content* or *practice* of faith. What, exactly, is the job to be done? How, exactly, will the world or our neighborhood be any different because we continue to exist?

These questions are only answered as we rev up the traction of inclusivity, spirituality, and intimacy. The more effectively churches facilitate this movement of hospitality, worship, and small groups around the axis of high trust, the more church members become sensitive to the needs of God's world and urgent about participating in God's mission. A merger is successful not because people want to preserve a tradition, but because they want *to make a difference.* Yes, their tradition can help them make a difference, but institutional success depends on the latter rather than the former.

Just as marriage partners can bring complementary gifts to a healthy marriage, so also can individual churches bring complementary strengths to a successful merger. One church may be better at hospitality, worship, or small groups than another church, but together they can generate more traction through the combination of their resources and abilities. No individual church has the critical mass of resource, participation, or talent to rev up the process of inclusivity, spirituality, or intimacy; but merged churches can do it together. This assumes, of course, that they can build a foundation of trust and commit to a culture of accountability that will carry a heavy load long distances, across the rough terrain of future mission.

In a motor vehicle, torque specifically transfers energy to rotate the wheels. In a church, the energy from the spiritual formation process is transferred to mission outreach. "Disciples" become "apostles": Those who have been blessed become agents of blessing.

Of course, if the process of spiritual formation weakens, the energy for outreach sputters. The more the rear wheels spin (lose traction), the less outreach is generated. The church not only loses momentum, but also loses any sense of direction. Outreach tends to occur in fits and starts, reacting primarily to unexpected emergencies or the sudden personal passions of individual members. Churches tend to slow down to a crawl or precipitously speed up. The church also wanders down the highway, swerves across lanes, plunges down side roads leading in the wrong direction, and eventually hits a tree.

Unfortunately, many churches wait too long to consider merger. They are already swerving recklessly across the lanes of the road to mission, or they are already dangerously off course, either of which makes merger incredibly difficult.

In the classic 1969 version of the movie *The Italian Job,* starring Michael Caine, there is a scene in which three Mini Coopers weave in and out of the alleys and sewers of Turin, narrowly missing obstacles and pedestrians, escaping the police at high speed. Later, each speeding vehicle hides from capture by dashing up the ramp of a moving truck to come to a screeching halt. In the background is a male chorus singing the jaunty verses of "We Are the Self-Preservation Society."

That is like the experience of merger for many churches. The movie scenes required expert stunt drivers to do the daring deeds. Churches imagine that they can do something similar with volunteer boards and clergy who were never trained to lead mergers in seminary. Such churches are like Mini Coopers veering down the road, narrowly missing obstacles and pedestrians, desperately hoping that they can find some larger ecclesiastical "truck" into which they can all dash to safety. And yes, they are all singing a song similar to "We Are the Self-Preservation Society"!

How to Steer in the Right Direction   **24**

The goal of a merger is to steer the church in the right direction.

Imagine that the bus that was stranded by the side of the road has now got traction and is moving again. All the passengers are cheering as the bus enters the stream of traffic on the road to mission. But then the bus driver begins changing lanes unexpectedly, drives erratically, takes the wrong exits, tries to negotiate low bridges, and winds up on dead-end streets. The public sees the bus go by and asks: *Where in the world are they going?*

Any Christians who happen to visit a church that is steered in the same manner will ask: *Who is driving that "bus" anyway?!* All the torque in the world will only lead to disaster if you aren't able to steer in the right direction. (Recall the bus in figure 23.1.)

Steering is the action of the front wheels of a motor vehicle that guides the vehicle forward. Steering is not only about aiming the vehicle in the right direction, but also monitoring speed and compensating for oncoming traffic and emerging obstacles. When a vehicle loses steering, it swerves across the highway, runs the risk of accidents, and fails to arrive at its destination.

Steering for a church is achieved by the actions of training, blessing, and mentoring as they spin around the axis (or "axle") of leadership accountability. (See figure 24.1.) If any of these activities are ineffective, or if the axis of leadership accountability breaks down, the wheels spin out of control. At best there is a terrible noise of screeching parishioners and a scramble of innocent pedestrians.

Figure 24.1.

If the rotation of the "rear wheels" works efficiently, then inclusivity, spirituality, and intimacy will generate passionate, urgent, driving energy to train, bless, and mentor. Translate this into more familiar, programmatic terms. The movement of radical hospitality, life-shaping worship, and spiritual growth through small groups generates an urgent need for Christian education or training . . . that equips social action to bless the world . . . that provides opportunities to mentor seekers in Christian faith.

Effective church mergers must emphasize the Christian formation of adults and training for leaders.

Any church that is serious about *movement*—and any churches seriously considering merger—must recapture the original purpose of Christian education. The original goals of education were to mature seekers in Christian faith and equip disciples for Christian mission.

This purpose was gradually eroded in the post Christendom world. And this has made it increasingly difficult for leaders to steer the church into the future. Three things have caused the church to lose steering.

First, Christian education has become a program primarily for children that effectively ended with membership. Once teenagers finished catechism or confirmation and were received into full communion or membership, they were not really expected to do any further intentional Christian development. The adults or parents are supposed to model continuous learning and daily devotional disciplines for children, and this has become increasingly rare.

Steering primarily depends on adult Christian education. Church governance, stewardship, and outreach only work if the core membership of adults is spiritually mature and striving for spiritual growth. Today only a small percentage of adults engage in any serious, ongoing, practice of education. Churches struggle to elect boards, who struggle to make faithful decisions. Churches struggle to raise money, with many adults giving less than 1% of their net income to the church. Churches fail to multiply volunteers, leaving 20% of the members to do 80% of the work.

Second, Christian education has become a program to satisfy curiosity or communicate political and ideological correctness. What little adult education exists is usually designed to acquire historical and sociological information, or explore alternative theologies and religions. It is also designed to address "hot" ethical issues, and indoctrinate participants in whatever point of view the denomination or clergy consider to be correct.

But steering depends on depth and breadth, not curiosities and issues. You can satisfy your curiosity about the engineering specs, and you can form an opinion about driving standards, but that doesn't mean you can actually drive the open road. You can have a PhD in Biblical Studies and set policy on ethical dilemmas, but that doesn't mean you can guide church through the complexities of the mission field.

Third, Christian education has become a process of social assimilation and conflict mediation. It is individually and organizationally therapeutic. Individuals can explore their personality type, and groups can resolve their differences. Harmony is preserved, and new members can adjust to the hidden values, local customs, and denominational expectations of the congregation.

Yet steering depends less on helping people "fit in," and more on helping people "step up." The future of the church depends on volunteers discerning their calling, vocation, personal mission, or place in God's plan. Discernment may actually increase friction within the body of the congregation. Yet the alignment between the individual calling of leaders, and the mission purpose of the church, must be perfect.

The original understanding of Christian education was to be engaged in intensive training. Paul compares it to athletic training (1 Corinthians 9:24–26, Philippians 2:16, Hebrews 12:1–3). It is a discipline that builds muscle, sharpens awareness, and equips the "athlete" to run the race and win the prize. It is primarily an *adult* regimen; it concentrates on a deeper understanding of planning, organization, and empowerment, and a broader sensitivity to emerging opportunities and obstacles; and it results in clarity about one's place in God's larger plan to bless and redeem the world.

> **Effective church mergers focus their energy on blessing a particular group of people outside the church membership in a very big way.**

Congregations find their way into the future because their heart bursts for people other than themselves. Imagine traveling in a vehicle in which the driver was constantly turning around to talk to the people at the rear of the bus, instead of paying attention to the road ahead. Also imagine a busload of passengers who were so intent on talking among themselves that they never looked out the windows. The bus could go around in circles and arrive at the same place from which they started—and no one would ever know!

That, of course, is what frequently happens with church mergers. Congregations are so obsessed with themselves and their survival that the merger simply returns them to where they had been—the situation in which they had previously declined. The process of decline will simply start all over again, because nothing has really changed. Such a merger simply postpones inevitable closure.

The problem is not solved just by admitting new people onto the bus; and church decline is not reversed by simply adding a few new people to membership each year. It is the fundamental "attitude of inwardness" that has to change. The church must learn to bless other people without any expectations of organizational rewards. There can be no strings attached. The act of blessing is an act of generosity, plain and simple. We do not bless people in order to receive a financial return, add volunteers to our programs, boost the careers of the clergy, or boast a broader influence in the community. We do it simply because we love those people out there, regardless of their mode of spiritual transportation.

Many churches make the mistake of blessing people through "random acts of kindness." They use up precious resources of volunteer time and energy, and organizational money and technology, spraying the mission field with minor generosities. Everybody gets a little, but nobody ever gets enough. This causes the church to lose its sense of direction. It is as if the bus zigzagged across an open field or turned down every side road, wandering all over the place, never arriving anywhere in particular, and ultimately losing any sense of direction.

The best strategy for a growing church—and especially for a church merger—is to target its outreach very carefully. Prayerfully discern the lifestyle segments for which your heart bursts; and strategically focus your resources to deliver the maximum impact for positive change. The best rationale for a merger is that the combined resources of multiple churches will exponentially increase outreach impact. By targeting a particular public, and meeting a specific need, the church knows exactly where it is going and what it will do when it gets there. It can focus on a specific result and even measure its progress to achieve it.

Effective mergers require a unity of purpose—a single-minded target—and a common heartburst. They concentrate their energy for a single, major, ongoing, outreach ministry that will have enormous and lasting impact to bless people beyond their congregations. This great philanthropic project concentrates on one of seven major outreach goals,[1] as shown in table 24.1.

Every lifestyle segment is primarily concerned with one or two of these needs. The church focuses on *those others'* needs rather the needs of the membership. It sacrifices its own sense of privilege for the sake of strangers to grace. It does not connect with the public in order to *use* the public for its own institutional needs, but in order to *bless* the public even at the sacrifice of its institutional comforts.

Random acts of kindness do not bring lasting positive change to a neighborhood, community, or mission field. Real change requires *deliberate* acts of kindness. Churches intentionally and strategically concentrate their resources to bring lasting change. This is why mergers today are often built around a signature outreach ministry that is a separately incorporated, faith-based, nonprofit organization. The merged church develops a 501(c)3 charitable organization that is governed by its own board. It functions according to the core values and bedrock beliefs of the church.

Table 24.1.   Lifestyle Preferences to Receive and/or Share Outreach

Survival	Focus on basic needs for food, shelter, clothing, employment, and basic health care. Often related to food banks, shelters, recycling, job placement, and medical clinics.
Recovery	Focus on addiction intervention, twelve-step support, and counseling. Often addresses addictions (alcohol, drugs, tobacco, gambling, pornography, etc.).
Health	Focus on mental and physical fitness, disease prevention, healing and rehabilitation, and therapy. Often related to counseling, healing therapies, diet/exercise disciplines.
Quality of Life	Focus on social well-being. Often related to crime prevention, safety, immigration, environment, conflict intervention, advocacy against violence, and peace.
Human Potential	Focus on personal/vocational fulfillment, education, and human rights. Often includes schools, training, career counseling, and intervention against discrimination.
Interpersonal Relationships	Focus on family life, marriage, sexuality, and healthy friendships. Often includes marriage counseling and enrichment, divorce counseling, parenting counseling and training, and advocacy for nontraditional relationships.
Human Destiny	Focus on repentance, conversion, stewardship, and alignment with God's purposes. Often includes revivals, witnessing, canvassing, Bible distribution, and prayer chains.

As a signature reveals the personality of an individual, so also the outreach ministry reveals the identity of the church. It establishes the reputation of the church in the community.

Many church members are personally volunteering in the outreach ministry. Prayers for the outreach ministry, and stories of positive change in the community are routinely shared in weekly worship. Financial donations to the church increase, not because people love the institution itself, but because people love the mission results that the institution accomplishes. The church itself has a practical, concrete purpose for which there are measurable results. It knows where it is going.

Effective church mergers not only share their hope, but also mentor seekers and believers to go ever deeper into faith.

Social action and evangelism are two sides of the same coin. Effective churches never do good work without sharing their faith motivation for doing it; and they never share their faith without doing good work. They know that the public is very suspicious of "do-gooders." The public will want to know why these church people are so generous, and will want reassurances that there are no hidden agendas or expectations in return. Social action brings lasting change because faith is part of the gift—perhaps even the most important part of the gift.

Remember this old saw: *Give hungry people a fish and feed them for a day; teach them to fish and they can feed themselves for a lifetime.* Churches understand that there is a third step. *Give hungry people a reason to hope, and they can endure a season of bad fishing.* Hope is really what outreach is all about. And hope must be communicated by word as well as deed.

Churches find their way into the future because they are just as intentional about giving people *hope* as they are about giving people *help*. Evangelism is not about handing out tracts, preaching on street corners, or confrontational advertising. It is simply about sincere conversation. Volunteers who are doing good work build relationships of trust, talk confidently about their beliefs, and share their reasons for hope in a troubled world. Hope is more important than doctrine. Relationship is more important than conversion.

This is why the activity we historically call "evangelism" is best understood as a process of mentoring. Mentoring relationships emerge from doing good work. People bond, talk, and share with one another. Churches with a clear sense of direction talk about their faith journey. They share where they have come from and where they are going. They confess their own life struggles, but can also talk about their spiritual victories. A mentor is just a pilgrim who is a bit farther down the road of faith, but has doubled back to help someone else behind him or her, or has paused to help someone who is stuck along the way.[2]

The best mentors are volunteers—not paid staff. The training that matured adults through Christian education and deployed volunteers in Christian service now equips them for Christian conversation. Volunteers are more authentic as mentors than clergy or other paid staff. They do not share life struggles and spiritual victories because they are obliged to do so, but because they want to do so. They are not theologians—just laity. They are ordinary people who risk rejection or ridicule simply because they love a stranger like their own brother or sister. They do not know everything, and do not claim to have all the answers. But they do know *something*, and they are willing to share that secret so others might live well.

Effective church mergers hold leaders accountable to a high standard of behavior and performance.

Once again, imagine the forward progress of a motor vehicle. The church is like a bus. Traction is gained as people spin round and round the cycle of inclusivity, spirituality, and intimacy. In practice, this means there is continuous movement as people cycle through radical hospitality, life-shaping worship, and small groups. Traction turns on an axle of trust, which generates the torque that transfers energy to the front wheels.

Steering is gained as people spin round and round the cycle of training, blessing, and mentoring. In practice, this means there is a continuous movement of people cycling through training, outreach, and evangelism. The axle around which this movement occurs is leadership accountability.

Clearly the axle of trust that gives a church traction and the axle of accountability that gives a church direction, are related. Accountability is *applied* trust. Leaders and volunteers hold one another accountable for the core values and bedrock beliefs that are the consensus of the church. Add in accountability for aligning all programs and ministries with the vision of the church and for prioritizing all programs and ministries to accomplish the mission of the church. All paid and unpaid leaders are hired (acquired), trained, evaluated, and if necessary fired (dismissed) using the same four criteria.[3]

Table 24.2 shows four keys to accountability that, when used consistently and universally through the church, give rise to a culture of accountability. Accountability is what comes naturally to the organization.

Too many churches fail to generate a culture of accountability. Some ignore it altogether. They allow the whims of individuals to change the priorities of the church, accept bad behavior from leaders and members without comment, accept mediocrity in program implementation without trying to improve skills, and even encourage a handful of individuals to burn themselves out doing all the work. Other churches practice account-

Table 24.2.   The Four Keys to Leadership Credibility

Attitude	Perfect alignment of job description or committee mandate with the vision and mission of the church.
Integrity	Routine modeling and articulating of the core values and bedrock beliefs of the church in both rehearsed and unrehearsed words; planned and spontaneous actions.
Competency	High standards of excellence to accomplish work that achieves the results that are used by the church to measure success.
Teamwork	Compatibility among staff and volunteers to work together in mutually supportive, respectful, and effective ways to get maximum mission results.

ability inconsistently. They are rigorous in their dealings with some people (usually those who are new or poorly connected members), and overly tolerant of other people (usually veterans or well-connected members). They are overly demanding in some programs (often related to music and children's ministries) and overly lenient in other programs (often hospitality and outreach ministries).

It is difficult for a "high accountability" church to merge with a "low accountability" church. It is difficult for churches that are indifferent or sporadic about accountability to merge as well. Their hidden habits of privilege and power take a long time to learn, and the journey toward unity is constantly hampered by unexpected quarrels over even the smallest issues. On the other hand, it is possible for a "high accountability" church to *absorb* a "low accountability" church, but only if the weaker church is willing to embrace the higher expectations of the stronger church.

The biggest benefit of a culture of accountability is that it raises the credibility of a church in the community. Breakdowns in accountability exponentially decrease inclusivity. It can take years to build up trust and confidence among publics that are essentially skeptical of organized religion, but it can all be lost in an instant because of some spontaneous deed or unrehearsed word that betrays attitude, integrity, competency, or teamwork. Mistakes happen. We are all sinners. The culture of accountability does not eliminate that. However, it does ensure that breaches in accountability will be rapidly, consistently, and urgently addressed. The church can be expected to take action to protect its reputation in the community.

Thrust

The traction of the rear wheels creates torque. The effectiveness of inclusivity (radical hospitality), spirituality (life-shaping worship), and intimacy (small groups) is measured by the weight of responsibility the organization can bear and the drive to advance God's mission in the world.

The steering of the front wheels creates *thrust*. The effectiveness of training (Christian education), blessing (targeted outreach), and mentoring (relational evangelism) is measured by the power and speed of the organization as it addresses or impacts the mission field. Thrust overcomes the "drag" of the institutional infrastructure. Most churches carry the weight of fixed costs for property and technology, personnel, insurance, civic or denominational taxes, and other aspects of institutional life. These all tend to "drag" the church back to a state of inertia.

As a church effectively connects training, blessing, and mentoring, the church creates thrust that overcomes the unavoidable drag of the institution. The mission moves forward, relying on the torque gained by the effectiveness of inclusivity, ecstasy, and intimacy. It's not that the institution or infrastructure is bad. After all, it is the "container" that carries the weight of increasing numbers of faithful disciples. The bus may weigh several tons, but the thrust generated by training, blessing, and mentoring overcomes inertia to maximize mission.

Trouble arises when small churches can no longer generate the thrust that overcomes the drag. In the absence of a culture of accountability, the cycle of training, blessing, and mentoring breaks down. Everyone becomes obsessed with just keeping the doors open, the heating bills paid, and the clergy retained full-time. The property and personnel costs absorb almost all budgets. The church tries to regain thrust by sending a few loyal volunteers to the back of the "bus" to start pushing. If the bus moves at all, it won't be far because the drag of the institution is just too much for the physical and financial energy of even the most faithful and sacrificial members.

The only lasting solution is to slowly but steadily get the cycle of training, blessing, and mentoring going again. Just as a bus goes through several gears to eventually produce enough power to move forward, so the church may have to proceed in several stages to produce enough thrust for forward movement. Unfortunately, this takes time. Churches that wait too long simply run out of time.

The result of thrust is both mission impact *and* church growth. The latter, however, is a by-product of the former. It is because the community experiences positive change that the church grows. People experience relevant social service and profound faith, and they are drawn into the cycle of inclusivity, spirituality, and intimacy within the church. As church people become role models and spiritual mentors, people ask: *How can I experience what you have experienced? How can I become a blessing to others as you have been a blessing to me? How can I get what you've got?* This is why in the Christian movement most people who come to a church for the first time are accompanied by a church member they have met in the mission field.

Why Some Mergers Succeed . . . 25
but Others Fail

The metaphor of the motor vehicle helps us understand the three main reasons churches merge. It also helps us understand why so many mergers fail and why other mergers can be gloriously successful.

The worst reason to merge is to pillage another church for spare parts. Your bus has broken down, new parts from the denominational factory are either unavailable or too expensive, and there are no more grants from historical societies. Too many "mergers" are really just acquisitions of technologies or staff from other churches that have all but closed. We sometimes refer to this as the "last man standing" approach to merger. Churches of the same denomination in a city or region endure as long as they can, while hoping their sister churches will collapse first and any remaining assets or volunteers will be transferred to their own church. The name might change with the addition of a hyphen to suggest a merger of institutions, but for all practical reasons one church has taken over another.

The challenge, of course, is to evaluate the crippled church to make sure the acquisition is a relative bargain. In other words, the assumption of debt and liability is a reasonable risk because the residual value left in the church provides exactly what your church needs. These are often called "maintenance driven" mergers, and they almost always fail.

They fail because they are so obviously self-serving. They do not really get the bus moving; they just create more comfortable seating for the few remaining passengers on the bus to enjoy each other's company for a little while longer. They create the illusion of movement. The seats are upholstered, the driver sits in his or her place, the engine is allowed to idle, and

the people even sing traveling songs—but the bus does not actually go anywhere. People seem perpetually ready to go. They may even show films
on the bus that tell great mission stories about somebody else, somewhere
else, but there is neither torque nor thrust. Neither traction nor steering is
really required, and indeed, it is not provided.

A more faithful reason to merge is to restore or create clarity of purpose. Churches merge around a common vision to bless a particular public
in a special way. This is really a merger based on *leadership and volunteer
energy* rather than *property and money*. New leaders and more energetic
participants bring with them a new attitude, a more poignant heartburst,
or a greater motivation to *get going*. You often see this happen today with
the merger of an established and long-standing congregation with a new
church plant. The former has resources and the latter has vision, and the
combination can have glorious results.

The vision, however, must be generated from within. It cannot be
imposed top-down. Therefore, it is very difficult for such a merger to
be legislated by a denomination or commanded by a bishop. The leaders
(pastors and boards) of each congregation must build their own relationship of trust. They start by expanding a united consensus over core values
and bedrock beliefs, and go further to build a culture of accountability that
focuses on God's mission and liberates the churches from dysfunctional
controllers who want to shape the merger around their personal needs and
preferences.

Such a merger does not necessarily presume that the vision and mission are already clear. That will become clear as the relationship between
pastors and boards deepens. What is necessary is *desire to surrender to God's
purpose*. It is the desire *not* to die, and the desire to be part of God's plan,
that drives the merger conversation. The litmus test of this desire is the
spiritual life or spiritual discipline of the pastors and board members who
commit themselves to that conversation.

If spiritual discipline is low, you will observe pastors and board members
who are sporadic in weekly worship, perfunctory in personal prayer, indifferent to Bible study, inarticulate about experiences of Christ, and immature
in faith. This reveals a low level of desire to be part of God's plan. The
merger conversation will take forever and not get anywhere. Soon the leaders who are most urgent to bless the community will leave, and find other
ways to serve; and the leaders who are most self-centered about membership
privileges will shift the conversation from mission to maintenance.

On the other hand, if spiritual discipline is high, you will observe
pastors and board members who are intentionally regular in weekly wor-

ship, serious about personal prayer, committed to Bible study, articulate about experiences with Christ, and eager to grow in faith. This reveals a high level of *desire* to be part of God's plan. The merger conversation will deepen and accelerate. It will not take long to broaden consensus over values and beliefs. In such a climate of spiritual waiting, God will reveal a compelling new vision that will capture the imaginations of the leaders. The leaders who are most self-centered will leave, but the leaders who are most mission-minded will stay *and* generate excitement that will attract new people.

Perhaps the most faithful and practical reasons to merge have to do with traction and steering. Churches merge because together they will be better able to achieve the torque or thrust necessary to move God's mission forward. There are many reasons for this. It may be that the churches involved have become too small, have been overwhelmed by demographic shifts in the mission field, or have been affected by denominational schisms that have created gaps in congregational programs.

Many churches have some clarity about their vision. They know the people they want to bless and the nature of the blessing they want to share. They may even have a plan to create the critical momentum to accomplish this. However, they also have problems, and they cannot solve these problems on their own.

One typical problem has to do with traction. The cycle of inclusivity, spirituality, and intimacy breaks down: the hospitality is not radical enough, the worship does not profoundly shape lives and lifestyles, or the spiritual growth of small-group experience is not widespread or is too modest. Churches merge because one church provides strength precisely where the other church is weak.

For example, Church A has great hospitality and reaches a broad demographic diversity in the community, but worship is dull and attendance sporadic. Church B has profound and powerful worship even though its hospitality is basic and its reach too homogeneous. As another example, a small struggling church plant offers multiple small groups that prompt great spiritual growth, but it has few resources for powerful worship; and an established church can generate profound and powerful worship, but does not understand the philosophy or strategy of midweek small groups.

Whenever the motivation for merger is to get traction, the greatest challenge is usually to build trust. Trust is the axle or hub around which the "rear wheels" turn. This is precisely where many small declining churches struggle: Trust has been replaced by personalities, and the consensus of the whole church around core values and bedrock beliefs has been replaced by the eccentricities, preferences, or privileges of a few strong families. And it is usually these very personalities who are leading the negotiations around merger. Therefore, each participating church needs to step back, rebuild its trust, clarify values and beliefs, and then explore compatibility based on church identity rather than membership privilege.

The second set of problems is about steering. The cycle of training, blessing, and mentoring is breaking down. Training may not be consistent and universal, outreach is vague and indifferent, or mentoring is nonexistent from tongue-tied or confused members and leaders. Churches merge because one provides strength where the other is weak.

For example, Church A provides inadequate training, even though it is deeply involved in social service. Church B is diligent and methodical in training. A merger makes sense because the combined organization can do social service without burning out volunteers. As another example, an older congregation that is very articulate about sharing faith merges with a younger congregation that is less mature but active in volunteer service. Together they can do social service and relational evangelism at the same time.

Whenever the motivation for merger is to improve steering, the greatest challenge is usually to build a culture of accountability. Accountability is the axle or hub around which the "front wheels" turn. This is precisely where many established churches and new church plants struggle. They fear being judgmental and do not know how to discipline staff or equip volunteer leaders properly. In the absence of accountability, people are exiting the church faster than other people are entering it. Bad behavior goes unchecked, planning is driven by crisis, and churches cannot recruit and keep quality board and team leaders. Therefore, each church needs to learn how to acquire, train, evaluate, and fire leaders. Once everyone is on the same page for due diligence in accountability, the churches can explore compatible mission statements and strategic plans.

The fundamental purpose of the church is to participate in Christian *movement*. We are a part of God's greater plan to bless and redeem the world. Therefore, merger is simply a strategy to accelerate movement. It is not about maintenance or survival. It is about getting the bus moving again, so that God's people can catch up with Jesus who is already far ahead on the road to mission.

Notes

1. Why Merge?
1. All biblical citations are from the New Revised Standard Version.

2. Unexpected Visions
1. Lifestyle segmentation is used by demographers to cluster groups of people around shared behavior patterns, attitudes, world views, and day-to-day priorities. It has emerged in the digital age, and is now the primary method of research used by strategic planners in all sectors.

3. Get Moving!
1. The seven distinct experiences are described in Thomas G. Bandy, *Worship Ways* (Nashville: Abingdon Press, 2014).

6. Trust
1. Thomas G. Bandy, *Christian Chaos* (Nashville: Abingdon Press, 1999).

7. Vision Team
1. See further explanation of the four keys to accountability in Thomas G. Bandy, *Spirited Leadership* (St. Louis: Chalice Press, 2006).

11. Compatibility
1. We use the classifications and segment or group names used by www.MissionInsite.com, and developed by Experian.

2. The report can be generated using the search engine, www.missioninsite .com.

3. Categories for ministry expectations by lifestyle segment regarding pastoral and lay leadership, hospitality, worship, Christian education, small groups, and outreach; facilities, technologies, and symbols; financial management and fund raising; and internal and external communication are developed in Thomas G. Bandy, *See, Know and Serve* (Nashville: Abingdon Press, 2013).

4. See Thomas G. Bandy, *Mission Impact* (www.missioninsite.com). The code in parentheses indicates lifestyle group (letter) and lifestyle segment (number) as defined by Experian, a multinational corporation that gathers such data.

5. See *Mission Impact* commentaries on all seventy-one lifestyle segments and nineteen lifestyle groups that describe ministry preferences in www.missioninsite .com.

6. See *Mission Impact* in www.missioninsite.com. For a complete summary of lifestyle expectations for ministry (leadership, hospitality, worship, Christian education, small groups, outreach, facility/technology, financial giving/management, and communication), see Bandy, *See, Know & Serve.*

12. Setting Priorities

1. See Thomas G. Bandy, *Accelerate Your Church*, available as a pdf workbook at www.missioninsite.com.

13. Stress Management

1. Thomas G. Bandy, *Coaching Change* (Nashville: Abingdon Press, 2004).

22. Critical Mass

1. See Thomas G. Bandy, *Moving Off the Map,* 2nd ed. (Nashville: Abingdon Press, 2005).

2. See Thomas G. Bandy, *Spirited Leadership* (St. Louis: Chalice Press, 2007).

3. See Thomas G. Bandy, *Worship Ways* (Nashville: Abingdon Press, 2014).

4. See Thomas G. Bandy, *95 Questions for the Future of Your Church* (Nashville: Abingdon Press, 2005).

23. How to Get Traction

1. See Thomas G. Bandy, *Worship Ways* (Nashville: Abingdon Press, 2014).

2. See Thomas G. Bandy, *Moving Off the Map* (Nashville: Abingdon Press, 1995) and Bandy, *Spirited Leadership* (St. Louis: Chalice Press, 2006), for further explanations of the process and the goal to build clarity and consensus over trust.

24. How to Steer in the Right Direction

1. See Thomas G. Bandy, *See, Know & Serve* (Nashville: Abingdon Press, 2013).

2. Thomas G. Bandy, *Christian Mentoring: Helping Each Other Find Meaning and Purpose* (Amazon, 2011).

3. See Thomas G. Bandy, *Spirited Leadership* (St. Louis: Chalice Press, 2006) for further explanation of these keys to leadership accountability.

Index

Note: Page references for figures and tables are italicized.

Made in the USA
San Bernardino, CA
04 April 2017